THE VARIABLE BODY
IN HISTORY

Chris Mounsey and Stan Booth (eds)

PETER LANG

Oxford · Bern · Berlin · Bruxelles · Frankfurt am Main · New York · Wien

Bibliographic information published by Die Deutsche Nationalbibliothek.
Die Deutsche Nationalbibliothek lists this publication in the Deutsche National-
bibliografie; detailed bibliographic data is available on the Internet
at http://dnb.d-nb.de.

A catalogue record for this book is available from the British Library.

Library of Congress Control Number: 2016942152

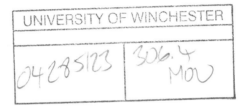

ISSN 2235-5367
ISBN 978-1-906165-72-7 (print) • ISBN 978-1-78707-100-1 (ePDF)
ISBN 978-1-78707-101-8 (ePub) • ISBN 978-1-78707-102-5 (mobi)

© Peter Lang AG 2016

Published by Peter Lang Ltd, International Academic Publishers,
52 St Giles, Oxford, OX1 3LU, United Kingdom
oxford@peterlang.com, www.peterlang.com

Chris Mounsey and Stan Booth have asserted their right under the Copyright,
Designs and Patents Act, 1988, to be identified as Editors of this Work.

This publication has been peer reviewed.

Printed in Germany

THE UNIVERSITY OF
WINCHESTER

Martial Rose Library
Tel: 01962 827306

To be returned on or before the day marked above, subject to recall.

QUEERING PARADIGMS · IN FOCUS

Series Editor

Bee Scherer, Canterbury Christ Church University, UK

PETER LANG

Oxford · Bern · Berlin · Bruxelles · Frankfurt am Main · New York · Wien

Contents

Figures

CHRIS MOUNSEY

Introduction: Speaking Forwards in History

In the introduction to my first collection of essays on disability, *The Idea of Disability in the Eighteenth Century*,[1] I explored the output of academic studies of disability in history until 2013, and in the interim I am happy to find over a hundred new publications in the field of disability studies. The same introduction also argued that it was now time for detailed studies of particular impairments and particular impaired people within their historical contexts, and that the time for general statements and theories was past. I was therefore a little saddened when researching for this new introduction that less than a tenth of the hundred outputs of the last two years concerned disability in history. Even David Bolt's excellent *Changing Social Attitudes to Disability*,[2] which is subtitled 'Perspectives from historical, cultural, and educational studies', gives us very little and a very short history. Although the first part of the book is intended to illustrate 'the fact that, though often neglected, an historical analysis of changing social attitudes toward disability is an important area of study',[3] history is reduced to an account of Darwinism, the changing nineteenth-century attitudes toward tuberculosis, and the Nazi extermination programme.

A more substantial contribution to a longer history of impairment has come from Allison P. Hobgood and David Houston Wood in *Recovering Disability in Early Modern England*.[4] The collection explores representations of disabilities in the early modern period in the same way my own *The Idea of Disability in the Eighteenth Century* centred on its academic period.

---

1   (Lewisburg, PA: Bucknell University Press, 2014).
2   David Bolt, *Changing Social Attitudes to Disability* (Abingdon: Routledge, 2014).
3   Bolt, *Changing Social Attitudes*, 7.
4   Allison P. Hobgood and David Houston Wood, *Recovering Disability in Early Modern England* (Columbus, OH: Ohio State University Press, 2013).

In the book, Hobgood and Houston Wood's contributors confronted me with theoretical approaches choreographed around Rosemarie Garland-Thomson's idea of 'the stare', and Mitchell and Snyder's 'narrative prosthesis', in what a review of the book by Elizabeth Bearden calls a:

> ... reassessment of medicalized models of disability in favor of ... a more inclusive and intersectional model favor[ing] a postmodern and postcolonial worldview.[5]

I am either being hopelessly old-fashioned, or trying to focus on a different goal, but importing a postmodern and postcolonial worldview to read Edmund Spenser, Ben Jonson, Thomas Hobbes and John Locke, the *Book of Common Prayer*, revenge tragedy, early modern scientific treatises, ballads and broadsides seems a little odd. This is not to say that this and the essays in Hobgood and Houston Wood's collection are unreadable or wrong.

I can understand them because I know enough about literary theory and enough about how literature works to read outside my period. But I learned a great deal more from their collection from the essays' contributions on specific historical information about the representations and experiences of impaired people than from its theoretical framework. It is true that the theoretical framework was intended to help understanding between periods of study, and here am I introducing a collection of essays which spans the medieval period to the early twentieth century. How can its essays hope to make a single point, or talk to one another if they do not hold in common a language of communication across the centuries?

Our academic love affair with periodization can be problematic. In order that we might be able to have meaningful conversations at our conferences and a focus for our publishing strategies we keep to our own periods and rarely if ever read outside our own century. This can become a trap because periodization means we can fail to communicate beyond our 'own' century, albeit that our topic itself might be narrow enough to allow for a wider historical base for debate: and the study of impaired people is just such a narrow topic, and I believe that it does not need to hide behind the rhetoric of a methodology in order to make sense. The language of the body,

5   *Journal of Literary & Cultural Disability Studies*, 8/2 (2014), 231–235.

the body of you or of me, or of any character in any piece of literature is the same language because it terminates upon the body and articulates it, albeit that the body in each case is different. But it must be remembered that each body is the 'same only different' from every other.

Thus I would argue that we can go farther than David Bolt or Hobgood and Houston Wood suggest. As important as theoretical study may be, it is important that a history of social attitudes towards impaired people is read as accounts of what was, in the terms deployed in the past, in order that they become a method of bringing the past into the present. Only in this way can cultural history be understood to 'speak forwards from history' to teach us now how to live with the same impairments with which people were living in the past. If we impose a modern methodology upon the language of the past we stand a good chance of listening only to an echo of ourselves, rather than to the accounts of the lives of our foremothers and forefathers.

It was just this problem of listening to personal accounts of impairments across history which was highlighted in the symposium 'Disability History: Voices and Sources', held at the London Metropolitan Archives on 22 March 2013. One of the papers told a typical story of the loss of the voice of disabled people in history, when the presenter, Phil Samphire 'had visited a local library in Manchester, and seen an exhibition about his old special school, in which the school's story was told entirely from the point of view of its governors.'[6] A number of projects were highlighted in the same symposium in which the voices of inmates are now beginning to be heard over the records of the nineteenth-century institutions: Earlswood and Normansfield, Bethlem Hospital, and the stately homes transformed into hospitals during World War One. However, apart from one account of a deformed man in the Norman period given by Simon Jarrett, all the voices of the disabled came from the nineteenth and twentieth centuries. It is true that these more recent historical voices are still faint, as Martha Stoddard Holmes argues of the voices of one Victorian group of individuals:

---

6   Emmeline Burdett, 'Disability History: Voices and Sources, London Metropolitan Archives', *Journal of Literary & Cultural Disability Studies*, 8/1 (2014), 97–103, 97.

The question of how people with intellectual disabilities were 'othered' – scientifically, linguistically, environmentally/spatially, socially, educationally, and sexually – through texts – including the scientific, the clinical, the educational, and the literary – has been underexamined and underhistoricized.[7]

David Bolt, Julia Miele Rodas and Elizabeth J. Donaldson have gone some of the way to fill in the gap in historicization of nineteenth-century impairment with their collection of essays concerning Charlotte Brontë's novel *The Madwoman and the Blindman: Jane Eyre, Discourse, Disability*,[8] which demonstrates that often the voices of the disabled in history are to be found in literary rather than historical texts.

Considering the contributions to the field of disability studies over the past two years, I am more and more convinced that the concentration on histories of impairments after 1784 is due to the fact that the theory of compulsory ableism which underlies much of the current work in disability studies is only comprehensible after that date. As Cornelia Dayton argues about the case of Joseph Gorham, a man with intellectual disabilities in eighteenth-century Cape Cod, '... lay opinion remained the most important factor shaping the designation of a person as mentally competent or incompetent.'[9] Dayton's ground-breaking work explores the way in which Joseph Gorham's mental capacity to make a will was not judged by an idea of compulsory ableism but by 'social accommodations and interpretive confusions.'

The probate appeal bequeathed to us a thick file containing testimony from twenty witnesses, all men. On one hand, they agreed that Joseph was not a fully active member of the community: he had never followed a trade, and, by family fiat and local consensus, he was not allowed to bargain. On the other, as a result of the parties'

---

7   Martha Stoddard Holmes, 'Intellectual Disability', in *Victorian Review*, 40/1 (2014), 9–14.

8   David Bolt, Julia Miele Rodas, and Elizabeth J. Donaldson, *The Madwoman and the Blindman: Jane Eyre, Discourse, Disability* (Columbus, OH: Ohio State University Press, 2012).

9   Cornelia H. Dayton, '"The Oddest Man that I Ever Saw": Assessing Cognitive Disability on Eighteenth-Century Cape Cod', *Journal of Social History*, 49/1 (2015), 77–99, 79–80.

lawyers scouting for witnesses to provide supporting evidence for their side, the deponents disagreed about the testator's capacities. Ten men described behaviors of Joseph which seemed to mark him as incompetent to dispose of his property, while ten claimed that, although Gorham was 'very Different from the Generality of Mankind,' he possessed sufficient rationality to write a valid will. These testimonies afford us a glimpse into the social accommodations and interpretive confusions that arose around a man whom one observer called 'the oddest man that I Ever saw.'[10]

While ten deponents appear to have believed that Gorham had to be at least not 'odd' in order to write a will, ten believed he could though he was 'very Different from the Generality of Mankind.' That said, I cannot go as far as Dayton's retro-diagnosing Gorham as autistic. But this is not because I believe that Gorham was impaired in a way specific to Cape Cod in the eighteenth century, but because the language we have of him in the historical records is all we have to go on. Why replace it with other? But then does it become impossible for impaired people to speak forwards from history? Will we fail to understand them as their context was so very different from our own? This is one of the basic questions of historiography, and is one which can and has been answered in a number of ways.

Ann Schmeising gives us a straightforward answer in her reading of *Grimm's Fairy Tales*[11] in which she focuses on literal disability, which allows her to explore the lived bodily experience of physical impairment. While her book is part of the project of disability studies, and therefore set against compulsory ableism, it challenges the brothers Grimm, who '... aspired to restore an organic wholeness to their tales ... [with Schmeising's] own prosthetic goal ... to restore disability to their tales by foregrounding it instead of – as has been the case too often in fairy-tale scholarship – reading over it or seeing it as valuable only insofar as it symbolizes something else.'[12] The lesson to learn from this approach is that we can and should read people in literature as well as people in history as people with bodies like ours. And furthermore, Schmeising urges us to understand disability not

10 Cornelia H. Dayton, '"The Oddest Man that I Ever Saw"', 78.
11 Ann Schmeising, *Disability, Deformity, and Disease in the Grimm's Fairy Tales* (Detroit, MI: Wayne State University Press, 2014).
12 Ann Schmeising, *Disability, Deformity, and Disease*, 186.

only as a social or political problem but focusing on the impaired person as having a life worth living and not as someone with a disease to be cured.

It might be argued that there is a problem with working with fairy tales, which being so ingrained into our culture may be in part responsible for the way we think. It is what makes fairy tales so important a locus of literary study. But when we read them are we reading ourselves, because these tales, told to us in whatever version at our cradle, formed the ways in which we now think about ourselves and our bodies? When the lived bodily experience of physical impairment speaks forward from the fairy tale, does it do so unimpeded by a shift in context because the fairy tale is the context of all our childhoods?

When speaking forwards from other less familiar histories and literatures, the impairment remains in its context of understanding and in its own words. This is why I argue against Dayton's suggestion that Joseph Gorham was autistic since there can be no real certainty in retrospective diagnosis from the indirect historical voices no matter how hard we attend to them, but also why I accept Dayton's work as ground-breaking since at bottom she is listening out *for* Joseph among, amid and through the legal documents *about* him. The difficulty of doing this, as expressed by Dayton's move towards retro-diagnosis says more about a twenty-first century desire to pigeon-hole ideas in a grid of scientific certainty, than the conclusions that can be drawn from the paucity of historical facts available about impaired people, that come from impaired people. And this might be another reason why so little work has been carried out on their histories farther back than 1784.

I choose 1784 with a wry smile, as it recalls the famous date of 1869 when Westphal first used the term homosexual, and so founded sexuality. 1784 was the date of the foundation of the first blind school in Paris by Valentin Haüy, the beginning of the great incarceration. Thus, it might be used as the date when we lost the views of those such as Phil Samphire, among countless others brought up in institutions, whose stories were told entirely from the point of view of the governors. I have argued elsewhere that this was undoubtedly the case for blind people, due to the fate of the Liverpool Blind School, the first of its kind in Britain, in 1792. The School was dreamed up by Edward Rushton, the blind anti-slavery writer, newspaper publisher and bookseller, as a friendly society into which all blind people would pay while they were employed so that they could draw a pension when they became unemployed or too old to work. However, when Henry Dannett brought the scheme to fruition it had mutated into a work-house where:

> That the employment be such, as gently to engage the mind without fatiguing it, and by diverting the attention of the blind from their unhappy lot, making them less a burden to *themselves*.[13]

The ground plan of the School, published nearly twenty-five years after it was founded, shows no classrooms at all. On the ground floor are a 'Women's Basket-weaving Room' and a 'Men's Basket-weaving Room', and on the first, 'Women's Looms' and 'Men's Looms'. Although there is a 'Music Room', and a number of people are mentioned – former inmates who have become organists and music teachers, presumably from lessons taught at the school – the writer of the pamphlet cannot refrain from hoping that the governors will 'improve the nature of the establishment ... to render it less an ASYLUM, and more approaching a SCHOOL',[14] as Katharine Kittredge tells us later in this collection.

In fact, the *Address in Favour of the School for the Blind* gives us accounts of the lives of only twenty-five former 'pupils' from among the 465 who came from around the whole country to find work in the Liverpool Asylum between 1792 and 1816, weaving baskets and cloth or making whips. Of these sixteen are simple statements that the former 'pupil' is now an organist at a named church. The voices of the nine remaining are heard in letters or short pieces written about four of them, and five by the former 'pupils' themselves.

These voices are very faint indeed and need to be read carefully. The voices of the impaired before this time need to be read even more carefully as they 'speak forward in history', and this is what the essays in this collection

---

13   *A Plan for Affording Relief to the Indigent Blind* (Liverpool: n.p., 1790), 1.
14   *An Address in the Favour of the School for the Blind* (Liverpool, G. F. Harris, 1817).

attempt to do, giving accounts of impaired people in an historical sweep from the medieval period to the twentieth century.

What holds together such an historically disparate group of essays is not a common methodology, although all essays eschew the Foucauldian approach to disability studies and the struggle against compulsory able-bodiedness. Instead, each essay begins with either an idea of or about the body (impaired or not) in a particular context, or by exploring a particular body within its historical and cultural context. Common to all essays is the move from the one methodology to the other: from ideas about bodies to bodies themselves. Thus, together the essays demonstrate the reciprocity between ideas about bodies and the physical experiential body, suggesting that the two are both contextually determined, and that neither focus of explanation is, by itself, capable of fully explaining embodiment in its variable forms.

The opening essay is by Irina Metzler. Her essay, 'In/Dis-Ability: A Medieval Perspective' begins by explaining that since not all impairments were consistently disabling in all cultures, we need both textual and materialist approaches to the historical study of disability: what she calls the cultural model of disability. Thus, examples in her essay explore St Martin and the iconography of his act of charity, asking to whom should charity be given? Who are the deserving? Which leads to discussions of work and the ability to work, and the manifestation of disability in the first forms of wheeled chairs and those who used them, as well as the choice of guide for blind people.

Adleen Crapo moves the argument forward into the pre-modern period. 'The Possibility of an Island: Colonialism, Embodiment and Utopia in Pre-Modern Literature' brings a similar combined argument to the body of Teresa de Cartagena, a deaf woman converted to Christianity who lived in fifteenth-century Spain, through a comparison with Shakespeare's Caliban. The essay brings idea and body together by combining the idea and experience of having a monstrous body with the desire for a utopia for people with disabled bodies: Caliban's famous island, and Teresa's *insula* for her and other disabled thinkers, rendering it a *locus amoenus* for disabled female creativity.

Emile Bojesen's essay explores the origins of the English public school, in particular from the perspective of the variety of boys who entered the system to be unified into civilized members of Queen Elizabeth's nation. But what the essay demonstrates is that just as the grammar school gave us Shakespeare, Richard Mulcaster, the headmaster of Merchant Taylor's and St Paul's Schools, who devised the grammar school curriculum, knew and understood that the process of education must necessarily retain the uniqueness in body and mind of its pupils in the diet of both.

Kevin Berland writes of 'Thersites and Deformity', and reverses the process of Adleen Crapo's essay, beginning with a detailed account of the idea of the link between the deformed body (*somatos*) and deformed mind (*ethos*) in the literary figure of Thersites. We learn that Homer does not link the two, but when the character moved into the early modern period, his deformed body is regarded to be an outward expression of his mind. Berland then shifts focus to a real deformed man, William Hay, and reads the experience of a real historical body in his society to explore how the idea fitted.

My own essay on Aphra Behn's seventeenth-century novel *The Unfortunate Bride: or, the Blind Lady a Beauty*, reads the changes in the depiction of the blind woman, from the butt of jokes in Sir Robert Howard's play *The Blind Lady* to become the heroine of Behn's novel. At the same time the essay notes the contemporary knowledge Behn demonstrates about the cures of blindness and their minute effects on the person cured: knowledge which suggests that either Behn herself was cured of a blinding condition, or that she knew someone who was.

Simon Jarrett's essay, entitled 'Laughing about and Talking about the Idiot in the Eighteenth Century', explores the way 'idiots' were perceived in the eighteenth century. The essay challenges Simon Dickie's assumption that those whom we'd now call people with learning difficulties were always deemed to the outcast of the Enlightened world. Instead, Jarrett finds that 'idiots', as they were known in the eighteenth century, were regarded as full members of society and used as examples of behaviour that might be improved for those who could.

Stan Booth offers a challenging new way of reading the impaired or diseased body in historical subjects. His essay rejects retro-diagnosis in favour of a 'cultural studies' approach to a specified subject: in this essay the paralysed Lady Elizabeth Smith-Stanley, Countess of Derby. The new method of reading makes the most of what little we know about her diagnosis and treatment, and binds together disparate information streams with chronology.

Miriam L. Wallace writes about the 'value' of the sexualized body of women in the eighteenth century. Wallace begins with satirical prints which offer prices for sex acts with different classes and races of married women. She then notes that these prices are based on the law of 'criminal conversation' (1670–1850), a law that gave a husband the legal right to claim money from another man who had sex with his wife. The argument is made towards the conclusion that the prints made fun of what was, in fact, a legal fiction, and that real husbands and wives valued their bodies over money.

Katharine Kittredge has searched the archives for the first time for the representation of blind children in literature, as well as in literature by blind children. Her ground-breaking essay tells of the change in the way blind children were 'used' before and after the setting up of the first blind school in the USA, the Perkins Institute. What is more, the essay takes account of the experiences of the first blind children to be educated, other than by their parents, to prepare them for life in the nineteenth-century world of work.

Clare Walker Gore reads two nineteenth-century novels by Dinah Mulock Craik, *Olive* and *A Noble Life*, both of which feature protagonists with more or less severe impairments. The study therefore argues against the idea that disabled characters are always marginalized in literature, and powerfully contends that the reading of a text about disability by a disabled reader – a reader who shares the experience with the protagonists – is an intersection between the social and embodied aspects of disability. Thus the essay offers a rare opportunity to peep through a window (or into a mirror) and see ourselves as we have been seen – or rather not seen.

Will Visconti returns to the sexualized body with a fascinating reading of La Gouloue (Louise Weber), the famous dancer of the Moulin Rouge in Paris (active between 1880 and 1920). The problem with La Gouloue's body, which has become so well known through Toulouse Lautrec's iconic portraits, is that her body disappears amid the gossip and misinformation that warped and impaired her representation over time, creating an image of her that has implicitly linked her with wickedness and made a morality play of her life. Visconti's essay attempts to relocate the body amid the historical fragments that read too much like the literature of desire – the way people wanted La Gouloue to be.

The collection ends with an epilogue from Bee Scherer, founder of the series in which this book finds a home, and of the 'Queering Paradigms' conference series. Scherer's essay opens up a dialogue between contemporary critical disability theory with Buddhist thought, noting the way in which the move away from reading 'disability' towards the more inclusive idea of variability, which this collection suggests, is inherent in the Buddhist religion: 'without judging, blaming, shaming, and guilt-tripping variable embodiments – mitigates the Buddhist karmatic views on "disability" or embodied variabilities: ... [Scherer argues] ... that that from a Buddhist point of view body variances express genealogies or actualizations of generic human potentials rather than essentialized, individual histories ...'.

Bringing together all these essays, if such a thing is possible, I would like to end on a misquote from Bee Scherer's epilogue. Together the voices from the individual essays, 'speaking forwards from history', seem to me to echo in the present: the time seems ripe for socially engaged 'Crip Liberation' and a fuller 'theology' of embodied variability.

IRINA METZLER

In/Dis-Ability: A Medievalist's Perspective

ABSTRACT

This essay discusses medieval and modern concepts of disability and how they might differ. One may note the medieval variability of labelling for 'disability' and the disabled. The conversation may highlight key concerns of today, by concentrating on two main themes: mobility and work (also working ability). The changing notions of poverty from the early to the later Middle Ages, from involuntary to voluntary poverty, demonstrate that inability to work becomes a key indicator of both poverty and disability. Personal mobility is a further key indicator, with differing types of mobility experienced by medieval disabled people. While mobility today is individualized and technologized, in contrast mobility in the past relied more on people than animals.

A beautifully executed fresco of St Lawrence distributing alms to the needy, made around 1449 by Fra Angelico for the Cappella Niccolina in the Vatican, depicts the classic stereotypical images of 'the disabled' as a group. However, this includes people who according to modern definitions are not physically impaired: widows and orphans; as well as those who are: the blind and crippled. Interpreting the representation of these figures from left to right, we find

- a widow with an infant
- an elderly crippled man
- an older widow with a small child
- an elderly man sitting on the ground supported with hand-trestles
- St Lawrence in the centre
- two small children (orphans?)
- a middle-aged blind man

- an old man with a long beard, who has no obvious impairment other than age
- a female pilgrim identifiable as such by her hat
- a middle-aged blind man with his cane.

All are shown with dignity and respect, they are certainly not caricatures. In fact, if any group label may be attached, 'the needy' may be more appropriate. To be classed as poor, or rather as 'needy', gave one the right to receive alms. In encompassing the sick, the disabled, the economically poor, the widowed and pilgrims, the *pauperes* who had a need for assistance were a multiform group,[1] a medieval total greater than the sum of its modernist categorical parts.

This essay will discuss medieval and modern concepts of disability, how they might differ and how the conversation may highlight key concerns of today, by concentrating on two main themes: mobility and work(ing ability). These two are some of the main themes of today for disability studies/ activists, but the interesting question is whether this was also true in the Middle Ages. It then raises the question of how the two periods differ. Following the theme of the recent 'VariAbilities' conference[2] which was 'history and representation of the body in its diversity', it is apt to draw attention to diversity of periods as well as of bodies within periods.

Thus I chose the play on words used for the title: in/dis-ability, because it arouses the question of when a simple inability becomes a disability, and what is the terminological differences. Who are 'the disabled'? As an all-embracing umbrella term, this is rather vague semantically, since it means all and sundry – physical, sensory and intellectual disability. Added to the conceptual mix is the growth of disabilities in the modern day where more and more conditions are being identified and pathologized, e.g. autism

---

1   On the concept of 'need' as essential element for charitable assistance given to these groups see J. Agrimi and C. Crisciani, 'Wohltätigkeit und Beistand in der mittelalterlichen christlichen Kultur', in M. D. Grmek, ed., *Die Geschichte des medizinischen Denkens. Antike und Mittelalte*r (Munich: C. H. Beck, 1996), 182–215.

2   'VariAbilities, the History and Representation of the Body in its Diversity', University of Winchester, 20–22 July 2015.

which was unknown prior to the 1960s, and arguably 'learning disabilities' is a misnomer for any historical period prior to the advent of universal schooling. This arouses further the question of the validity of umbrella terms more generally. Do they include too much? And what do we mean by disability? In our society it usually means two things: possessing a physical/mental impairment and benefitting from certain legal and/or social rights but also suffering from social and economic restrictions.

So what does 'disability' mean for other cultures? The starting point for discussing disability is to be clear about the very valuable distinction between the different models of disability. In the medical model, anatomical difference automatically and invariably equates to social and cultural difference as well. So the physically impaired are always also the disabled, at all times past and present. In the social model, by contrast, impairment is taken purely as an anatomical phenomenon and is distinguished from disability (this need not exclude 'intellectual' impairment either, especially considering the genetic basis discovered so far for a number of conditions, Down's syndrome being the most well known). Disability then relates to the social, cultural or economic perception of people. Ultimately, disability is a social construct that is laid on top of the somatic condition of impairment.

Back in 1970s Britain the following definition was suggested:

> Impairment. Lacking part or all of a limb, or having a defective limb, organ, or mechanism of the body. Disability: The disadvantage or restriction of activity caused by a contemporary social organisation which takes no or little account of people who have physical impairments and thus excludes them from the mainstream of social activities.[3]

In other words, to paraphrase Simone de Beauvoir's famous statement on women, one may be born impaired but one is made disabled. The notion of the social construction of disability therefore permits historical investigation and analysis. If disability is a social construct, as times and societies change so too should notions of what is and what is not disability.

---

3   Union of the Physically Impaired Against Segregation, *Fundamental Principles of Disability* (London, 1976), 3–4, cited in C. Barnes, G. Mercer and T. Shakespeare, *Exploring Disability: A Sociological Introduction* (Cambridge: Polity Press, 1999), 28.

Yet impairment is ubiquitous in human society, and as far as we can tell from the archaeological record, has been so in past human societies.[4] It has even been demonstrated to exist in other vertebrate animals, as a number of archaeological finds of osteological pathologies in animal bones testify.[5] The World Health Organisation suggested that approximately 10 per cent of the world's population is either physically or mentally impaired at any given time,[6] which means that we may assume a similar proportion for past societies as well with the Middle Ages being no exception. Impairment therefore is and has been a factor in a large number of people's lives, so one can study the implications and effects of impairment, in past as well as present societies.

Armed with the distinction between impairment and disability, the historian can then set off on the discovery of disability in past times, and can discover how, why, and in what way impaired people may or may not have been regarded as disabled by their cultures. This distinction allows us to observe and research change over time and between cultures – change in attitudes to and therefore treatment of impaired people. All too often historians have assumed unquestioningly that all physically or cognitively impaired people were also always disabled, no matter which culture they lived in. It is therefore important to note that not all impairments were consistently disabling in all cultures.

A new addition to the variegated growth in disability models has been Edward Wheatley's 'religious model' of disability.[7] At first glance this constitutes an attractive proposition for the medievalist looking at medieval

---

4   See D. Brothwell and A. T. Sandison, eds, *Diseases in Antiquity* (Springfield, IL: C. C. Thomas, 1967), which examines all kinds of pathologies from skeletal evidence with a wide-ranging geographical and historical scope.

5   Skeletons of severely arthritic dinosaurs, to name but one example, have been discovered.

6   P. H. N. Wood, *International Classification of Impairments, Disabilities and Handicaps: A Manual of Classifications Relating to the Consequences of Disease* (Geneva: Springer, 1980).

7   For example, Edward Wheatley's unpublished talk 'Does Sin Cause Disability? Some Medieval Perspectives', at the 'Symposium on Disease and Disability in the Middle Ages and the Renaissance', Newberry Library, 20 February 2010.

disability, since religion obviously played an important role in medieval culture, to the extent that the period was popularly called the 'Age of Faith'. But herein lies the problem: Wheatley does not resolve the contradiction between his interpretation of blindness as defined by human negotiation, presumably meaning culture, and religion as something 'outside' of culture, which is evidently nonsense. Religion is a sub-set of culture, as any ethnologist, archaeologist or historian could have pointed out. I take the 'social' in the social model of disability to relate to religious factors as much as to legal, political, literary, and economic in – other words 'culture'. The distinction between religion and economics that we make nowadays was far less apparent in medieval times. There was a far more complex relation between health and wealth, religiosity, disability, economics and social structures than a reduction to a purely religious model of disability would allow.

The postmodern critique of history has focused the historians' gaze on the world of language and texts, and allowed historians to develop more complex analyses, as well as to take a heightened interest in previously disregarded topics (of which disability is one example). There is a danger, though, that the 'linguistic turn'[8] in the discipline of history may make us ignore the very real facts of illness, poverty, death, and so on, which are not simply reducible to textuality alone. One postmodern author, Elizabeth Deeds Ermarth,[9] has reduced everything to pure text and discourse, thereby eliminating notions of time or society as anything other than linguistic constructs. Criticism of the 'linguistic turn' has come from historians such as Richard J. Evans, who argues against the 'postmodernist concentration on words [which] diverts attention away from real suffering and oppression and towards the kinds of secondary intellectual issues that matter in the physically comfortable world of academia.'[10]

But purely materialist interpretations of disability in western society, as advocated by David T. Gleeson and others, are not sufficient as an

8   This concept and the critique of it are discussed by R. J. Evans, *In Defence of History* (London: Granta, 1997), 184–185.

9   Elizabeth Deeds Ermarth, *Sequel to History: Postmodernism and the Crisis of Historical Time* (Princeton: Princeton University Press, 1992).

10   Evans, *In Defence of History*, 185.

explanation. Materialist theory has been criticized by Colin Barnes as 'an aid to understanding rather than an accurate historical statement'[11] which is therefore 'simplistic' in that it assumes simple relationships between the mode of production and the perceptions or experiences of disability, whereas the impact of ideology or culture is just as great as (if not greater than) the materialist situation. The adoption of a cultural angle aids an analysis far more. 'Culture' is here used in the sense Mary Douglas[12] described it, as a 'communally held set of values and beliefs'.[13] It is cultural ideas that create the myth of bodily perfection, or the discourse of the able-bodied ideal, if one so prefers, whereas the materialist approach completely ignores such notions. Therefore, we need both textual and materialist approaches to the historical study of disability – perhaps what might be called the cultural studies model of disability.

In the rest of the essay I will follow medieval terminology by talking of 'cripples' and 'dumb' people, rather than attempting retrospectively to impose modern medical diagnoses onto conditions we can only guess at. After all, the Middle Ages did not even have a word 'disabled' (according to the *Oxford English Dictionary*, 'disability' first appears in the sixteenth century).

Some physical impairments that we would now call 'disabilities' were recognized as such by medieval people, in other words the crippled (*contracti, defecti, decrepiti*), blind (*caeci*), mute (*muti*) or deaf (*surdi*) people, epileptics (*epileptici* or people with *morbus caducus*)[14] and children born with congenital deformities. The non-specific invalids, the *infirmi*, are

---

11   Colin Barnes, 'Theories of disability and the origins of the oppression of disabled people in western society', in L. Barton, ed., *Disability and Society: Emerging Issues and Insights* (London and New York: Longman, 1996), 47.

12   See Mary Douglas, *Purity and Danger: An Analysis of Concepts of Pollution and Taboo* (London and New York: Routledge, 1966).

13   Barnes, 'Theories of disability', 43.

14   Epilepsy is sometimes referred to as *gutta caducus* (in thirteenth- and fourteenth-century English manuscripts), so that even though *gutta* mostly refers to the more specific gout, *gutta* can also mean an ailment in general. See R. E. Latham, *Revised Medieval Latin Word-List from British and Irish Sources* (London: British Academy, 1965), s.v. 'gutt/a'.

probably the nearest thing the Middle Ages had as an equivalent to the modern umbrella-term 'disabled'. Besides *infirmus*, there were any number of other vague references to disability as a concept, e.g. *deformans, impotens, debilitans, defectus*. So apart from the direct, precise terms, we can never be too certain that the vaguer terms actually imply the notion of disability, as they would in modern parlance. Where we accept the distinction between the two terms 'impairment' and 'disability' as being contrasting notions, the important historical question is raised: What constitutes a disability, or an ability for that matter, in an historical culture? To answer this the crucial point to be borne in mind is that 'disability' is a cultural construction. Disability has no 'inherent meaning'[15] outside of a particular culture: one cannot therefore speak automatically of all impaired persons as disabled at all times, in all places. However, there are certain cultural similarities in which the Middle Ages did, in fact, have a concept of 'disability' akin to the modern notion, namely an idea of disability as something that is tied up with social, legal and economic status, not just with meta/physical phenomena.

In the theological terms of the twelfth to fifteenth centuries, poverty and the poor possess neither dignity (*dignitas*) nor authority (*auctoritas*).[16] 'Paupers, according to canon law, were those who passively received alms as a right,'[17] which placed them at the bottom of the social hierarchy and therefore without authority. Without authority, a person was also impotent. How some of this concept may have filtered down from the refined intellectual circles of theologians and scholastics to 'ordinary' people can be seen in literary texts. In Chaucer's *Troilus and Criseyde*, for example, the staff that is used as a crutch by a mobility impaired character is called

15   M. L. Evans, 'Deaf and Dumb in Ancient Greece', in L. J. Davis, ed., *The Disability Studies Reader* (New York and London: Routledge, 1997), 29.

16   Miri Rubin, *Charity and Community in Medieval Cambridge* (Cambridge: Cambridge University Press, 1987), 68. See also, *Decretum magistri Gratiani*, in *Corpus Iuris Canonici I*, E. Friedberg, ed. (Leipzig, 1877), at C.2 q.1, X.20.32, X.1.6.22.

17   Janet Coleman, 'Property and Poverty', in J. H. Burns, ed., *The Cambridge History of Medieval Political Thought, c.350-c.1450* (Cambridge: Cambridge University Press, 1988), 607–648, 627.

his *potente*[18] – this is a rare word in Middle English, and probably derived from the Latin *potentes*. Interestingly, the T-cross used since the late twelfth century by the Antonite order as an emblem of St Anthony is in German also called the *Krückenkreuz* ('crutch cross') or Latinized as *potentia*.[19] Here the material prop used as a crutch literally becomes the thing that gives power to the person, in this case the power of movement, since it empowers both physically and nominally. The opposite, where a person is described as impotent due to the lack of ability of movement, can be found in a will dated 2 August 1400. Sir Richard de Scrop, lord of Bolton, leaves a sum of money to people who are 'lame, blind or impotent, being bedridden'.[20] Semantically, we therefore have a small range of looser or unspecific terms like *infirmi*, *debiles*, *impotentes* associated with what we would now term 'disability'. Of these, *impotentes* is likely the nearest equivalent to modern 'disability' as an umbrella term. But one must not forget that only the specific terms allow the modern historian to make accurate reconstructions of whether a source is referring to an impaired person as we understand it.

To elucidate something about the mentality of medieval 'disability', I wish to turn to the iconography of my favourite saint and to a miracle – of sorts – because this image represents the most materialistic of medieval miracles. St Martin is an unusual saint, because he rarely performs anything supernatural, that is thaumaturgic miracles, but instead is very down-to-earth. In the *vitae*, first composed by Sulpicius Severus in the fourth century, taken up by Gregory of Tours in the sixth, and then spread further in the thirteenth through the extremely popular *Legenda aurea* of James of Voragine, with the saint's most famous 'miracle' is described thus:

18   Geoffrey Chaucer, *Troilus and Criseyde*, book 5 line 1222.

19   Guillaume le Roux (†1181), fourth master of the order of St Anthony of Vienne, had introduced this crutch-cross as emblem of the order; it was also the ownership sign branded onto the pigs belonging to the order. See Marie-Luise Windemuth, *Das Hospital als Träger der Armenfürsorge im Mittelalter* (Sudhoffs Archiv Beihefte 36) (Stuttgart, 1995), 62.

20   Item cuilibet ... claudum, secum [caecum], vel impotentem, in cubiculo jacentem, xiijs iiijd'. Testament of Sir Richard de Scrop, cited in J. Fowler, 'On a window representing the life and miracles of S. William of York, at the north end of the eastern transept, York Minster', *Yorkshire Archaeological and Topographical Journal*, 3 (1873–1874), 260.

As a young Roman soldier Martin (316/17–397) meets a freezing beggar outside the town walls of Amiens with whom he shares his cloak. During the following night he dreams a vision in which Christ appears robed in the same piece of cloak he had given to the beggar. The insight that charity is the prime Christian virtue became a key experience for Martin. He asked to be baptized and even achieved the bishopric of Tours in 373. The cloak donation came to symbolize charity as such, and Martin's conduct provided the template for episcopal virtue. Martin divides his cloak, a material object, to share with a needy person. The 'miracle' only happens after the main event, namely the vision Martin has later that night in his dream of Christ visiting him with the fragment of robe Martin had given the beggar. The story was originally told purely as a textual narrative, but came to be depicted in art from the central Middle Ages onwards, gaining in popularity as a motif towards the later Middle Ages, especially so north of the Alps, in Germany. The basic visual elements – Martin, horse, sword, cloak and beggar – remained unchanged, but social and religious concepts changed which influenced artistic representation.

The iconography of St Martin and the beggar provides an interesting case study of how attitudes to disability changed in the course of the Middle Ages. The oldest known imagery of Martin's donation dates from the end of the tenth century, in a Benedictine manuscript, the so-called *Fulda Sacramentary*. Here and in the earlier iconographic tradition generally, the beggar shown alongside the saint is physically healthy, even robust and strong, and often the figures of saint and beggar are even drawn the same height (a significant convention in the medieval hierarchy of imagery). In some depictions the symbolism of the cloak donation is emphasized as the act recognized directly by God or Christ, with the additional representation of Martin's dream. During the twelfth and thirteenth centuries the topos of Martin's gift begins to change. The beggar may not yet be depicted as a cripple, but he is shown with caricatured, distorted or ugly facial features. However, from about the first half of the fourteenth century, the figure of the beggar comes to be represented with the physical characteristics of orthopaedic impairment, which becomes so entrenched as an artistic routine that by the fifteenth century in northern European art the beggar is always and only shown thus. Iconographically, the cripple came to symbolize the deserving poor person *per se* – the beggar has become a 'cripple' as well as a symbol. So much for the outline of art historical developments, which arouses questions: Why did this change in iconography take place? And how did changes and developments in medieval society in general influence or reflect the iconography? To answer these questions, one must turn to socio-cultural aspects of medieval notions of disability, poverty and charity.

Here it is important to recognize that definitions of poverty change over time. Poverty is nowadays seen primarily as a consequence of non-work. If ability to work is one of the main themes in disability concerns today, then lack of work resulting in poverty surely validates any discussions of poverty then and now. To examine this assumption, we need to look a little closer at medieval concepts of poverty.

Medieval notions of poverty distinguished between voluntary poverty, which was understood as part of a religious vocation and was praised, and involuntary poverty, which was seen as resulting from a situation of social distress and increasingly came to be despised.[21] The phrase the 'poor of Christ' (*pauperes Christi*), meaning the religious poor, becomes frequent from the eleventh and twelfth centuries onwards.[22] Apostolic poverty was

---

21   However, O. G. Oexle has argued that the contrast between voluntary, religious poverty on the one hand, and involuntary, economic/social poverty on the other hand, has been exaggerated; furthermore poverty had come to be defined through manual labour in the high Middle Ages, so that in the case of St Elisabeth her aspirations to voluntary poverty included the real, involuntary poverty and physical work of the lower orders (O. G. Oexle, 'Armut und Armenfürsorge um 1200. Ein Beitrag zum Verständnis der freiwilligen Armut bei Elisabeth von Thüringen', in *Sankt Elisabeth: Fürstin, Dienerin, Heilige: Aufsätze – Dokumentation – Katalog* (Sigmaringen: Thorbecke, 1981), 78–100, 79 and 92).

22   See Karl Bosl, 'Potens und Pauper. Begriffsgeschichtliche Studien zur gesellschaftlichen Differenzierung im frühen Mittelalter und zum "Pauperismus" des Hochmittelalters', in *Frühformen der Gesellschaft im mittelalterlichen Europa. Ausgewählte Beiträge zu einer Strukturanalyse der mittelalterlichen Welt* (Munich and Vienna: R. Oldenbourg Verlag, 1964), 106–134, 121. On poverty and the mendicant orders in particular, see David Burr, *Olivi and Franciscan Poverty: The Origins of the Usus Pauper Controversy* (Philadelphia, PA: Pennsylvania University Press, 1989); also Hervaeus Natalis, *The Poverty of Christ and the Apostles*, John D. Jones, trans. (MSDT 37) (Toronto: PIMS, 1999).

something to be imitated voluntarily by those people who according to their original status (one may here think of St Francis the wealthy merchant's son) were neither materially poor nor socially powerless. In the recent interpretation by Sharon Farmer, the involuntary, economically poor can be associated with the flesh, while the voluntary, religious poor can be associated with the spirit.[23] Because the involuntary poor, who had not chosen to be poor, resented being in that state and desired change, in particular desired wealth, such desire, even if for just a modicum of possessions and money, endangered the spiritual health of the poor.

According to Thomas Aquinas 'spiritual danger comes from poverty when it is not voluntary, because a man falls into many sins through the desire to get rich, which torments those who are involuntarily poor.'[24] Hence it was argued that it was better to give alms to the voluntary poor, since they did not fall into the sin of cupidity, whereas the involuntary poor were consumed by desire. Already in the fourth century St Jerome had stated it was preferable to give alms to the voluntary poor than the involuntary ones 'among whose rags and bodily filth burning desire has domain.'[25] Being poor was therefore a most problematic state to be in during the high and later Middle Ages, since one's moral condition does not sit well with one's entitlement to charity.

And in economic terms, the crises of the early to mid-fourteenth century, coupled with rising numbers of the poor and beggars, narrowed the amount of charity the rest of society was able/willing to provide; fear of

23 Sharon Farmer, 'Introduction', in Sharon Farmer and Barbara H. Rosenwein, eds, *Monks and Nuns, Saints and Outcasts: Religion in Medieval Society: Essays in Honor of Lester K. Little* (Ithaca, NY and London: Cornell University Press, 2000), 13.

24 Thomas Aquinas, *Summa theologiae*, 2a 2ae, quaest. 186, art. 3, resp. ad 2, Blackfriars, ed. and trans. (Oxford: Oxford University Press, 1973), vol. 47, 108–111, cited by Sharon Farmer, 'Manual Labor, Begging, and Conflicting Gender Expectations in Thirteenth-Century Paris', in S. Farmer and C. B. Pasternack, eds, *Gender and Difference in the Middle Ages* (Medieval Cultures, vol. 32) (Minneapolis: University of Minnesota Press, 2003), 261–287, 273.

25 Jerome, 'Against Vigilantius', 14, in *The Principal Works of St. Jerome*, W. H. Freemantle, trans. (The Nicene and Post-Nicene Fathers, 6) (Grand Rapids, MI: Christian Classics Etherial Publisher, 1954), 422, cited by Farmer, 'Manual Labor', 273.

'fraudulent' beggars became common, and miracle cures of sick or disabled people became subsumed into the discourse of fraud. Stories surrounding fake cures started to circulate, which invalidated the 'real' healing miracles. What worried later medieval people was the fake body, the body that pretends to be one thing but is in fact quite another:[26] the theatrical delusion of the fraudulent beggar's artificially disabled body.

In *Piers Plowman* there were many such deceiving types.[27] Late medieval society accused the poor of fraud, duplicity and faking, assuming that they begged even though they did not have an actual need for it. Begging had to be legitimated through need, and physical impairment could be regarded as one such legitimization. Many depictions of the poor in fifteenth-century art therefore show the 'type' of the disabled, mainly the orthopedically impaired beggar, as we have seen in connection with

26   This is why hermaphrodites are regarded as possessing worrying bodies, because they are positioned outside of the established concepts of male/female, and a male body can turn out to have female characteristics and vice versa. See Irina Metzler, 'Hermaphroditism in the western Middle Ages: Physicians, Lawyers and the Intersexed Person', in S. Crawford and C. Lee, eds, *Bodies of Knowledge: Cultural Interpretations of Illness and Medicine in Medieval Europe* (Studies in Early Medicine, 1) (Oxford: Archaeopress, 2010), 27–39.

27   Geoffrey Shepherd, 'Poverty in Piers Plowman', in T. H. Aston, P. R. Coss, C. Dyer and J. Thirsk, eds, *Social Relations and Ideas: Essays in Honour of R. H. Hilton* (Cambridge: Cambridge University Press, 1983), 169–189, 173. But the character of Piers the ploughman, trying to discern between rightful and fraudulent alms-seekers, learns in the course of 'B' passus VI 'that he is not in a position to determine who is deserving or not ... all beggars ... are answerable to God individually. The onus is on the receiver.' Anne M. Scott, *Piers Plowman and the Poor* (Dublin: Four Courts Press, 2004), 109. On the terminology used of fraudulent beggars, see Kellie Robertson, *Keeping Paradise: Labor and Language in Late Medieval Britain* (Basingstoke: Palgrave Macmillan, 2004). On beggars, vagabonds and other non-settled marginal types in general in England, see D. B. Thomas, ed., *The Book of Vagabonds and Beggars* (London, 1932); J. J. Jusserand, *English Wayfaring Life in the Middle Ages*, Lucy Toulmin Smith, trans. (London: T. Fisher Unwin, 1888); and G. T. Salisbury, *Street Life in Medieval England* (London: n. p., 1939). More general is Jose Cubero, *Histoire du vagabondage du Moyen Age à nos jours* (Paris: Imago, 1998).

St Martin.[28] By the high Middle Ages the notion of indiscriminate charity was becoming refined. High medieval canonical theory tried to make ethical differences: only the 'just', the 'honest' and the 'shameful' poor were to receive charity. In such a way the giving of alms came to be connected more closely with exhortations to make oneself useful[29] – the notion of *utilitas* became more important, as expressed in the New Testament verse 'who does not work shall not eat'.[30] The categorisation of persons according to their ability to work (begging forbidden) or inability (begging allowed) constituted a paradigmatic underpinning of the discourse pertaining to concepts of deserving and undeserving poor.[31] In short, to that degree by which the value of work increased, the status of beggars decreased ('In dem Maße, wie der Wert der Arbeit stieg, sank das Ansehen der Bettler').[32] Disability thus legitimized need and impairment and could become loaded with certain cultural values. In this case possession of a physical impairment established a certain right, the right to legitimate receipt of charity.

In the twelfth century the corpus of papal laws and decrees known as *Decretals* included a passage that prohibited the giving of alms to 'followers of infamous professions'.[33] The *Glossa ordinaria*, another canon law text and basic commentary on the *Decretum*, 'cautioned against one who can

28   Others have also observed this trend. Jütte argues that in the sixteenth century the
      pauper 'was no longer characterized by physical deformities but was designated by
      begging gesture and a pathetic condition. This change reflects a new attitude to the
      poor. It was no longer a physical handicap that denoted a beggar, but something less
      concrete, less tangible: a gesture, a way of behaving, in short the physical and moral
      condition.' Robert Jütte, *Poverty and Deviance in Early Modern Europe* (Cambridge:
      Cambridge University Press, 1994), 14.

29   Arnold Angenendt, *Religiosität im Mittelalter* (Darmstadt: Primus, 1997), 595.

30   2 Thess. 3:10.

31   On poverty and the increased value placed on work see K. Bosl, 'Armut, Arbeit,
      Emanzipation', in *Beiträge zur Wirtschafts- und Sozialgeschichte des Mittelalters.
      Festschrift für Herbert Helbig* (Cologne and Vienna: Böhlau, 1976), 128 ff.

32   Frank Meier, *Gaukler, Dirnen, Rattenfänger. Außenseiter im Mittelalter* (Ostfildern:
      Jan Thorbecke, 2005), 39.

33   Quote in Jütte, *Poverty and Deviance*, 159, citing Brian Tierney, 'The decretist and the
      deserving poor', *Comparative Studies in Society and History*, 1 (1958/1959), 363–364.
      The 'unlawful professions' are derived from Augustine, in *Decretum magistri Gratiani*,

work and earn his bread and chooses not to, but rather 'plays all day long with dies and cubes' (Set hic intelligitur in eo casu cum quis potest laborare et suo labore sibi victum querere et non vult, set tota die ludit, in alea vel taxilis).[34] Teutonicus, a contributor to the *Glossa*, stated that 'the Church need not provide for those who can work. One must take into account wholeness of body (*integritas membrorum*) and strength of constitution (*robur membrorum*) when alms are dispensed' (Et qui potest laborare, non debet ecclesia providere. Integritas membrorum enim et robur membrorum in conferenda elemosyna est attenda).[35]

One crucial aspect of disability therefore revolves around the issue of work. An indicator of 'disability' in our society can be observed in the relationship between an individual's impairment and the degree to which that individual is deemed incapable of earning their living. In some ways this relationship forms the main definition of 'disabled' in modern western society, as has been pointed out in Herzlich and Pierret's study of illness and social attitudes:

> In a society in which we define ourselves as producers, illness and inactivity have become equivalents. That is why today we have come to perceive the sick body essentially through its incapacity to 'perform', rather than through the alteration of its appearance.[36]

With regard to work, then, one's ability or in/dis-ability to perform work of all kinds has become the measuring stick by which charity (in the later Middle Ages and early modern period) or welfare state benefits (in contemporary society) have been allocated. Being able to 'perform' in society has become crucial.

We can observe this in present-day Britain, where a conservative government is pressing for changes to health and social security benefits, and

---

in *Corpus Iuris Canonici I*, E. Friedberg, ed. (Leipzig, 1877), D.86 cc.7–9, 14–18; also see Rubin, *Charity and Community*, 69.

34   Cited in Rubin, *Charity and Community*, 69, from the *Glossa ordinaria ad* C.5.q.5.C.2.

35   Cited in Rubin, *Charity and Community*, 69., *Glossa ordinaria ad* D.82 ante C.1

36   C. Herzlich and J. Pierret, *Illness and Self in Society*, E. Forster, trans. (Baltimore, MD: Johns Hopkins University Press, 1987), 85.

placing greater emphasis on 'means-testing', arguing that spiralling welfare costs mean support will still be provided but that people need to be properly entitled to such support. As the late Umberto Eco so succinctly put it: We are still living in the Middle Ages.[37] Culturally, we are heavily influenced by the endurance of medieval inventions and institutions, such as universities, banks, loans and credit, hospitals, charitable aid, the value of work and so forth, not to mention books, buttons, or spectacles.[38] The adjective 'medieval', so often used in a pejorative sense by modern commentators, should in many ways be more appreciated, not just because it is written here by a medievalist, but because so many elements of our contemporary cultural norms and attitudes are carry-overs from the Middle Ages, albeit generally unrecognized for what they are. Substitute the modern term benefits for the medieval word charity, or claimant for beggar, and the modern continuity with the medieval approach to poverty, charity and disability becomes apparent.

Let me now turn to the second of the themes of this essay, the question of mobility. Why was there (apparently) no wheelchair in the Middle Ages? What sparse scholarship there is on the history of the wheelchair mentions the wheelbarrow as an early form of mobility aid. Supposedly wheelchairs as we know them were not in evidence before the sixteenth century, when small rollers or wheels were added to normal household furniture such as upholstered chairs. These were then primarily intended for easier movement of the piece of furniture rather than of the person.[39]

However, an intriguing device is mentioned in connection with one of the popes, Honorius IV (d. 1287) who had severe gout and was already very old when he came to office. He could only celebrate mass with the aid of a special chair made for him, which contemporary accounts describe thus:

37   See the seminal essay by the late Umberto Eco on concepts of the Middle Ages in popular and academic culture in contemporary Western society, 'Dreaming of the Middle Ages', in *Travels in Hyperreality*, W. Weaver, trans. (London: Harvest, 1987), 61–72.

38   An allusion to Chiara Frugoni, *Books, Banks, Buttons and Other Inventions of the Middle Ages*, William McCuaig, trans. (New York: Columbia University Press, 2003).

39   Herman L. Kamenetz, 'A Brief History of the Wheelchair', *Journal of the History of Medicine and Allied Sciences*, 24 (1969) 205–210.

'the gouty sickness had taken away almost all the bones of his feet and hands; whence he was sitting in a chair, which was artificed thus that he solemnly celebrated the Mass.' (Cui pedum ac manuum fere ossa abstulerat artetica aegritudo; unde sedendo in sella, ad hoc artificiose facta missarum solemnia celebravit).[40] Some scholars are of the opinion that this sounds very much like a modern Zimmer frame, but, since a Zimmer frame is nothing like a chair, and does not allow the user to sit down, this is unlikely.[41] Rather, I think this is the closest candidate we have for a medieval wheelchair, since a wheeled chair, with its fluid movement, would have allowed Honorius IV to be moved around appropriately for the solemn rites (*solemnia*) during Mass. Constructing a wheelchair in something like the modern form would certainly not have been beyond the technical capacity of the later thirteenth century, hence the question arises of why such chairs were apparently not made in greater numbers. The answer must lie with suitability and infra-structure. Wheelchairs of the modern variety require a flat, level surface to be practical. In the absence of such surfaces in the rutted streets, tracks and uneven roads of medieval Europe, a wheelchair would have been no use. The interior of St Peter's in Rome, where Honorius IV officiated, would of course have had level paving, but outside of this edifice even he must have relied on other mobility aids.

That technically a wheel(ed) chair was possible can be demonstrated from examples of similar, but not identical, medieval contraptions. In the *miracula* of St William, an impaired girl was brought to Norwich by her father 'in a wheeled vehicle of the kind called a litter (civière)' (in uehiculo rotatili aduehitur, quod ciueriam appellant), and on the same day her miracle cure occurred, a lame boy was brought by his father 'also in a litter with wheels' (itidem in ciueria aduehitur rotatili).[42] The fact that the *miracula*

---

40 Willelmi Rishanger, quondam monachi S. Albani ... Chronica et Annales, A.D. 1259–1307, *Rolls Series*, 28 (London, 1865), 109.

41 Peter Linehan, *The Ladies of Zamora* (Manchester: Manchester University Press, 1997), 1.

42 *The Life and Miracles of St William of Norwich by Thomas of Monmouth*, A. Jessop and M. R. James, eds and trans (Cambridge: Cambridge University Press, 1896), miracle VII.xvi. 'Civière' in modern French can mean a stretcher, litter or wheelbarrow in

text specifies wheels on the litters means these were not the regular litters, carried by two men, which begs the question: what exactly were they?

One possibility is suggested from artistic sources. A variable range of mobility aids is depicted in a series of paintings associated with the stories of hermits in the Thebaid, set during the time of the early church but depicted according to the dress, surroundings etc. of the artists' own later medieval times. These show varieties of a 'wheeled chair' as used by hermit saints. One such painting by Grifo di Tancredi, made c.1280–1290, depicts 'Scenes of the Lives of the Hermits'. It is part of a triptych with hermits in the centre, while the wings contain scenes from the Passion of Christ. In the centre of this panel is shown a hermit with a halo, sat in a wheeled chair made of wicker, the wheels of wood with spokes; and towards the lower left is the depiction of another hermit with a halo carried by two able-bodied hermits in a chair placed on a litter. On a panel painting of the Florentine School, the 'Death of St Ephraim and Other Scenes from the Lives of the Hermits', made anonymously c.1480–1500, one may observe several depictions of hermits seated in wheelbarrows, who are pushed by another hermit behind each barrow, and one elderly hermit who is sitting in a wheeled cart pulled by a lion.[43]

A further device resembling a modern-day armchair made out of wicker and fitted with two large wheels can be seen in a panel painting of about 1410 made by Gherardo Starnina, possibly for a predella, depicting more hermits.[44] An elderly hermit is seated in this chair, reading, while he is being pulled along by an animal harnessed to his vehicle. The overall scene may be highly imaginary, but since many other realistic elements are depicted, such as another hermit transported in the more conventional

---

English. The fluidity of the term implies that it was perhaps not the most common word, and that Thomas of Monmouth, author of the *St William* narrative, as well as his nineteenth-century editors, were struggling to describe the device used as mobility aid.

43 Both of these paintings are exhibited in the National Gallery of Scotland, Edinburgh.

44 *Thebaid*, by Gherardo Starnina, now in Florence, Uffizi Gallery. A predella is the platform or step on which an altar stands (*predel or *pretel, Langobardic for 'a low wooden platform that serves as a basis in a piece of furniture'). In painting, the predella is the painting or sculpture along the frame at the bottom of an altarpiece.

wheelbarrow, or two more hermits carried in litters resembling the canvas stretchers used today by ambulance crews, the little wicker wheel(ed) chair is a distinct possibility.

This brief survey of modes of transport demonstrates the differing types of mobility experienced by medieval disabled people. Undoubtedly social status and economic position was reflected in the mode of transport, so that those lower down the scale were more likely to use the cheaper alternative of being carried by a relative or friend, while those with more material means had access to horse-drawn vehicles or servants who could take them to places, mainly shrines, and wheel(ed) chairs were the prerogative of a select few. The wide variety of transportation also shows how people tried to make do according to their circumstances. In the Middle Ages, before the confirmed invention of the wheelchair, mobility of the disabled was not necessarily curtailed or restricted, but relied on improvisation, making the most use of already existing transportation methods – the ubiquitous crutches, carts, baskets and handbarrows – and adapting them for the specific needs of the impaired.

Finally, with regard to mobility I wish to debunk the assumption that guide dogs for the blind were an innovation or the preferred means of assistance in medieval times. Medieval literature and art describe a number of episodes concerning the interaction between blind people and their guide dogs. The elusive hunt for medieval guide dogs for the blind has turned up a few isolated textual references and a couple of images. It seems in the hierarchy of mobility aids, from sighted adult guide, via child guide to dog, guide dogs were regarded as a last resort, because of their unreliability – they are literally mis-leading the blind. Art historian Moshe Barasch cited an early fourteenth-century marginal image in a Flemish manuscript, of a blind man with his staff being 'led' on a rope by a dog who is additionally holding the man's begging bowl in its muzzle, as an example of this presumption in favour of guide dogs.[45] Against Barasch, I am inclined to regard this dog simply as

---

45   Moshe Barasch, *Blindness: The History of a Mental Image in Western Thought* (New York and London: Routledge, 2001), 100, referring to *Psalter-Hours*, c.1315–1325, made in the region of Ghent, now in the Baltimore, Walters Art Museum, MS 82, fol. 207r. The fifteenth-century wing of an altar from the workshop of Johann

a 'companion animal' or pet in the modern sense, and not in any way as a trained guide dog, since the blind man navigates primarily by use of his staff. The dog is jumping away and dragging the unfortunate blind man with him, which is turning this visual mini-story into a tragi-comic episode.

Two elderly blind men on other fifteenth-century images also appear to have companion animals rather than guide dogs (one also holding a begging bowl for his master).[46] Where dogs do appear in conjunction with blind people, they are always depicted in images and described in texts as additional to the stick or cane – no blind person has just a dog to guide them. Dogs for the blind seem to have been better at holding the begging bowl than at guiding.

Bartholomew the Englishman, working in the 1240s, wrote what would become the first encyclopaedia in the modern sense, including listing items in alphabetical order to make it easier to locate entries. On blindness he had this to say:

> Among all the sufferings and evils affecting sense perception, blindness is the worst. Without any actual bond, blindness is a prison to the blind. ... The blind man's wretchedness is so much that it makes him not only subject to a child, or to a servant, for ruling and leading, but also to a hound. The blind person is often brought

---

Koerbecke, *Legend of St Leonard*, depicts a kneeling blind man who holds a small dog by the leash, while a second blind man, possibly representing blind Lucillus from the *Legenda aurea*, is guided to this scene (cf. exh. cat. *Westfälische Maler der Spätgotik 1440–1490*, Landesmuseum Münster, 1952, no. 102 and plate 26); and in the *Bible of Jaromér* (see Bohatec, *Schöne Bücher*, Prague, National Museum, XII A 10, fig. 112) of second half of the thirteenth-century date, where we finds the depiction of a blind man with his staff but also holding a dog on a long leash 'der sicher als Blindenhund gedient hat.' (See Georg Wacha, 'Tiere und Tierhaltung in der Stadt sowie im Wohnbereich des spätmittelalterlichen Menschen und ihre Darstellung in der bildenden Kunst', in *Das Leben in der Stadt des Spätmittelalters* (Vienna: Veröffentlichungen des Instituts für mittelalterliche Realienkunde Österreichs Nr. 2, 1977), 229–260, 243.

46 The first painting is by the Sienese school, Master of the Osservanza, made in the second quarter of the fifteenth century, now in Washington, National Gallery of Art; the blind old man accompanied by his dog holding his begging bowl is a detail of 'Procession', workshop of Rogier van der Weyden, c.1440, British Museum, Department of Prints and Drawings.

to such great need, that to pass over and escape the peril of a bridge or of a ford, he is compelled to trust in a hound more than in himself.[47]

The reason generally given is that dogs (and children) are too readily distracted, so that if a dog, who is meant to be guiding a blind person, sees a bone, the dog will drag the blind person with him into the mud. Hence the dog, mis-guiding the blind man (pilgrim or beggar) in the manuscript known as the *Smithfield Decretals*,[48] is actually a fox: the arch-trickster. The elusive guide dog for the blind in the Middle Ages can be regarded as an example of the medieval non-individuated approach to disability in contrast to modern times. Human guides are preferred to dogs since the medieval guide dog is literally mis-leading. The change may have come about in the late nineteenth century as a consequence of the introduction of universal schooling, which resulted in drying up of the former pool of child labourers available as guides for the blind. Structured training of guide dogs for the blind only happened after World War One.[49]

In summary one may note the medieval variability of labelling for 'disability' and the disabled. The changing notions of poverty from the early to the later Middle Ages demonstrate that inability to work becomes a key indicator of both poverty and disability, and that mobility is a further key indicator. Finally that while mobility today is individualized and technologized, in contrast mobility in the past relied more on people than animals.

---

47   Robert Steele, ed., *Medieval Lore: An Epitome of the Science, Geography, Animal and Plant Folk-Lore and Myth of the Middle Age: Being Classified Gleanings from the Encyclopedia of Bartholomew Anglicus on the Properties of Things* (London: Elliot Stock, 1893), Book VII, ch. xx, 58–59; See Barasch, *Blindness*, 100. Barasch follows Gudrun Schleusener-Eichholz, *Das Auge im Mittelalter*, PhD diss., University of Münster, 1975, 2 vols (Munich: W. Fink, 1984), I, 508; Dietrich Schmidtke, *Geistliche Tierinterpretationen in der deutschsprachigen Literatur des Mittelalters (1100–1500)* (Berlin, 1968), 318.

48   Marginal illumination, *Smithfield Decretals*, British Library MS Royal 10 E.iv, fol. 110r, made c. 1330 at Toulouse and London.

49   See the work on guide dogs for German veterans by Monica Baar, 'Prosthesis for the Body and for the Soul: The Origins of Guide Dog Provision in Interwar Germany', *First World War Studies* (in press, 2015).

ADLEEN CRAPO

The Possibility of an Island: Colonialism, Embodiment and Utopia in Pre-Modern Literature

ABSTRACT

This essay considers the implications of disabled bodies in colonized spaces by juxtaposing the work of Teresa of Cartagena with Shakespeare's *Tempest*. The essay demonstrates that the disabled body insistently gestures to the need for utopian spaces. In her treatises *The Grove of the Infirm* and *Admiración Operum Dei*, Teresa of Cartagena, a disabled nun, created a discursive space for herself, a cloister within a cloister. Though her identity as a *conversa* posed a threat to nascent ideas of Spanishness, or Hispanitas, her allegorical grove enabled artistic creation for those left out of the body politic. In contrast, the character of Caliban in *The Tempest* reminds readers of the utopia which the island was before contact. It is only to Europeans that Caliban is a monster, the product of an insalubrious island. Although colonialism can prove a disabling force, the response of disabled people can also underline the utopias possible in both memory and creation.

The pre-modern depictions of disability discussed in this essay involve a utopian space, one that only comes into existence in response to both ableist and colonial discourses. In the *Grove of the Infirm* and the subsequent *Admiration of the Works of God*, works of life-writing by the deaf medieval nun Teresa de Cartagena, she devises a utopian island or *ínsula* for her and other disabled thinkers, rendering it a *locus amoenus* for disabled female creativity.[1] As Cartagena was a *conversa*, or descendant of Jewish converts to Christianity, she remained outside the accepted ideal of Spanish Gentile Christianity. Part of her literary project included forging a rhetorical space

---

1   Dayle Seidenspinner-Núñez, *The Writings of Teresa de Cartagena: Translated with Introduction, Notes, and Interpretive Essay* (Cambridge: D. S. Brewer, 1998).

for those whose heritage and bodies foreclosed their access to the Spanish cultural mainstream. In this essay I juxtapose Cartagena's writing with the depiction of Caliban from *The Tempest*, whose role as the play's deformed and racialized Other has been the object of much critical scrutiny. What has not yet been considered alongside Caliban's experience of race and deformity is his evocation of the utopian island space he inhabited pre-contact. This essay will explore the relationship of disability to utopian spaces in both metropole and periphery.[2] By comparing Teresa de Cartagena's medieval Spanish text with Shakespeare's later intervention, and Cartagena's hoped-for future utopia with Caliban's nostalgic past, I will demonstrate that disabled bodies insistently evoke, require, and cry out for utopian spaces of creation and spaces of plenty.[3]

Teresa of Cartagena was one of Spain's earliest-known women writers. Born in 1425, her family were prominent *conversos* or Jewish converts to Christianity, having produced two high-ranking churchmen and a guard de corps for Juan II.[4] Significantly, Dayle Seidenspinner-Núñez notes that 'while the Cartagenas were active agents of history, they were more importantly *writers* of history [...].'[5] Sometime after joining her convent, Cartagena lost her hearing during a prolonged illness. She subsequently used this experience as the basis for an autobiographical and consolatory treatise on her deafness, *Arboleda de los enfermos*, or *Grove of the Infirm*.

Teresa de Cartagena was thus marginalized three times over 'by her gender, by her deafness, and by her status as a *conversa*'[6] as she was writing around the time of the *converso* Toledo uprising of 1449, when non-Gentiles were met with suspicion. At a moment when Spain's burgeoning national project was beginning to require *limpieza de sangre* of its subjects,

---

2   Although the terms 'metropole' and 'periphery' are anachronistic, they remain suited to the texts' respective cultural contexts: Cartagena's convent in Burgos, the ancient capital of the Spanish heartland, and Caliban's faraway island, inspired by accounts of Bermuda.

3   This essay complements Silvia Federici's *Caliban and the Witch*, a feminist work on the history of the female body in the context of early modern capitalism.

4   Seidenspinner-Núñez, *The Writings of Teresa de Cartagena*, 5.

5   Seidenspinner-Núñez, *The Writings of Teresa de Cartagena*, 7.

6   Seidenspinner-Núñez, *The Writings of Teresa de Cartagena*, 3.

or proof of one's purely Christian (and not Jewish, or Moorish descent), Cartagena's body represented an internal threat to nascent and soon-to-be hegemonic ideas of Hispanitas, or Spanish identity. It would be erroneous to assume that the cloister served as a kind of female and utopian space for Cartagena; in fact, she repeatedly demonstrates that the cloister is in fact far from idealized depictions of monastic living. In the *Arboleda de los enfermos*, Cartagena underlines this inadequacy by focusing on the evils of idleness and feminine gossip which beset her convent. The benefit of writing her autobiographical treatise is largely 'avoiding solitude and idleness'.[7] Later, she declares her desire to 'make war on idleness, occupying [herself] in this small work [...]'.Anticipating anxieties about idle disability, Cartagena eagerly refutes the idea that the invalid knows only rest. In fact, the truth is the contrary, that 'the invalid is always busy in worthy and secret labors, hidden without doubt from all human praise'.[8] The work of an invalid is more intensive than 'a worker who keeps his hand to the hoe from morning to night'.[9]

The theme of the active, invalid life continues in the second treatise, the *Admiración Operum Dei*. The feminine nature of idleness renders it especially dangerous for women in convents, but a deaf woman writer like Cartagena can avoid its traps. While she does emphasize the dichotomy between masculinity and femininity, noting that 'males are strong and valiant and of great spirit and daring and of more perfect and sound understanding and women, to the contrary, are weak and cowardly, faint hearted and fearful'[10] a further examination of her embodied metaphors shows how a disabled woman can avoid such traps. Cartagena's repeated discussions of disability, in contrast to her reliance on traditional gender norms, demonstrate the anxiety underlying the text: it is not (and she herself realizes this) that physical impairments have disabled her, rather, it is being a woman that constrains her. The body from which she longs to escape is hampered, not by the impairment of chronic illness or deafness. Rather,

---

7   Seidenspinner-Núñez, *The Writings of Teresa de Cartagena*, 25.
8   Seidenspinner-Núñez, *The Writings of Teresa de Cartagena*, 61–62.
9   Seidenspinner-Núñez, *The Writings of Teresa de Cartagena*, 62.
10   Seidenspinner-Núñez, *The Writings of Teresa de Cartagena*, 91–92.

it is gender roles that have her truly confined, and in need of carving out a new space for creation. This space is one which she must herself fashion, through a recurring set of alternative locations. She does so, as the critic Victoria Rivera-Cordero describes, by the use of embodied metaphors:

> [Deafness] triggers her writing and she renders it visible by metaphorically 'giving body' to it. In *Arboleda* Cartagena narrates her own perception of the world through the deafness that modifies the space in which she is inscribed. Yet, her deafness also allows her to create a substitute world.[11]

From the discussion of illness in general, from which she draws her authority, Cartagena passes to a detailed and precise depiction of disability. The ailments she describes 'goad us with their spurs, making us run along the narrow path [...]. Although it may seem that the afflicted stays still at home, he traverses more roads than we think and, even bedridden, in the grip of a fever or some other painful affliction, he walks more, I believe, than a fifty-day journey'.[12] Cartagena delineates her own particular and subjective experience by claiming that 'the painful spurs of my great suffering have forced me, to my dismay, to travel more day-journeys than from here to Rome'.[13] Though Cartagena mentions Rome, a frequent site of medieval pilgrimages, in fact she is going someplace further and more necessary, her *ínsula*, or utopic island.

Although Rivera-Cordero also notes that Cartagena's *Grove* describes the creation of a *locus amoenus*, she neglects to discuss the importance of work in this utopia. For Cartagena, as I have demonstrated, utopia is filled with important work, not idleness. In the heart of an increasingly homogenous Castile, Cartagena creates a utopia through her account of deafness by going into the deepest cloister possible. By figuring disability as a pilgrimage that brings similar benefits as a trip to Rome, Cartagena is able to recreate an idea of disability as an active state. More importantly, by

11   Victoria Rivera-Cordero, 'Spatializing Illness: Deafness in Teresa of Cartagena's *Arboleda de los enfermos*,' *La corónica: A Journal of Medieval Hispanic Languages, Literatures, and Cultures*, 37/2 (2009), 61–77, 68.

12   Seidenspinner-Núñez, *The Writings of Teresa de Cartagena*, 53.

13   Seidenspinner-Núñez, *The Writings of Teresa de Cartagena*, 55.

choosing to portray disability as a spiritual and Christian undertaking, she renders a public action sanitized and appropriate for a *conversa*. Although Cartagena's deafness (and her cloistered status) would make physical pilgrimage exceedingly difficult, through writing she can reclaim the experience of deafness and re-cast it, avoiding enforced and non-generative idleness. In both the *Arboleda* and the *Operum*, Cartagena manoeuvres between the various impairments that could have kept her from writing and sharing her efforts publicly. She anticipates a utopian state that is one of true cloistering, in which disability allows a kind of productiveness and creativity foreclosed to those who are not typically thought fit for active pursuits, such as *conversas*.

In contrast to Cartagena, Shakespeare's *The Tempest* evokes another aspect of disabled utopian creation.[14] Though Shakespeare's text belongs to a different genre, Caliban's focus on a *locus amoenus* of the past allows for a similar vision of a utopian and disabled space, one that existed before the Eurocolonial project came to disrupt it. Prospero's abject slave remembers and recreates verbally for European colonizers the ideal island of the past when his mother, Sycorax, ruled. The reader experiences Caliban entirely through the eyes of the European characters who meet him with disgust, such as Prospero: he describes Caliban as 'this mis-shapen knave'.[15] Caliban's moral failures link up very clearly with his appearance, or at least they do for his European masters. As Prospero condemns Caliban: 'He is as disproportioned in his manners / As in his shape'.[16]

The Europeans who meet Caliban in Act 2, Scene 2 demonstrate a change in attitudes to race and embodiment. Whereas Cartagena and her contemporary *conversos* would not always have been seen as inhabiting strictly 'Jewish' bodies, by the time of the early modern period, once-confused or indistinct ideas of race and embodiment were beginning to

14   William Shakespeare, *The Tempest* (New York: Signet., 2005).
15   Shakespeare, *Tempest*, 5.1.268.
16   Shakespeare, *Tempest*, 5.1.291. Until recently, most contemporary disability theorists such as Lennard J. Davis insisted that the early modern period focused mainly on deformity and its implications of moral turpitude; what *The Tempest* demonstrates is that this idea was operative in colonial contexts, and not necessarily for everyone.

calcify.[17] Moreover, Stephano always discusses both Caliban's heritage and his monstrousness in the same breath, implying his conflation of the two concepts:

> ... Have we devils here? Do you put tricks upon's with savages and men of Ind, ha?
> I have not 'scaped drowning to be afeard now of your
> four legs. Or it hath been said, 'As proper a man as
> ever went on four legs cannot make him give ground,'
> and it shall be said so again while Stephano
> breathes at' nostrils.[18]

The monstrosity of Caliban's body derives from his presentation through European eyes: to intruders, on a strange island, the foreign body cannot be comprehended and reads as 'deformed'.

In the same breath, Stephano declares:

> ... I will give him some
> relief, if it be but for that. If I can recover him
> and keep him tame and get to Naples with him, he's a
> present for any emperor that ever trod on neat's leather.[19]

Stephano's suggestions reflect a hyperawareness of early modern practices with indigenous bodies, in which 'monstrous' indigenous people were taken to Europe to be looked at and objectified in court. It has been well-documented that continental royal ceremonies, for example, often revolved around the display of Amerindigene bodies in *tableaux vivants*.[20] The economic benefits would be enormous: 'I will / Not take too much for him. He shall pay for him that / Hath him, and that soundly'.[21] Trinculo's musings seem to veer in a similar direction:

17   See the works of Ania Loomba on Race and Colonialism for more on this subject.

18   Shakespeare, *Tempest*, 2.2.57–63.

19   Shakespeare, *Tempest*, 2.2.65–70.

20   For more on ceremonial entries featuring indigenous bodies, please see Richard Cooper's essay 'The Theme of War in French Renaissance Entries', in J. R. Mulryne, Maria Ines Aliverti, Anna-Maria Testaverde, eds, *Ceremonial Entries in Early Modern Europe: The Iconography of Power* (London: Routledge, 2015).

21   Shakespeare, *Tempest*, 2.2 75–77.

> Were I in England now,
> As once I was, and had but this fish painted,
> Not a holiday fool there but would give a piece
> Of silver: there would this monster make a
> Man; any strange beast there makes a man:
> When they will not give a doit to relieve a lame
> Beggar, they will lazy out ten to see a dead
> Indian.[22]

Trinculo's statement appears ambiguous. Does Caliban incarnate the lame beggar stereotype? He could also (like many indigenous people taken back to Europe) eventually fit the description of a 'dead Indian' since the Northern European climate and disease did not spare Amerindigenes removed from their homes. What both Europeans' discussions above have in common is their collapse of the categories of disability and race, as well as a desire to take Caliban out of the context of the island, to make him the object of other Europeans' stares. However, neither realizes that the process of colonialism has already rendered Caliban out of context, even in his birthplace.

The Europeans' descriptions of Caliban's bodily malaise call back to his relationship with the island and his physical environment and serve a similar ideological purpose. Stephano's description of Caliban as '[s]ome monster of the isle with four legs, who / Hath got, as I take it, an ague'[23] implies not only that Caliban has a tremor, which would lend itself to spectacular displays, but also that he suffers from a malarial illness.[24] The reference to Caliban's being 'in his fit now', which reinforces the implication of malaria, also implies a deeper connection between his body and his physical environment. Caliban understands between body and environment when he 'calls down upon Prospero 'all the infections that the sun sucks up / From bogs, fens, flats',[25] since, as Heninger notes, '[e]vaporations from

22 Shakespeare, *Tempest*, 2.2.27–33.
23 Shakespeare, *Tempest*, 2.2.66–67.
24 'ague, n.' *OED Online* (Oxford: Oxford University Press), September 2015. Web: 12 October 2015.
25 Shakespeare, *Tempest*, 2.2.1–2.

fens were thought to incorporate the infectious qualities inherent in such places, so that Caliban means precisely what he says'.[26] Trinculo's summation of Caliban's appearance, that he is 'legged like a man and / His fins like arms'[27] ends in the conclusion that Caliban is 'an islander, that hath lately suffered by a thunderbolt'.[28] Heninger notes that 'lightning was thought to have immediate and violent effects on men. It was dangerous to some extent if seen only at a distance' such that some early moderns described the effects a 'face [that] swelleth', for some, while others 'become lepers'.[29] Caliban's European beholders agree that the environment of the island must have produced him through its meteorological effects. Caliban also subscribes to the idea that the environment can deform a body, and wishes this misfortune on Prospero – clearly it is in reaction to his natural environment that Caliban has become who he is. But perhaps this is a meteorological misinterpretation as well. In fact, though Caliban is shown to have a close relationship with the island's physical environment, and although his body seems to be made for and by it, perhaps it isn't the island that has 'disabled' him.

Prospero's earlier condemnation of Ferdinand highlights quite baldly how the European arrival has effectively deformed Caliban. Prospero tells Miranda that Ferdinand is in fact deeply ugly, and that her inexperience with the wider world has misled her: 'To the most of men this is a Caliban / And they to him are angels'.[30] Prospero's meaning is clear, however, his statement holds important and unintended racial implications: much like disability, beauty exists on a continuum and people are thought more beautiful or less beautiful with reference to others' looks. On an island of inhabited by spirits, where he is the sole enfleshed creature, why would Caliban be thought ugly? If no Europeans existed to decree his speech corrupt, to

26   S. K. Heninger Jnr, *A Handbook of Renaissance Meteorology: With Particular Reference to Elizabethan and Jacobean Literature* (Durham, NC: Duke University Press, 1960), 39.

27   Shakespeare, *Tempest*, 2.2.33–34.

28   Shakespeare, *Tempest*, 2.2.36.

29   S. K. Heninger Jnr, *A Handbook of Renaissance Meteorology*, 79.

30   Shakespeare, *Tempest*, 1.2.481–482.

teach him to curse, to criticize the way he moves or to enslave him, Caliban would simply continue his life as before. He portrays his prior existence as being one in which he has no disability, on the contrary, he is uniquely able to benefit from all of the island's bounty.

This impression of physical and natural harmony and abundance is clear in Caliban's evocations of the island and the contrast in his pre- and post-contact lives:

> ... When thou camest first,
> Thou strokedst me and madest much of me, wouldst give me
> Water with berries in't, and teach me how
> To name the bigger light, and how the less,
> That burn by day and night: and then I loved thee
> And show'd thee all the qualities o' the isle,
> The fresh springs, brine-pits, barren place and fertile:
> Cursed be I that did so [...]
> For I am all the subjects that you have,
> Which first was mine own king: and here you sty me
> In this hard rock, whiles you do keep from me
> The rest o' the island.[31]

This description gestures to both his past bucolic ease and Prospero's present-day tyranny, echoing the rhetoric of both pastoral poetry and utopian political theory.

Caliban's evocation of the past can be subtler, such as in Act 2, Scene 2, where he declares to Trinculo his interest in taking on a new European master and offers to 'show thee the best springs; I'll pluck thee berries; / I'll fish for thee and get thee wood enough'.[32] The land described, much like Bermuda on which *The Tempest* is thought to be set, seems to have plenty even by the most avaricious standards. Caliban implores his interlocutors:

> ... let me bring thee where crabs grow;
> And I with my long nails will dig thee pignuts;
> Show thee a jay's nest and instruct thee how

31 Shakespeare, *Tempest*, 1.2.332–344.
32 Shakespeare, *Tempest*, 2.2.160–161.

To snare the nimble marmoset; I'll bring thee
To clustering filberts and sometimes I'll get thee
Young scamels from the rock. Wilt thou go with me.[33]

The space is one of sufficiency: unlike the grasping power plays of Europeans
Alonso, Antonio, and Prospero, which speak to a kind of scarcity mentality, on the island there is *enough*, even for a second (albeit small) group of
European newcomers. Clearly, Caliban knows and fully enjoys the island.
His unusual way of walking hardly impinges on his ability to explore and
benefit from it all has to offer. The *locus amoenus* Caliban describes predates
the arrival of Prospero, whom he calls a 'tyrant', and has ceased to exist.

Caliban's situation on the island, compared to his nostalgic evocations
of Edenic past, call attention to his plight as an indigene that has suddenly
been made to be out of place, animalistic, a potential spectacle, a freak. The
monstrousness of his body also has potential, however, as theorists such as
Laura Knoppers and Joan Landes have noted:

> As portent signifying divine wrath and imminent catastrophe, monsters evoked
> horror: they were *contra naturam*, violations of both the natural and the moral orders.
> As marvels, they elicited wondering pleasure; they were praeter naturam, rare, but
> not menacing, reflecting an aesthetic of variety and ingenuity in nature as well as
> in art. As deformities or natural errors, monsters inspired repugnance: they were
> neither ominous nor admirable but regrettable, the occasional price to be paid for
> the very simplicity and regularity in nature from which they shockingly deviated.[34]

If we take a pre-modern reading of this variable pre-modern body, what
kind of message does Caliban's body send us? When placed back into the
context of his island, without the European interlopers, he enjoys pastoral
ease, occupying his time not in slavery, but in living off of what he can gather
in his explorations. Early modern Europeans often felt, in their encounters
with the new world and its inhabitants, that the people they were seeing

---

33   Shakespeare, *Tempest*, 2.2.167–172.
34   Laura L. Knoppers and Joan B. Landes. *Monstrous Bodies/Political Monstrosities in
      Early Modern Europe* (Ithaca, NY: Cornell University Press, 2004), 11.

were contemporary ancestors,[35] or examples of Europeans in a pre-lapsarian context. European political theory of the time often depended on evocations of Eden, the fall, and possible solutions to humanity's post-lapsarian issues. As I have demonstrated, it becomes apparent that, although his creator is a European man, Caliban's body and his words evoke an earlier time on the island, a kind of utopia where there was self-sufficiency without the artificial disability of ugliness, or of walking on all fours. More importantly, it gestures at two of the most pronounced problems of eurotyranny: the fact that colonialism renders indigenous people out of context in their own countries, and the scarcity mentality which drives colonialism ever onwards.

The relationship of disabled body and space comes across quite clearly in these pre-modern texts. By focusing on the depictions of racialized and disabled Others, it becomes apparent the extent to which the European colonial project worked as a disabling force. However, it is also in the depictions of impaired pre-modern bodies that the possibilities of different spaces become apparent. Although Eurocolonialism and nationalism made the existence of racialized Others dangerous, narrow, and difficult, a consideration of disabled bodies also allows us to conceive of pre-modern utopian spaces in which there is both creation and plenty.

35   Mary Nyquist, 'Contemporary Ancestors of de Bry, Hobbes, and Milton', *University of Toronto Quarterly*, 77/3 (2008), 837–875, 837.

EMILE BOJESEN

'This so low a purpose': Richard Mulcaster and the Aims of Public Education in Sixteenth-Century England

ABSTRACT

This chapter briefly explores an example of what Norbert Elias calls the 'civilizing process' in grammar school education in sixteenth-century England. Through a close reading of Richard Mulcaster's published texts on education, the aims of public education as an education towards public service are given voice. A desire for uniformity is seen to be coupled with an attention to variability – a responsiveness to the variability of learners being necessary to producing a uniform outcome. A sensitivity to variability if shown to be crucial for Mulcaster's educational theory – not to preserve it but to take it into account so that individuals can be better groomed for public service.

There are not many different ways to conceive of what Norbert Elias calls 'the civilizing process'[1] in terms of sixteenth-century grammar schooling. Even if the proclivities of a headmaster like Richard Mulcaster might have leaned in particular directions which were not completely at ease with the common doctrines of education, the authority of the state in its regulation meant that grammar school education was, as Mulcaster argued it should be, remarkably similar in terms of the content that was taught. Equally, the ways in which this content was taught, and the means by which students were guided to learn it, stuck to a model which can be traced to Cicero and Quintilian. What is remarkable, however, is the way in which variable

---

1   Norbert Elias, *On the Process of Civilisation*, Stephen Mennell, with Eric Dunning, Johan Goudsblom and Richard Kilminster, eds (Dublin: University College Dublin Press, 2012).

natures were accommodated and responded to in educational theory and practice. There was clearly no attempt to stifle variability if it was found to be germane to ones' service to the state and public life in general. And the point of judgement, on which the relationship between education and variability meet, is key to consideration of variability and education today. What comes first, the preservation of an individual's nature or the turning of their nature to be of use in society? If the former, how do we avoid a situation where an individual falls between the cracks of society, finding themselves in prison or unemployed? If the latter, how can we ensure that the 'civilizing process' does not create an extremely unhappy and unsatisfied person? These decisions fall to the individual and often intuitive judgement of the teacher. The teacher-student relation is the location at which the civilizing process comes most acutely under stress and is at the greatest need of a sensitivity towards variability, even if the aim of public education was uniformity.

In *Shakspeare's Small Latine and Lesse Greek*, T. W. Baldwin provides a long and convincing analysis of sixteenth-century grammar schooling and its profound direct and/or indirect influence on Shakespeare. What is ostensibly a book on Shakespeare, is also at one and the same time an ode to schooling, and especially sixteenth-century English grammar schooling. Baldwin's respect for the influence the grammar school had on Shakespeare is at once a critique of those who locate his entire genius in his nature, as well as a reminder to teachers of the significance of their task:

> One does not acquire such knowledge and proficiency by inheritance, inspiration, transcendentalism, etc., etc. This is Art, not Nature. Critics may conceivably be forgiven for overlooking this fundamental fact, but schoolmasters cannot, for their very existence depends upon it.[2]

For Baldwin, 'the grammar school gave Shakespeare at least an elementary grasp upon the fundamental doctrine and method of literary composition in his day, the theory and practice of imitation' wherein the goal was to

---

2   T. W. Baldwin, *William Shakspeare's Small Latine and Lesse Greeke*, 2 vols (Urbana, IL: University of Illinois Press, 1944), 672.

'analyze the old that by imitative synthesis the old might be reincarnated in the new'.[3] Baldwin then asks 'With our romantic theories of originality by transcendental inspiration, have we yet succeeded nearly so well?'[4] We might then also ask, does a focus on variability in education – if it is at the cost of knowledge and proficiency – actually get in the way of educating variable natures to fruition?

Today we find it uncomfortable to conceive of education as being a civilizing process, due to its various negative implications (the blinkered perception of the supremacy of Western civilization; problematic Enlightenment ideals; internal social hierarchies of nations), which usually ignore its contextual specificity. Perhaps even more disturbing to us, though, is the thought that public education exists to serve the state, rather than ourselves. But, as a reading of Richard Mulcaster – the originator of the term 'public education' – shows, this is a misconception of its history and purpose. For Mulcaster:

> *Education* is the bringing up of one, not to live alone, but amongst others, (bycause companie is our natural cognisaunce) whereby he shall best be able to execute those doings in life, which the state of his calling shall employ him unto, whether *publike* abroad, or *private* at home, according unto the direction of his countrie whereunto he is borne, and oweth his whole service.[5]

His system, then, provides the means by which to think a version (or spurt, in Norbert Elias's terms)[6] of the 'civilizing process' in sixteenth-century England. It is little surprise that Merchant Taylor's School, for whom he was the first headmaster, have made reference to part of this quote in their recent Curriculum Policy document, designed to address the Independent Schools Inspectorate's Regulatory Requirements (effective from February 2016) Part 1, Paragraph 2. (1) and (2). Mulcaster did not see schooling as being to do with 'anie naturall inclination, but of artificiall helps', which

---

3   Baldwin, *Small Latine*, 677.
4   Baldwin, *Small Latine*, 678.
5   Richard Mulcaster, *Positions Concerning the Training Up of Children*, William Barker, ed. (Toronto: Toronto University Press, 1994), 186.
6   Elias, *Civilisation*, 422.

are '*reading, writing, drawing, singing*, and *playing*'.[7] Therefore, even though Mulcaster was more explicitly drawn to physical education than most of his contemporaries, his conception of education was very much in fitting with that which Baldwin ascribes to grammar schooling in sixteenth-century England in general. However, for Mulcaster the 'artificiall helps' that education provides are crucial in making the most of one's nature, regardless of its variability:

> Take exercise awaie, what then is the bodie, but an vnweildie lump? what vse of it hath either cutrie [country] in defence, or it self in delite? Remoue precept and practis, and where then is vertew, which neither knoweth, what to do, if it be not directed, neither doth when it knoweth, if it faill of practis? Set these fiue principles apart, what can the vnlearned eie judge of? the untrained hand deal with? the vnframed voice please with?[8]

In terms of education today the prevailing feature of Mulcaster's educational theory and practice is its promotion of uniformity of means. This uniformity is the result of an acute awareness of the variability of individual teaching and learning contexts, the most significant issue within which, for Mulcaster, is bad teachers with bad methods. Variability of individuals is unquestionable for Mulcaster, arguing that '*nature* engraffe *private* differences for distinction sake, as *reason* in man to part him from a beast, yet that difference remaineth one still, by cause there is none better'.[9] But preservation of these differences is not Mulcaster's concern, instead regarding public education as tool to bring children effectively into service of the state. The art of education does not eliminate the individual differences provided by nature, neither in terms of teacher or student. For Mulcaster, there will always be differences in teachers' judgements, but 'wheras *difference* in judgement worketh *varietie*: *consent* in knowledge will plant *uniformitie*'.[10] Uniformity is an opportunity to increase the success of public

---

7   Richard Mulcaster, *Elementarie*, E. T. Campagnac, ed. (Oxford: Clarendon Press, 1925), 5, 27.
8   Mulcaster, *Elementarie*, 29.
9   Mulcaster, *Positions*, 187.
10   Mulcaster, *Positions*, 261.

education and ensure that, despite individual differences, an appropriate level of education is provided to students to make them of service to the state. The guiding principle for this uniformity is to educate so that each student, no matter their difference, would be taught a set body of content by teachers who used relatively similar methods of teaching:

> Whereby all the youth of this whole Realme shalle seeme to have bene brought up in one school, and under one maister, both for the matter and manner of traine, though they differ in their own invention which is private and severall to every one by nature, though generall and one to every one by art.[11]

While Mulcaster might already be considered 'holistic' in terms of his interest in a broad range of educational subjects, especially physical education,[12] he was also broadly of the mind that the 'soul' of the child could be observed and facilitated to grow by their own inclination through an educational process. He humbly suggests that he did not mean to

> make any anatomie, or resolution of the soule his partes and properties, a discourse, not belonging to this so low a purpose, but onely to pick out some natural inclinations in the soule, which as they seeme to crave helpe of education, and nurture, so by education, and nurture, they do prove very profitable, both in private and in publicke.[13]

The inclinations of the soul are, then, located specifically to be helped by education in becoming more profitable to the state and also to the individual person. Despite the fact that inclinations of the soul to be of profit in private is likely to be very much a secondary concern for Mulcaster, he sees 'the soule and bodie being comparteners in good and ill, in sweete and sowre, in mirth and mourning, and having general a common sympahthie, and a mutuall feeling in all passions'.[14] Thus, not to take the soul into account in the educational process might potentially upset the inner workings of children and make them less effective servants of the state and of themselves. However, this concern for the soul should not be overestimated

---

11   Mulcaster, *Positions*, 260.
12   Mulcaster, *Positions*, 51.
13   Mulcaster, *Positions*, 38.
14   Mulcaster, *Positions*, 51.

in Mulcaster's educational theory. There are few pointers given on how to attend to the soul, beyond those already recounted and he warns his reader to focus more explicitly on the body as

> the powers of the soule come to no proofe, or to verie small, if they cannot be fostered by their naturall traine, but wither and dye, like corne not reaped, but suffered to rotte by negligence of the owner, or by contention in challenge.[15]

And though Mulcaster states that 'I deale with the bodie but once, and that onely here, wheras I entreat of the soule, and the furniture therof in what so ever I meddle with, in my whole course hereafter,'[16] it is not entirely clear that he does so. The soul receives little further mention in the text, suggesting that Mulcaster either intended to write further on it and then did not, or, more likely, that he assumed attention to the soul was given more generally through all intellectual rather than physical educational pursuits. This suggestion leads to a further implication, which is that if we are to think of intellectual education as attending to the soul in general, then attention to individual souls has been left by Mulcaster up to individual judgement, rather than uniform practice. However, this individual judgement is still at the behest of a uniform aim: the enhancement of an individual's capacity for public service. In the *Elementarie* Mulcaster writes that 'publik vse ... is the naturall vse of all learning,'[17] to only turn inwards and towards one's own interest with one's learning is 'the priuat abuse of a publik good.'[18] Although 'if infirmitie let his choice then infirmitie is his pardon'.[19]

Public education in sixteenth-century England had none of our contemporary romantic trappings which promote the educational growth of the individual as their priority. A sensitivity towards variability or physical and mental disability was required, not to reward and facilitate difference, but rather to respond differently to produce a relatively uniform result. However, this sensitivity to variability should not be underestimated,

---

15   Mulcaster, *Positions*, 51.
16   Mulcaster, *Positions*, 52.
17   Mulcaster, *Elementarie*, 13.
18   Mulcaster, *Elementarie*, 14.
19   Mulcaster, *Elementarie*, 14.

especially in terms of Richard Mulcaster's educational theory. Uncommonly among his contemporaries, he was deeply concerned with physical educa- tion and wrote extensively on the subject in *Positions*. His interest in this subject provoked him to expand on the physical variability of students otherwise ignored in educational texts in sixteenth-century England:

> Now as all constitutions be not of one and the same mould, and as all partes be not moved alike, with any one thing: so the exercise must alter, and be appropriate to each: that both the constitution may be continued in her best kinde, and all the partes preserved to their best use, which exercises being compared among themselves one to an other, be more or lesse, but being applyed to the partie kepe alwayes in a meane, when they meane to do good.[20]

This sensitivity to physical variability in an educational context indicates a desire to adapt the means to be able to better reach the end. Influenced by Galenic thought, Mulcaster understands that ignoring physical variability can obstruct educational success. Interestingly, physical variability is never described as problematic, but rather as a given, to be taken into account through educational means. This is not the case for Mulcaster's evaluation of the 'kinde of witte I like best for my country'.[21] Unlike physical variability, intellectual variability becomes one of the loci for a practical judgement on whether or not a child should be admitted to school: 'it seemeth to me verie plaine that all children be not to be set to schoole, but onely such as for naturall wittes, and sufficient maintenance.'[22] For Mulcaster there is a 'want of provision', leading him to ask, rhetorically, 'For the rowmes which are to be supplied by learning being within number, if they are to supply them, grow on beyound number, how can yt be but too great a burden for any state to beare?'[23] Mulcaster's dilemma is not our own; there is not only sufficient provision but that provision is itself enforced on students in England up until the age of eighteen. However, Mulcaster's stratification of 'wittes' does play into the contemporary arguments of selection and

20   Mulcaster, *Positions*, 56.
21   Mulcaster, *Positions*, 145.
22   Mulcaster, *Positions*, 145.
23   Mulcaster, *Positions*, 139.

streaming, as well as posing a dangerous question to our contemporary norms: should we be schooling everyone, even if we can afford the provision? And does a sensitivity to variability endorse rather than proscribe such a perspective? The rhetoric of contemporary education has moved a long way from Mulcaster's definition of its purpose as being the building of individual capacities for service of the state. Social mobility, equality of opportunity, and individual flourishing, are the words with most purchase in the contemporary educational debate. And yet, is it truly possible to believe that these are the aims of contemporary public education? Or is it rather that the notion of an education designed to 'civilize' and provide one with the capacity for public service might be unsavoury to the general public?

Juan de Vives, a leading humanist intellectual cited by Mulcaster in *Positions*,[24] pioneered this civilizing aspect of education. In *Christian Humanism and the Puritan Social Order*, Margo Todd explains that 'Vives' works on education had consistently argues that society can be improved to a significant degree by laws and teaching which repress man's evil impulses and foster his good ones.'[25] This perspective, as Todd shows, was hugely popular and influential in England, Vives significantly outselling (both in Latin and in English translation) other similar authors in the same time period, such as Thomas More.[26] Richard DeMolen details the influence of Vives on Mulcaster in his *Richard Mulcaster and Educational Reform in the Renaissance*[27] and argues, 'In contrast to Vives and Mulcaster, Erasmus, Elyot, Ascham, and Montaigne focused their attention on society's privileged few.'[28] Thus, however unpopular Mulcaster's (and Vives') view, that that education should primarily be directed towards social welfare, might

---

24   Mulcaster, *Positions*, 256.
25   Margo Todd, *Christian Humanism and the Puritan Social Order* (Cambridge: Cambridge University Press, 1987), 40.
26   Todd, *Christian Humanism*, 94.
27   Richard DeMolen, *Richard Mulcaster (c.1531–1611) and Educational Reform in the Renaissance* (Nieuwkoop: De Graaf, 1991), 45–52, 92–96.
28   DeMolen, *Mulcaster*, 49.

be in terms of contemporary rhetoric, they were themselves combatting an even less socially generous form of educational practice.

In Norbert Elias' famous formulation, it is not difficult to evaluate the relative success or failure of what he calls the 'civilizing process', which we can see in Mulcaster and sixteenth-century grammar schooling in England. Elias writes that:

> In the successful case, after all the pains and conflicts of this process, patterns of con-
> duct well adapted to the framework of adult social functions are finally formed, an
> adequately functioning set of habits and at the same time – which does not necessarily
> go hand in hand with it – a positive pleasure balance. In the unsuccessful, either the
> socially necessary self-control is repeatedly purchased – at a heavy cost in personal
> satisfaction – by a major effort to overcome opposed libidinal energies, or the control
> of the these energies, the renunciation of their satisfaction is not achieved at all; and
> quite often no positive pleasure balance of any kind is finally possible, because the
> social commands and prohibitions are represented not only by other people but also
> by the stricken self, since one part of it forbids and punished what the other desires.[29]

Elias does not attack or defend the 'civilizing process' but rather outlines its tendencies and presents evidence to support his claims. He also does not suggest that there are many individuals for whom the civilizing process is particularly 'favourable or unfavourable', arguing instead that there are 'relatively few cases at the end of each scale. The majority of civilized people live midway between these two extremes. Socially positive and negative features, personally gratifying and frustrating tendencies, mingle in them in varying proportions.'[30] As such, the 'civilizing process' affects individuals variably and forms variable individuals. Equally, there are, of course, variable means of civilizing people (different families, schools, communities, jobs, courts and prisons). These statements rest at the precipice of the platitudi-nous. However, drawing attention to these facts allows for a consideration of why it might be appropriate to civilize (for example, to avoid religious strife or educate employable citizens), who has made arguments in favour of the civilizing process (Mulcaster has been our model), what were their

29 Elias, *Civilisation*, 416–417.
30 Elias, *Civilisation*, 417.

means of civilizing (the grammar school), and how they accounted for variability, during and at the end of this process. For Mulcaster the response to this final concern is the most pertinent in terms of variability. In his argument, uniformity in teaching methods reduces the likelihood of bad teaching, and increases the likelihood of being able to respond to variable natures in a manner which will develop them most effectively for public service. Elias does not see the civilizing process as following a 'straight line' of linear development.[31] It is instead a long sequence of 'spurts and counterspurts'.[32] One of the contemporary features of which is the diminishing contrast between upper and working classes.[33] One does not have to look too hard to see Richard Mulcaster as one of the more notable representatives of the civilizing spurt that was sixteenth-century grammar schooling in England. But in looking a little closer, it is also clear that this 'so low a purpose' – of directing public education towards public service – has an attentiveness to variability as its prerequisite.

31   Elias, *Civilisation*, 423.
32   Elias, *Civilisation*, 422.
33   Elias, *Civilisation*, 423.

KEVIN BERLAND

Thersites and Deformity

ABSTRACT

Shifts in the early modern interpretation of Homer's 'misshapen' haranguer Thersites provide an insight into what writers meant when they wrote about deformity. Homer and his earliest English translators avoided positing a causal link between a deformed body and deformities of mental or moral character. Others, however, maintained that a crooked body and a crooked mind were inextricably linked. Pope's Thersites is a case in point, for despite a tendency among modern critics to read empathy into Pope's version, in fact his Thersites is the most severely burdened by somatic determinism of them all. Following a brief investigation of *forma*, 'deformity', and the early modern notion of balance in the human constitution, the study concludes with a discussion of William Hay's principled answer to those who assume that *somos* determines *ethos*.

The Deformity of Satyr/Satire

In 1681 Thomas Durfey satirized rival playwright Thomas Shadwell in his play *Sir Barnaby Whigg*. The Tory satirist's exemplary Whig, Sir Barnaby is ranting, greedy, sanctimonious, loud, corpulent, corrupt, cowardly, and inconstant. He has also been a plagiarist and a hack satirist, but now that he has run out of Molière plays to rifle and his wit has worn out, he declares he will leave poetry for music. He sings:

> I got Fame by filching from Poems and Plays,
> But my Fidling and Drinking has lost me the Bays;
> Like a Fury I rail'd, like a Satyr I writ,
> *Thersites* my Humour, and *Fleckno* my Wit.

> But to make some amends for my snarling and lashing
> I divert all the Town with my Thrumming and Thrashing.[1]

Durfey mocks Shadwell with a redoubled antonomasia: he is a Thersites for humour, a Flecknoe for wit. His audience and readers would immediately have recognized and savoured these allusions – Homer's Thersites is the archetype of the sour, sharp-tongued complainer. In acknowledging 'Fleckno my Wit', Sir Barnaby bows in the direction of that very prince of Dullness who (as Dryden establishes in *Mac Flecknoe*) was Shadwell's mentor in the art of writing free of sense. Durfey sets forth the character of a poet-aster, whose traits include misplaced ambition, vanity, plagiarism, moral dissolution, false wit, and indiscriminate aggression against other writers. Sir Barnaby resembles the crabbed Thersites in his 'snarling and lashing', activities that originate in his 'humour' – his constitutional temperament.

But what precisely does Durfey mean by this association? A brief review of the source, and of some later interpretations, should prove useful. In the second book of the *Iliad*, Homer introduces the sharp-tongued Thersites, who mocked and railed against the warrior chiefs and even against King Agamemnon. Ulysses is offended and thumps him with a scepter, and eventually Achilles tires of being harassed and kills Thersites with a single blow on the ear. Homer's Thersites is not only verbally combative, he is strikingly deformed: hunchbacked, low in stature, weak-legged, squint-eyed, with a misshapen head crowned with thin, straggling hair. Homer combines two streams of description – *somatos* and *ethos* – but significantly he does not specify an explicit causal link. Indeed, many early commentators are careful to preserve the separation, as when Plutarch distinguishes between Homer's detailed description of Thersites' body and the poet's minimal account of the hatred that drives him:

---

1   Thomas Durfey, *Sir Barnaby Whigg, or, No Wit like a Womans: A Comedy* (London: Printed by A. G. and J. P. for Joseph Hindmarsh, 1681), 28. For Durfey's lampoon of Shadwell, see Christopher J. Wheatley, 'Shadwell, Durfey and Didactic Drama', in Susan J. Owen, ed., *A Companion to Restoration Drama* (Oxford: Blackwell, 2001), 340–354, and María José Mora, 'The political is personal: The attack on Shadwell in *Sir Barnaby Whigg*', *Sederi*, 15 (2005), 115–128.

> And the Poet *Homer* describing the deformitie of *Thersytes* his bodie, depainted his defects and imperfections in sundrie parts of his person, and by many circumlocutions; but his perverse nature and crooked conditions he set downe briefly and in one word in this wise:
>
> > Worthy *Achilles* of all the host
> > And sage *Ulysses*, he hated most.
>
> for he could not chuse but be starke naught and wicked in the highest degree, who was so full of hatred unto the best men.[2]

Thus, according to Plutarch, the problem with Thersites springs from his detestation for those men who shine in the Achæan company. He is careful to distinguish the two descriptive strains, maintaining that in Homer there is no causal connection between the body of Thersites and his moral character.

Some early modern writers focus on what Thersites actually does, rather than on internal cause or motivation. In this aspect he appears as a straightforward negative example of the great fault of intemperate speech: railing, haranguing, intemperate chiding, disrespect for authority, and vain chatter. For instance, in an essay on tempering the tongue, Jacques Hurault comments, 'Among the vices of *Thersites*, *Homer* blameth chiefly his ouermuch babling.'[3] For Dryden, Thersites' language was somewhat worse than babbling – it was railing (persistent and vehement complaint). In Dryden's translation of Ovid, Achilles explains, '*Thersites* tax'd the King, and loudly rail'd, / But his wide opening Mouth with Blows I seal'd.'[4]

It is interesting to note how often early modern writers describe the double deformity of Thersites without positing an explicit causal link. For instance, Richard Brathwaite, writing in 1613 of dangerous civil commotions and warning that 'Iniuries ript vp, haue oftentimes hazarded states', adduces Thersites as the type of a civil troublemaker:

---

2   Plutarch, 'Of Envie and Hatred', *The Philosophie, commonlie called, the Morals written by the learned Philosopher Plutarch of Chaeronea*, Philemon Holland, trans. (London: Printed by Arnold Hatfield, 1603), 235.

3   Iaques Hurault, *Politicke, Moral, and Martial Discourses*, Arthur Golding, trans. (London: Printed by Adam Islip, 1595), 336.

4   John Dryden, *Fables Ancient and Modern; Translated into Verse, from Homer, Ovid, Boccace, & Chaucer* (London: Printed for Jacob Tonson, 1700), 466.

Thersites, as deformed in minde as body (for so *Homer* characters him) was euer kindling the flame of ciuil combustion betwixt *Achilles* and *Agamemnon* at the siege of *Troy*, about the rape of *Breseis*, euer harping vpon that string to set them together by the eares.[5]

Brathwaite's focus is on Thersites' actions, not his motivation: tracing the cause of his conduct to his physical state does not occur.

Remarkably few early modern commentators – if any – consider whether Thersites' criticism might have had merit. This reluctance is pervasive; even today most translators tend to adopt the warriors' point of view, explaining who hated Thersites, but not whom Thersites hated and why.[6] Some twentieth-century critics have proposed that his contempt for authority represents an egalitarian critique of aristocratic privilege and established power, but this refinement does not appear among early modern writers until near the end of the eighteenth century.[7]

---

5   Richard Brathwait, *The Schollers Medley, or, An Intermixt Discovrse Vpon Historicall and Poeticall Relations* (London: Printed by N. O. for George Norton, 1614), 23. Brathwait frequently mentions Thersites in a proverbial sense; for instance, he reflects on unmerited aspersions 'by such, whose tongues are ever steeped in calumnie', similar to 'the contemptuous person of *Thersites*; whose character was, *More deformed in minde than bodie*', *The English Gentleman* (London: Printed by Iohn Haviland, for Robert Bostock, 1630), 43.

6   W. H. Rouse renders the passage thus: 'Achilles hated him heartily, and so did Odysseus, for he was always badgering them', *The Iliad* (1938; New York: Signet, n.d.), 27. Similarly, E. V. Rieu declares nobody hated Thersites more than Achilles and Odysseus, 'who were his favourite butts'. *The Iliad* (Harmondsworth: Penguin, 1966), 45. Robert Fagles, too, translates, 'Achilles despised him most, Odysseus too – for he was always abusing both chiefs', *The Iliad* (New York: Penguin, 1990), 106. Richard Lattimore simplifies, noting: 'Beyond all others Achilles hated him, and Odysseus', again without saying why, *The Iliad of Homer* (Chicago: University of Chicago Press, 1951), 82. No modern translator into English I have located has rendered Homer's words as an explanation for Thersites' disordered discourse.

7   Will Durant, for instance, discovered traces of 'class war' in Thersites' grievances, *The Life of Greece* (New York: Simon and Shuster, 1939), 47. For counterarguments, see Abraham Feldman, 'The Apotheosis of Thersites', *The Classical Journal*, 42/4 (1947), 219–221. For reflections on the history of hostile and sympathetic views, see N. Postlethwaite, 'Thersites in the "Iliad"', *Greece & Rome*, 2nd ser., 3/2 (1988),

How did the significance of Thersites move from his function as a classical exemplar of injudicious speech to the exemplar of a temperamental inclination to railing? One important clue may be discovered in the relation between physiology and mental temperament which many writers assumed. If the natural state of the human constitution was physical and mental health, disease was a falling-away from this ideal state. Accordingly, the English terms *disorder* and *distemper* indicate an imbalance in physiological condition. Disorderly behaviour is also traceable to a kind of imbalance. Sir Thomas Pope Blount notes that the belief that temperament produces legible marks of character gave rise to the saying *'Whom God hath Markt, let Man Mark.'* Blount sees in Homer's description and characterization of Thersites a unity of purpose: 'And therefore *Homer*, speaking of the several ill Qualities of *Thersites*, takes care to fit him with a Body suitable to such a Mind.'[8]

And so we may return to what Durfey meant by linking Sir Barnaby's temperament with that of Thersites. Sir Barnaby's confession is best understood in the light of the ongoing controversy about the nature and origin of satire. Is it a traditional rhetorical form or device used deliberately to promote critical judgement, or is it the production of the satirist's constitutionally sour nature? Proponents of the former argument maintain that satire is not personal: it is simply a literary device fitted to the task of exposing vice and folly. Proponents of the latter define satire as a matter of temperament, a kind of overarching mental ugliness, splenetic, corrosive, and spiteful. Such a temperament produces attacks aimed not at

---

123–136; and W. G. Thalmann, 'Thersites: Comedy, Scapegoats, and Heroic Ideology in the *Iliad*', *Transactions of the American Philological Association*, 118 (1988), 1–28. Typifying the view of Thersites as a voice for equality, Frederic Ahl calls Thersites 'Homer's blunt critic of the powerful', suggesting his 'judgment of the warrior kings is not unlike the judgment we ourselves might want to pass on them', though his 'criticism is not done in the right way by the right person.' See 'The Art of Safe Criticism in Greece and Rome', *American Journal of Philology*, 105/2 (1984), 174–175. See also Siep Stuurnamn, 'The Voice of Thersites: Reflections on the Origins of the Idea of Equality', *Journal of the History of Ideas*, 65/2 (2004), 171–189.

8   Sir Thomas Pope Blount, *Essays on Several Subjects* (London: Printed for Richard Bently, 1697), 160.

appropriate targets, but at people or cultural phenomena that personally displease the satirist. Satire, these critics insist, is both the production and symptom of moral deformity. Durfey's Sir Barnaby is obviously not a man of principle. Indeed, he declares he has been dedicated to railing – that is, to carping and criticizing – and to satire. Sir Barnaby's admission – '*Thersites* my Humour' – binds together his spiteful temperament and spiteful literary production.

The Origins of Invective

For those who wished to trace the origin of Thersites' bitter speech to a physiological source, there were strong precedents. That *somatos* affected *ethos* was a key element in Aristotle's understanding of human nature. The relation between inward constitution and outward form was well-expressed by the *Physiognomonica* long attributed to Aristotle:

> Mental character is not independent of and unaffected by bodily processes, but is conditioned by the state of the body[...]. And contrariwise the body is evidently influenced by the affections of the soul – by the emotions of love and fear, and by states of pleasure and pain.[9]

Thus the outward appearance is a sign – or a composite of signs – of the inward condition.

It is this understanding of human nature that informed the conflation of *ethos* and *somatos*, the two streams of Homer's description of Thersites, to produce for early modern writers a cogent example of mental character blighted by a deformed body. To make such an argument, it must be stressed, translators and critics moved beyond Homer. At first the movement toward

---

9   *Physiognomonica*, 805a; *The Complete Works of Aristotle*, Jonathan Barnes, ed.,
     T. Loveday and E. S. Forster, trans, vol. 1 (Princeton, NJ: Princeton University Press
     [Bollingen Series, 71, 2], 1984), 1237.

linking *ethos* with *somatos* was gradual. The earliest English versions of the *Iliad* still preserved some degree of separation, in 1581, Arthur Hall opened with Thersites' snarling, and then added a catalogue of his ugly features:

> This *Thersits* was a surly knaue, and eke a dogged swine,
> Not knowing honor nor his good, and alwaies spent his time,
> And tooke delight to mocke and scorne, and vse with trifling toyes
> Euen the chiefe: and in such trickes consisted al his ioyes:
> Thinking that it became him wel, when he did them contrary:
> And worse: he was the vgliest beast, that ere the earth did carry.[10]

Though it is possible for readers to infer a connection between surliness and ugliness, Hall offers no such explanation. A few years later, George Chapman's translation has begun to erase Homer's separation:

> Thersites onely would speake all. A most disordered store
> Of words he foolishly powrd out, of which his mind held more
> Than it could manage – anything with which he could procure
> Laughter he never could containe. He should have yet bene sure
> To touch no kings. T'oppose their states becomes not jesters' parts.
> But he the filthiest fellow was of all that had deserts
> In Troy's brave siege: he was squint-eyd and lame of either foote,
> So crook-backt that he had no breast, sharpe-headed, where did shoote
> (Here and there sperst) thin mossie haire. He most of all envied
> Ulysses and Æacides, whom still his spleen would chide,
> Nor could the sacred king himselfe avoid his saucie vaine.[11]

While Hall's Thersites simply delights in the discomfiture of others, Chapman's is driven by envy, his chiding stemming from maladjusted humours, an excess of spleen producing jealousy, discontent, and resentment. Thomas Hobbes's translation focuses on the laughter Thersites provokes by his ludicrous speech, but his appearance seems to be almost an afterthought:

---

10 *Ten books of Homers Iliades, translated out of French, by Arthur Hall* (London: Imprinted by [Henry Bynneman for] Ralph Nevvberie, 1581), 25.
11 *Chapman's Homer: The Iliad*, Allardyce Nicoll, ed., vol. 2 (Princeton, NJ: Princeton University Press [Bollingen Series XLI], 1998), 181–191, 51–52.

Thersites only standeth up and speaks.
One that to little purpose could say much,
And what he thought would make men laugh, would say.
And for an ugly fellow none was such
'Mongst all the *Argives* that besieged *Troy*.[12]

Dryden, explaining Juvenal's use of the name *Thersites* to indicate an inappropriately uncivil complainer, notes that the original was 'an Impudent, Deformed, Ill-Tongu'd Fellow ... who accompany'd the *Grecian* Army to the Siege of *Troy;* where he took a Priviledge often to rail and snarl at the Commanders.'[13] Although Dryden's phrase suggestively places impudence and deformity in close proximity, he does not in this instance insist upon a causal connection.

Pope goes much further even than Chapman in establishing an explicit link between Thersites' physical deformity and his clamorous discourse:

Thersites only clamour'd in the Throng,
Loquacious, loud, and turbulent of Tongue:
Aw'd by no Shame, by no Respect controul'd,
In Scandal busie, in Reproaches bold:
With witty Malice, studious to defame,
Scorn all his Joy, and Laughter all his Aim.
But chief he glory'd with licentious Style
To lash the Great, and Monarchs to revile.
His Figure such as might his Soul proclaim;
One Eye was blinking, and one Leg was lame:
His Mountain-Shoulders half his Breast o'erspread,
Thin Hairs bestrew'd his long mis-shapen Head.
Spleen to Mankind his envious Heart possest,
And much he hated All, but most the Best.
Ulysses or *Achilles* still his Theme;
But Royal Scandal his Delight Supreme.
Long had he liv'd the Scorn of ev'ry *Greek*,
Vext when he spoke, yet still they heard him speak.

12   *Homer's Iliads in English*, Thomas Hobbes, trans. (London: Printed by J. C. for William Crook, 1676), 20–21.

13   *The Satires of Decimus Junius Juvenalis. Translated into English Verse by Mr. Dryden and Several other Eminent Hands* (London: Printed for Jacob Tonson, 1693), 235.

> Sharp was his Voice; which in the shrillest Tone,
> Thus with injurious Taunts attack'd the Throne.[14]

This passage exemplifies Pope's well-known method of translating the classics: he felt little constraint to follow the original text literally. Rather, he built on Homer's narrative superstructure, preserving a great deal of Homer's descriptive and figurative language, but at the same time expanding creatively along lines that made sense to him. The key line of this passage – 'His Figure such as might his Soul proclaim' – decisively establishes the link between *somatos* and *ethos*, far beyond what Homer actually stated. Pope's intensified characterization of Thersites has largely escaped critics intent on tracing connections between Pope's works and his own physical condition, attracted by his candid private self-descriptions – as when he writes to Swift that 'the wretched carcase I am annexed to' makes a visit to Dublin impossible – and by his public references to 'this long Disease, my Life'.[15] But it does not necessarily follow that Pope's feelings about his own physical condition would be expressed in the characterization of figures in his translation of Homer.

During Pope's lifetime his enemies made a point of connecting his outer and inner form, as with Lady Mary Wortley Montagu's ferocious lines, 'And with the Emblem of thy Crooked Mind, / Mark'd on thy Back, like *Cain*, by God's own Hand / Wander like him, accursed through the Land.'[16] Such attacks may have increased Pope's sensitivity, as Frederick M. Keener has

14   Alexander Pope, *The Iliad of Homer, translated by Mr. Pope*, vol. 1 (London: Printed by W. Bowyer, for Bernard Lintott, 1715), 102–103.

15   Letter LXXIII (December 19, 1734), *The Works of Mr. Alexander Pope, in Prose*, vol. 2 (London: Printed for J. and P. Knapton, C. Bathurst, and R. Dodsley, 1741), 150. *An Epistle from Mr. Pope, to Dr. Arbuthnot* (London: Printed by J. Wright for Lawton Gilliver, 1734), 7 (line 127).

16   Lady Mary Wortley Montagu, *Verses Address'd to the Imitator of the First Satire of the Second book of Horace* (London: Printed for A. Dodd, [1733]), 8. On Pope's physical condition, see Marjorie Nicolson and G. S. Rousseau, *'This Long Disease, My Life': Alexander Pope and the Sciences* (Princeton, NJ: Princeton University Press, 1968); Maynard Mack, '"The Least Thing like a Man in England": Some Effects of Pope's Disability on his Life and Literary Career', in Maynard Mack, *Collected in Himself* (Newark, NJ: University of Delaware Press, 1982), 372–392; and Helen Deutsch,

suggested, so that certain features of Pope's translation indicate 'personal discomfort with misshapen Thersites'. Pope does not indulge in mockery of lame Hephæstus (Vulcan), as his predecessors do, nor does he turn up the heat on 'the Trojan complainer Polydamus.'[17] Such critical conjectures evidently originate with the opinion that it would be natural enough for Pope to feel for Thersites. Brean Hammond, for instance, maintains that Pope had 'empathy' for the 'misshapen' Thersites.[18] Be this as it may, it is not easy to determine where such empathy is to be found in practice, for Pope's version cannot be reconciled with personal discomfort or empathy. In truth, Pope not only follows the tradition associating physical and moral deformity, but he extends the association well beyond the authority of Homer's original narrative. Pope's rendering of Thersites deliberately fuses Homer's parallel descriptors into a single pathology.

Some of Pope's contemporaries recognized how far Pope's translation strayed beyond his original. The poet Thomas Cooke wrote anonymously in the 26 April 1728 edition of *The Daily Journal*, complaining that Pope had completely misunderstood Homer, mistaking 'a very good Character of Humour for a Wit'. Homer's Thersites 'was Master of many Words to Excess, and would wrangle with the Princes rashly and with no Grace', but, according to Cooke, Pope errs by representing Thersites as a satirical wit, studious in malice and licentious attack. Pope was apparently confident that his view of Thersites came directly from Homer, observing, 'Our Author has shewn great Judgment in the Particulars he has chosen to compose the Picture of a pernicious Creature of Wit.'[19] But, Cooke protested, half

---

'The "Truest Copies" and the "Mean Original": Pope, Deformity, and the Poetics of Self-Exposure', *Eighteenth-Century Studies*, 27/1 (1993), 1–26.

17   Frederick M. Keener, 'On the Poets' Secret: Allusion and Parallelism in Pope's "Homer"', *Yearbook of English Studies*, 18 (1988), 163. Jed Wentz points to Pope's praise for Homer's delicacy in not emphasizing Vulcan's lameness, which Pope describes only as 'auwkard grace', unlike Chapman and Dryden. See 'Deformity, Delight, and Dutch Dancing Dwarfs: An Eighteenth-Century Suite of Prints from the United Provinces', *Music in Art*, 36/1–2 (2011), 161.

18   Brean Hammond, *Pope* (Brighton: Humanities Press International, 1986), 9–11.

19   Alexander Pope, 'Observations on the Second Book', *The Iliad of Homer, Translated by Mr. Pope*, vol. 1, 155.

of Pope's version of Thersites is 'no Translation' at all, while the other half contains 'but faint Glimmerings of his Author's Meaning'. Specifically, the critic maintains, the sense of Pope's line – that the figure of the 'deformed Wretch' proclaims his soul – 'is not to be found in the *Greek*'. Thersites is not at all a scornful, witty satirist intent on provoking laughter. Rather, he is a crudely contentious, grumbling, cavilling nuisance. His behaviour springs from his humour, 'a restless, malignant Temper, always growling at, and wrangling with, his Superiors, but without a Spice of Wit'. He is properly understood not as the agent but the object of ridicule. Pope mistakenly transforms Thersites into a caustic wit, whereas Homer designed him not as satirist, but as an exemplar of excessive peevishness. His railing, therefore, is not a conscious and deliberate rhetorical performance, but the emanation of an internal condition. Cooke concludes that Thersites properly belongs not to the comedy of wit but to the comedy of humours, explaining that the comic spectacle 'not so designed by the Person in whom it is, cannot be beheld without creating Mirth in the Spectator'.[20] Still, although Cooke questions Pope's transformation of Thersites from complainer to satirist, the assumption of a somatic origin remains.

The Construction of Deformity

What is deformity, after all? The etymological root is *forma*, the Latin word both for beauty and for essential structure (form, pattern) and appearance. The addition of the negative prefix *de* indicates an aberration from beauty or ideal form. The *OED* defines the most frequent usages:

20　*A Compleat Collection of all the Verses, Essays, Letters and Advertisements, Which Have been occasioned by the Publication of Three Volumes of Miscellanies by Pope and Company* (London: Printed for A. Moore, 1728), 37–38. Cooke extended his criticism of Pope in 'Thersites, from the second Book of the Iliad', in *Tales, Epistles, Odes, Fables, &c. With translations from Homer and other antient Authors* (London: Printed for T. Green, 1729), 173–185.

1) The quality or condition of being marred or disfigured in appearance; disfigurement; unsightliness, ugliness.
2) The quality or condition of being deformed or misshapen; *esp.* bodily misshapenness or malformation; abnormal formation of the body or of some bodily member ... .
3) Moral disfigurement, ugliness, or crookedness.

In every case in which a socially recognized norm (*forma*) serves as a standard to measure divagation and distance from the ideal (deformity), both norm and instances of measuring up or falling short are socially constructed. It has been proposed that the construction of deformity is an attempt to understand a visible disruption in an ordinary (or expected) pattern of harmony. Helen Deutsch has observed, 'Deformity encapsulates the paradox of a visible sign of unintelligibility, a fall from form written by God or nature on the body[...]. At once sign and story.' There are two ways the sign or story may be read, either based on the notion of 'the body as a transparent index of the mind', or on 'an apparently more stable natural law of cause and effect.' In either case, the forces of causation are not inevitable, and may be 'interrupted by individual agency'. That is to say, a deformed person is not fated to behave in negative ways as observers might expect.[21]

In his essay 'Of Deformity', Francis Bacon acknowledges interrelatedness: 'Certainly there is a Consent between the Body and the Minde.' The term 'consent' implies an effective process, but the outcome is not always determined: there is room for agency. Bacon continues, 'And where Nature erreth in the One, she ventureth in the Other.' While man clearly experiences 'a Necessity in the Frame of his Body', necessity may be counterbalanced by 'an Election touching the Frame of his Minde'. Thus, while disease, a weakened physical state, deformity, or certain natural inclinations may be troublesome, discipline and virtue can produce better results than these limitations would seem to predict. In this respect Bacon follows Cicero, who in *De Fato* notably took the position that we are not limited and

---

21   Helen Deutsch, 'Deformity', in Rachel Adams, Benjamin Reiss, David Serlin, eds, *Keywords for Disability Studies* (New York: New York University Press, 2015), 52.

determined by natural inclinations or bodily conditions.[22] Bacon subtly proposes that deformity should be seen not as a sign, but as a cause, and the consequences are not always negative. Indeed, he argues, deformity may produce positive effects, for it often leads individuals to redoubled effort, to industry, and to wit.[23]

And yet few writers on deformity follow Bacon's advice. A survey of the image of Thersites in English writers from the sixteenth to the late eighteenth century reveals a strong tendency to essentialize deformity as a determining quality inherent in the object under view. It is illuminating to compare this tendency with the approach taken by modern disability theorists such as Lennard J. Davis, who have established the ways in which the notion of deformity and disability arise. The main stream of early modern social construction begins with the assumption of an essential link between inward and outward constitution. This premise may be seen clearly in a representative sample of writers, beginning with Nicholas Udall.

The title character of Udall's comedy *Thersites* (1537) apparently owes as much to the Roman tradition of the *miles gloriosus* as to Homer, a purveyor of hyperbolic self-praise, ill-favoured and constantly chiding. Udall describes him in terms repeated a few years later in his translation of Erasmus's *Adagia*:

> Thersites a pratleer bee ye sure,
> Without all facion, ende or measure.
> What soeuer came, in his foolishe brain,
> Out it should, wer it neuer so vain.
> In eche mannes bote, would he haue an ore,
> But no woorde, to good purpose, lesse or more:
> And without all maner, would he presume
> With kynges and princes, to cocke and fume.
> In feactes of armes, naught could he dooe,

22 Marcus Tullius Cicero, *De Fato* V.10, H. Rackham, ed. (Cambridge: Harvard University Press, 1927).

23 Francis Bacon, *The Essayes or Counsels, Ciuill and Morall, of Francis Lo. Verulam, Viscount St. Alban* (London: Printed by Iohn Haviland for Hanna Barret, 1625), 255.

Nor had no more herte, then a gooce therunto.
All the Grekes did hym, deride and mocke,
And had hym, as their commen laughyng stocke.
Squyntyied he was, and looked nyne wayes.
Lame of one leg, and lympyng all his dayes.
Croump shouldreed, and shrunken so vngoodly,
As though he had had but halfe a bodye.
An hedde he had (at whiche to ieste and scoffe)
Copped like a tankarde or a sugar lofe.
With a bushe pendente, vndernethe his hatte,
Three heares on a side, like a drouned ratte. [24]

In Udall's interlude, the foolish soldier Thersites has somehow lost his armour. A hyperbolic magnifier of his own valour, he cajoles the smith-god Mulciber into fashioning a new outfit of heroic gear suitable to a man of his narrative vigour. However, when pressed he runs from a snail he describes as a monster 'with an armed browe', hides behind his mother's skirts from the disgusted challenge of an ordinary foot-soldier, and attempts to placate Ulysses by begging his mother to prepare a deworming potion for the warrior king. Here Udall stresses the repugnant folly of empty bragging, a kind of social deformity, entirely submerging the Homeric association of physical and moral deformity.

A generation later, Shakespeare, in *Troilus and Cressida*, also focuses on Thersites' railing, from the time in the first act when Nestor describes Thersites:

A slave whose gall coins slanders like a mint,
To match us in comparisons with dirt,

---

24   *Apophthegmes, that is to saie, prompte, quicke, wittie and sentencious saiynges* (London: typis Ricardi Grafton, 1542), 180–181. On Erasmus's treatment of Thersites, especially as a figure of the ancient's loathing for garrulity, see Jessica Wolfe, *Homer and the Question of Strife from Erasmus to Hobbes* (Toronto: University of Toronto Press, 2015). See also Marie Axton, *Three Tudor Classical Interludes* (Cambridge: D. S. Brewer, Rowman & Littlefield, 1982), and Robert Hornback, 'Lost Conventions of Godly Comedy in Udall's *Thersites*', *SEL*, 47/2 (Spring 2007), 281–303. Axton and Hornbeck both indicate Udall drew on the early sixteenth-century dialogue, *Thersites*, by Ravisius Textor.

To weaken and discredit our exposure,
How rank soever rounded in with danger.[25]

It is a constitutional abnormality – an excess of gall – that compels Shakespeare's Thersites to rail against the Greek leaders; thus Achilles names him 'core of envy'. His railing takes the form of bitter, witty sniping. When Ajax threatens to beat him into 'handsomeness', Thersites retorts he would prefer to rail Ajax into 'wit and holiness', but such an attempt he knows would be futile, for the Greek leaders have more strength than intelligence, a 'valiant ignorance', just as a great deal of Achilles' wit 'lies in his sinews'. Agamemnon, though 'an honest fellow enough', does not have 'so much brain as earwax'. Thersites thus functions as fool and chorus. But while his disparaging remarks about his betters are shrewd and entertaining, in the sardonic tradition of the truth-speaking fool, his interventions disrupt the order and degree Ulysses praises, and his complicit bitterness about lechery and corruption in the last act is far less attractive. [26]

In Thomas Heywood's Trojan play *The Iron Age* (1632), Thersites disdains the life of a courtier, embracing the role his physical deformity necessitates:

Still suiting my conditions with my shape,
And doe, and will, and can, when all else fayle:
Though neither sooth nor speak wel: brauely rayle,
And that's *Thersites* humour.[27]

For Dryden, the humour of this character goes beyond railing, and in his revision of Shakespeare, *Troilus and Cressida, or, Truth Found too Late*

25   William Shakespeare, *The History of Troilus and Cressida*, I.iii.192–196.
26   See Robert Kimbrough, 'The Problem of Thersites', *The Modern Language Review*, 59/2 (1964), 173–176. See also W. W. Bernhardt, 'Shakespeare's *Troilus and Cressida* and Dryden's *Truth Found too Late*', *Shakespeare Quarterly*, 20/2 (1969), 129–141.
27   Thomas Heywood, *The Iron Age, Contayning the Rape of Hellen: The siege of Troy: The Combate between Hector and Aiax: Hector and Troilus slayne by Achilles: Achilles slaine by Paris: Aiax and Vlisses contend for the armour of Achilles: The death of Aiax, &c.* (London: Printed by Nicholas Okes, 1632), sig. F.II.r.

(1679), Ulysses deems Thersites beneath consideration, an ungrateful para-
site, practically subhuman:

> Who feeds on *Ajax*: yet loves him not, because he cannot love.
> But as a *Species*, differing from mankinde,
> Hates all he sees; and rails at all he knows;
> But hates them most, from whom he most received.
> Disdaining that his lot shou'd be so low,
> That he shou'd want the kindness which he takes.[28]

Dryden's Thersites embodies discontent. His oppositional conduct goes
against the general admiration for epic heroes and warrior kings. His contempt for rank and authority is fundamentally seditious.

With the Restoration, however, Thersites' bitter railing came to signify antimonarchism, and so the name Thersites became a sign for rebellion, just as physical deformity became emblematic of revolution. In 1670,
for instance, the *London Gazette* reported that the Cossack rebel Stepan
Razin had become 'as famous for his deformity of body, as his success in his
rebellion.'[29] The emblematic linkage of physical deformity and a seditious
temperament inevitably became proverbial. In 1763, a letter published in the
London Chronicle effected a comparison of Wilkes and Thersites by quoting
Pope's Homer,[30] a strategy carried on at length in Joseph Cradock's satirical
Life of Wilkes (1773). After a long passage of hyperbolical praise, Cradock
noted, with affected tones of shock and disapproval, 'And yet some one
was base enough to apply the following character to him' – followed by a
ten-line extract from Pope's description of Thersites in his *Iliad*.[31] Similarly,
in 1778 a correspondent in the *Morning Post and Daily Advertiser* attacked
the Duke of Richmond for his sympathy with the American colonies.

---

28   John Dryden, *Troilus and Cressida, or, Truth Found too Late. A Tragedy* (London:
      Printed for Abel Swall and Jacob Tonson, 1679), 20.
29   *London Gazette*, Issue 520 (7 November 1670). I have not been able to locate other
      references to Razin as having any sort of physical deformity.
30   *London Chronicle*, Issue 1020 (7 July 1763).
31   Joseph Cradock, *The Life of John Wilkes, Esq; In the manner of Plutarch*, 2nd end
      (London: Printed for J. Wilkie, 1773), 7.

The author pretended to contrast the Duke's loyalty to King George with the example of '*an unprincipled republican*, like Thersites, *who gloried in insolence to the King*.'[32] The same target and the same argument appears in Joseph Galloway's *Considerations on the American Enquiry*; after a discussion of the Duke's turbulence, Galloway muses, 'The following lines have unaccountably strayed into this note' – lines from Pope's *Iliad*, with the author's emphasis on Royal Scandal.[33] Still later, conservative writers found it useful to dismiss anyone whose criticism threatened the monarchy as 'another Thersites'. In 1793, John Wilde charged Thomas Paine with the sophistical method of making the good appear bad, and with railing like Thersites. In 1795, Helen Maria Williams called Marat 'the Thersites of the convention', and in 1796 Mirabeau also became a demagogue along the lines of Thersites.[34]

By far the most common appropriation of Thersites is the use of the figure of the twisted satirist as a stick to beat satire in general or satirists in particular. One polemical example of the conflation of *somatos* and *ethos* should suffice. In 1719, John Breval ridiculed the master-satirist Pope in his farce *The Confederates*:

> Thus in the *Zenith* of my Vogue I Reign,
> And bless th' Abundance of my fertile Vein;
> My pointed Satire aim alike at All,
> (Foe to Mankind) and scatter round my Gall:
> With poyson'd Quill, I keep the World in Awe,
> And from My Self my own THERSITES draw.

32 *Morning Post and Daily Advertiser*, Issue 1705 (7 April 1778).
33 Joseph Galloway, *Considerations upon the American Enquiry* (London: printed for J. Wilkie, 1779), 9.
34 John Wilde, *An Address to the Lately Formed Society of the Friends of the People* (London: Printed for T. Cadell and Peter Hill, Edinburgh, 1793). Helen Maria Williams, *Letters Containing a Sketch of the Politics of France, from the Thirty-first of May 1793, Till the Twenty-eighth of July 1794*, vol. 1 (London: Printed for G. G. and J. Robinson, 1795), 127–128.

Breval glossed the name Thersites as '*A Character in* Homer, *of an Ill-natur'd, Deform'd Villain*', and he uses Pope's own translation of the *Iliad* to characterize Pope reflexively:

> Aw'd by no Shame, by no Respect controul'd,
> In Scandal busie, in Reproaches bold:
> Spleen to Mankind his Envious Heart possest,
> And much he hated All, but most the Best. [35]

It is especially unpleasant (and clever) to turn Pope's words against him – unpleasant but not uncommon. Simon Dickie has commented on the dynamics of the eighteenth-century fascination with physical deformity in English jest-books, which typically exhibit 'a frank delight in human suffering. They suggest an almost unquestioned pleasure at the sight of deformity or misery – an automatic and apparently unreflective urge to laugh at weakness simply because it is weak.'[36] Dickie traces this comic pleasure to the Hobbesian sense of 'sudden glory', the reflexive sense of well-being attendant upon the perception of the misfortune of another. Roger Lund has gone further, tracing the assumptions underlying the wide-spread acceptance that the crippled and deformed naturally evoke repugnance and contempt. In a created world characterized by order and beauty, the imperfect is perceived as a violation of natural harmony.[37] The monstrous is unseemly, producing what Lennard J. Davis has called 'a disruption in the sensory field of the observer.'[38] Lund expands Davis's notion by referring to the definition of *deformity* in *Chambers' Cyclopædia*: 'A displeasing or painful Idea excited in the Mind on Occasion of some Object, which

35   John Breval, *The Confederates* (London: np , 1719), 1–2.
36   Simon Dickie, 'Hilarity and Pitilessness in the Mid-Eighteenth Century: English Jestbook Humor', *Eighteenth-Century Studies*, 37/1 (2003), 1–22.
37   See Roger Lund, 'Laughing at Cripples: Ridicule, Deformity, and the Argument from Design', *Eighteenth-Century Studies*, 39/1 (2005), 95–114.
38   Lennard J. Davis, 'Dr. Johnson, Amelia, and the Discourse of Disability in the Eighteenth Century', in Helen Deutsch and Felicity Nussbaum, eds, '*Defects*': *Engendering the Modern Body* (Ann Arbor, MI: University of Michigan Press, 2000), 56–57.

wants of the Uniformity, that constitutes *Beauty*.'[39] Examining Chambers' definition, it appears that deformity operates as the converse of the Platonic conception of καλοκαγαθία (kalokagathia), the principle that beauty reliably signals good nature. As Sir Thomas Pope Blount observed:

> It was a received Opinion among the Ancients, That outward Beauty, was an infallible Argument of inward Beauty; and so on the contrary, That a deformed Body was a true Index of a deformed Mind, or an ill Nature.[40]

This polarity was a convenient marker for physiognomists who worked to establish a science of reading character in the face. And yet the marker was famously unreliable, as Cicero pointed out in *De Fato*, telling the story of the physiognomist Zopyrus who pronounced Socrates stupid, thick-witted, and addicted to women. When the disciples laughed, Socrates corrected them, explaining this had been his character before he learned to cast out his vices by means of reason.[41]

Resisting the Connection

Thus, two radically different versions of the significance of Thersites flourished simultaneously during the period of this study. As we have seen, an impressive array of writers insists on a causal connection between his physical deformity and his temperament – that is, they believe that his tendency toward envy, bitter invective, and disruption of the social order is grounded in the physiological disruption of the deformed body. Still,

---

39   Lund, 'Laughing at Cripples', 95.

40   Blount, *Essays on Several Subjects*, 159.

41   Marcus Tullius Cicero, *De Fato*, J. E. King, trans. (Cambridge: Harvard University Press, 1927), 203–205. On the place of the Zopyrus tale in non-deterministic physiognomy, see my chapter, 'Inborn Character and Free Will in the History of Physiognomy, in Melissa Percival and Graeme Tytler, *Physiognomy in Profile: Lavater's Impact on European Culture* (Newark, NJ: University of Delaware Press, 2005), 25–38.

counterarguments also abound. Bacon's essay, while it shifts its ground to approach the topic from different angles, nonetheless emphasizes that what may appear to be a 'Necessity in the Frame of his Body' may be altered by 'Election touching the Frame of his Minde'.[42] By disciplined focus on moral improvement, an individual can overcome any innate predispositions visibly apparent in their external form and prove the marks of their character no longer accurate.

The tension between innate predispositions and ameliorating efforts of will stimulated intense interest among serious thinkers, as may be seen in the dialogue of the 'Virtuosi of France' on the question 'Whether the manners of the Soul follow the temperament of the body'. The opening speaker offers a familiar explanation: 'the extream variety of men's actions and manners cannot proceed from the diversity of their souls' (because all souls are equal). Rather, difference arises from the diversity of bodies, 'wherein according to the various tempers thereof the soul produces that variety of manners'. The second speaker disagrees, maintaining that:

> the soul informs and perfectionates the body, and begets in it the habit which pro-
> duces the manners and actions .... Besides, if the body and the humours thereof were
> the author and cause of manners, an ignorant person could never become learned ....
> The examples of many grand personages sufficiently ill furnish'd with graces of the
> body, evidence what certainty there is in arguing from the out-side of the corporeal
> structure to the furniture of the soul; and that the signs of malice, remark'd in some,
> as in *Zoilus*, from his having a red beard, a black mouth, and being lame, and one-
> ey'd; of *Thersites*, and *Irus*, from their having sharp heads, rather shew the malice or
> ignorance of such as make these remarks, then prove that these dispositions of body
> are the true cause of malice; we see people of the same temper, hair, stature, features,
> and other circumstances, very different in their manners and inclinations.[43]

This view elevates the factor of individual choice and discipline over the merely physical, opening the possibilities of personal amelioration. Similarly, Samuel Pufendorf insists that the proper judgement of moral actions must

---

42   Francis Bacon, *Essayes or Counsels*, 255.
43   [Théophraste Renaudaut], *A General Collection of the Discourses of the Virtuosi of France, Upon Questions of All Sorts of Philosophy, and other Natural Knowledg*, G. Havers, trans. (London: Printed for Thomas Dring and John Starkey, 1664), 495–496.

originate in an evaluation of volition and must exclude effects of those physical conditions over which the individual has no control. 'Hence no Man can be fairly reprehended for a weak, a tender, or a diminutive Body; for distorted, or for maim'd Limbs, or for want of Strength, provided that none of those Infirmities were contracted by his Default.' Pufendorf notes Aristotle's distinction between voluntary and involuntary conditions since natural deformity and unsightliness resulting from disease are not subject to blame, 'for Men will not reproach, but rather pity his Blindness who had it from Nature, or from a Distemper, or from an honorable Wound.' Pufendorf cites Plutarch's reading of Homer, noting that Ulysses upbraided Thersites only for his 'Scurrillity and Impudence', and not his physical deformity. 'Thus the wise Poet silently derides those who are asham'd of Lameness, Blindness, or the like Defects; it being his Judgment, that nothing can be Blameworthy which is not Vicious, and nothing Vicious the Cause of which is in Fortune, not in ourselves.'[44]

It is Homer himself who set the moral standard, Pufendorf maintains. To laugh at physical deformity is a grave moral fault. Generally it originates with a false sense of superiority. In social contexts it is a fault that, according to William Whitehead, belongs to the vulgar mob:

> Resign we freely to th' unthinking Crowd
> Their standing Jest, that swells the Laugh so loud,
> The Mountain Back, or Head advanc'd too high,
> A Leg mis-shapen, or distorted Eye;
> We pity Faults by Nature's Hand imprest,
> *Thersites'* Mind, but not his Form's the Jest.[45]

It remained for one figure to embody the difference between form and mind. William Hay (1695–1755), the poet, politician, and essayist, achieved a remarkable degree of success despite his physical deformities: he was born a dwarf with curvature of the spine resulting in a hunched back, and

44 Samuel Pufendorf, *Of the Law of Nature and Nations*, Basil Kennet, trans., 3rd edn (London: Printed for R. Sare, et al., 1717), 48.

45 William Whitehead, *An Essay on Ridicule* (London: Printed for R. Dodsley, and sold by M. Cooper, 1743), 13.

in his early twenties he was partially blinded and marked by smallpox.[46]
Hay studied at the Middle Temple, served as a justice of the peace, and
was a Whig member of parliament for twenty years, where he actively
sought to reform the poor laws. He married well, had four children, and
to a great extent lived a 'normal' life by contemporary social standards.
He is best known for his *Deformity: An Essay* (1754), a fusion of personal
memoir and meditation on the meaning of his physical condition. Much
has been written by modern theorists who have found *Deformity: An Essay*
an invaluable source for theorizing eighteenth-century disability: it is not
my intention to survey or comment on their positions.[47] Rather, I would
like to add to the literature on Hay some observations on his philosophy
as it concerns the discourse of deformity of character as physically determined or otherwise. Critics writing about *Deformity: An Essay* have not
often accorded Hay's other works much attention, though his forthright
account of his own condition is informed by the philosophical account of
human nature in his 1753 *Religio Philosophi: Or, the Principles of Morality
and Christianity*. In *Deformity: An Essay*, Hay employs his own story as an
example of the integrity of the individual soul even as it is held captive in a
body that invites condescension and contempt from a bigoted public. The
stoicism he displays in the essay is grounded on a view of human nature

46   On William Hay's life, see Stephen Taylor, 'Hay, William (1695–1755)', *Oxford
      Dictionary of National Biography* (Oxford: Oxford University Press, 2004), accessed
      15 September 2015, and Betty Adelson, *The Lives of Dwarfs: Their Journey from Public
      Curiosity Toward Social Liberation* (New Brunswick: Rutgers University Press, 2005),
      60–62.

47   On Hay's essay, see Kathleen James-Cavan, '"[A]ll in me is nature": The values of
      deformity in William Hay's *Deformity: An Essay*', in Brenda Jo Brueggemann and
      Marion E. Lupo, eds, *Disability and/in Prose* (Abingdon: Routledge, 2008), 17–28;
      and William Hay, *Deformity: An Essay*, Kathleen James-Cavan, ed. (Victoria:
      University of Victoria Press [English Literary Studies Monographs, 92], 2004);
      Helen Deutsch, 'The Body's Moments: Visible Disability, the Essay and the Limits
      of Sympathy', in Brueggemann and Lupo, eds, *Disability and/in Prose*, 1–16; Lund,
      'Laughing at Cripples'; David M. Turner, *Disability in Eighteenth-Century England:
      Imagining Physical Impairment* (New York: Routledge, 2012); and Chris Mounsey,
      'Variability: Beyond Sameness and Differences', in Mounsey, ed., *The Idea of Disability
      in the Eighteenth Century* (Lewisburg, PA: Bucknell University Press, 2014), 8–14.

that emphasizes the potential for amelioration. *Religio Philosophi*, which combines theology and moral philosophy with natural philosophy, emphasizes the power of the human faculty of reason, declaring that 'the Soul of Man is capable of perpetual Improvement.' God has:

> given him an Understanding to comprehend the Nature of Things, a Freedom of Will to chuse what he will do, and a Freedom of Action to do what he chuses. And the better to guard his Actions, God has given him Reason (or a Power of exercising his Understanding) to examine and compare Things, the better to judge of their Qualities and Relations, and of the Consequences of his own Actions with regard to them, and to himself. And if a Man employs his Reason before he acts, he will seldom err in his Moral Duty; for the Nature of Things, the most common and necessary to be known, is generally very obvious and plain.[48]

Most of *Religio Philosophi* is devoted to orthodox Anglican views of scripture history, the significance of Christ's ministry, the reconciliation of scientific and religious truths, and the moral duty of men, discernible through the application of reason to religious principles.

Hay opens *Deformity: An Essay* with an emphasis on interiority: 'Bodily Deformity is visible to every Eye; but the Effects of it are known to very few; intimately known to none but those, who feel them; and they are generally not inclined to reveal them.'[49] In the pages that follow this observation, Hay reflects on these effects, on cultural assumptions about them, and on his own personal experience, engaging along the way with Bacon's views on the subject. For instance, he questions Bacon's assertion that deformed persons have little feeling for others, even as he recognizes some truth in his own composure when confronted with the discomfort of others.[50] Hay responds to Bacon's claim that deformed persons are bold, first in their own defence and then habitually, by allowing this to be true 'among the inferiour Sort, who are in the Way of continual Insults',

---

48   William Hay, *Religio Philosophi: Or, the Principles of Morality and Christianity, Illustrated from A View of the Universe, and of Man's Situation in it* (London: Printed for R. Dodsley, 1753), 12, 40.

49   William Hay, *Deformity: An Essay* (London: Printed for R. and J. Dodsley, and Sold by M. Cooper, 1754), 2.

50   Hay, *Deformity: An Essay*, 43.

since a deformed person's return of verbal abuse is 'a natural weapon of self defence'.[51] Hay's observations about the abuse to which deformed persons are exposed are cogent:

> Such Contempt in general, joined with the Ridicule of the Vulgar, is another certain Consequence of bodily Deformity. For men naturally despise what appears less beautiful or useful: and their Pride is gratified, when they see such Foils to their own Persons. It is this Sense of Superiority, which is testified by Laughter in the lower sort, while their Betters, who know how little any Man whatsoever hath to boast of, are restrained by good Sense and good Breeding from such an Insult. But it is not easy to say why one Species of Deformity should be more ridiculous than another, or why the Mob should be more merry with a crooked Man, than one that is deaf, lame, squinting, or purblind.

However, instead of pursuing Bacon's discussion of the response of deformed persons to such abuse, Hay pointedly reverses the topic and challenges the abuser:

> To upbraid a Man with a personal Defect, which he cannot help, is also an immoral Act, and he who does it, has reason to expect no better Quarter, than to hear of Faults, which it was in his power not to commit.

Hay is not personally inclined to pursue this course of self-defence, for he is not bold at all, but afflicted with 'an unbecoming Bashfulness'.[52] Implicitly, then, Hay dismisses the standard claim that physical deformity inevitably produces a splenetic disposition, his own example being a case in point. As for literary exemplars of this disposition, Hay dismisses Thersites as 'a Child of a Poet's Fancy'.[53] Passing from a rational interrogation of one popular supposition about deformity to another, constantly adducing his own experience, Hay models in practice the principles he wishes to establish. Just as Juvenal recommends praying for a sound mind in a sound body, so Hay adds, 'every deformed Person should add this Petition ... for an upright

51   Hay, *Deformity: An Essay*, 53.
52   Hay, *Deformity: An Essay*, 53–54.
53   Hay, *Deformity: An Essay*, 4.

Mind in a crooked One'.[54] Indeed, he even suggests that deformity may afford an advantage in moving toward amelioration:

> Another great Advantage of Deformity is, that it tends to the Improvement of the Mind. A Man, that cannot shine in his Person, will have recourse to his Understanding: and attempt to adorn that Part of him, which alone is capable of Ornament: when his Ambition prompts him to begin, with *Cowley*, to ask himself this Question:
> > '*What shall I do to be for ever known,*
> > *And make the Age to come my own?*'[55]

Though many avenues to fame may be barred, some remain open through the avenue of self-correction and virtue. Hay preserves his good humour, joking at the close of his essay that Hogarth's *Analysis of Beauty* establishes that a crooked body is an example of beauty, for Hogarth 'proves incontestably, that it consists in Curve Lines: I congratulate my Fraternity; and hope for the future the Ladies will esteem them *Des Beaux Garçons*'.[56] His wit underscores the exemplary self-presentation of the essay, for he is sufficiently secure in estimation of his own worth to make himself the subject of mild ridicule – and the fact that his jest is otherwise victimless substitutes a benevolent humour for the cruelty of personal ridicule.

In thus turning the tables on the humour of deformity, Hay is consistent in his program of subverting negative cultural assumptions. His approach is at once personal and rational, always demonstrating the many fallacies of the deterministic approach to deformity. 'And let every deformed Person comfort himself with reflecting' that tho' his Soul hath not the most convenient and beautiful Apartment, yet that it is habitable'.[57] In this temporary dwelling, every deformed person has the option to choose between allowing opinions of the unthinking mob to determine his or her character, or to resist by electing to pursue benevolence and virtue. In *Religio Philosophi*, Hay maintains, 'The only true Christian is he, who with a benevolent Temper, and sincere Disposition, conforms himself to the

---

54 Hay, *Deformity: An Essay*, 58.
55 Hay, *Deformity: An Essay*, 68–69.
56 Hay, *Deformity: An Essay*, 82.
57 Hay, *Deformity: An Essay*, 72.

best of his Understanding to the moral and general Rules of the Gospel.'[58] His essay recounts his own struggles to achieve this elevated standard. Hay implicitly calls upon his readers to examine their presuppositions and to learn from his example that deformed persons are worthy of benevolent consideration.

And so Hay, with elegance, just consideration, a touch of self-mocking humour, and an exemplary life sunders the deterministic connection of *somatos* and *ethos*. Instead of tracing the mental and moral character of deformed persons to physical causes, Hay provides an alternative approach, one that is benevolently respectful of human potential.

---

58   Hay, *Religio Philosophi*, 184–185.

CHRIS MOUNSEY

Aphra Behn's 'Blind Lady': Reading Impairment/ Impairing Reading

ABSTRACT

This essay argues that Aphra Behn, writing during the Restoration, was able to combine an understanding of the impaired body as a lived experience, with a political metaphor: Varronian satire. The combination, the essay argues, set off Behn's career as a playwright in her attack on the Whig Robert Howard's play *The Blind Lady*, in a satire *The Unfortunate Bride: or, the Blind Lady a Beauty* that was not published until after Howard's death in 1698, which has skewed the chronology of her writing and our understanding of Behn's career in the theatre.

Introduction

One of the major problems of studying historical texts is the question of how to study them. As scholars of English we move from theory to theory, sometimes inventing our own, sometimes using old theories in new ways, but the question remains when we use whatever reading method we do, have we captured what the text meant to the readers for whom it was written? Or are we getting something out of the text (or perhaps putting something into it) that was never there.

Aphra Behn's *The Unfortunate Bride: or, the Blind Lady a Beauty*[1] is a case in point. As with most of Behn's posthumously published novels, it has a very short bibliography of secondary sources, in fact I can locate no

---

1   Aphra Behn, *The Unfortunate Bride: or, the Blind Lady a Beauty* (London: Printed for Samuel Priscoe, 1698).

secondary sources in any of the readily available academic databases. But where it is reduced to a mere mention in a feminist account of the author by Ros Ballaster in 'Aphra Behn and the Female Plot', an essay in *Re-reading Aphra Behn*,[2] the 'blind lady' of the title is explained as a metaphor within the twentieth-century struggle for women's rights as a feminist challenge to male specularity, thus we are told:

> Behn ... presents physical disability in a woman as a means of dramatising masculine specularity and narcissism.[3]

An online article gives us the only Disability Studies account of Behn's *Unfortunate Bride* but here the 'blind lady' is explained as 'a narrative tool that subverts and disrupts the characteristics of normalcy of dominant ideologies (Mitchell and Snyder 51)',[4] and as such she becomes a justification of the Foucauldian approach to Disability Studies: a methodological 'blind lady' who also serves the feminist cause.

Both these readings might be thought very odd indeed (and I shall go on to argue that they entirely miss the import of the novel from the point of view of the readers for which it was originally written) when read in the terms of a story that questions sight and metaphors of sight throughout. For it is not the women who are the object of male specularity, rather it is the men who are looked at by the women. Behn begins with a description of Wildvill as 'admired for outward qualifications, as strength and manly proportions', and Frankwit as having 'a much softer beauty ... [and who is attractive] for his inward endowments'.[5] Likewise, Celesia, the 'blind lady', who initially cannot see the men, ends up cured and married to Frankwit the hero, in whose 'inward endowments' lie his beauty, rather than his 'manly proportions'. To be sure, Celesia has said some lovely things about Frankwit's 'inward endowments' while blind. But they marry not because

---

2   In Heidi Hutner, ed., *Re-Reading Aphra Behn: History Theory and Criticism* (Charlottesville, VA: University of Virginia Press, 1993), 191–203.

3   Ros Ballaster, 'Aphra Behn and the Female Plot', 199.

4   David Mitchell and Sharon Snyder, *Narrative Prosthesis: Disability and the Dependencies of Discourse* (Ann Arbor, MI: University of Michigan Press, 2000).

5   Behn, *The Unfortunate Bride*, 4.

she's in love with him, or 'seen' his inward beauty while blind, but because it is her friend Belvira's dying wish after she's been killed by her husband Wildvill with a sword thrust that passes first through Frankwit's arm.

In the novel, the fact that Behn points to but always seems to miss the expected outcomes of her metaphors might suggest this is a slight piece or an apprentice work. But the novel really is very silly indeed, and there is no getting away from its silliness. But nor, I shall argue, should we try to get away from silliness, as silliness is the main tool of Varronian satire, the form by which Rachel Carnell argues a seventeenth-century 'author signals her Tory values ... understood in its day as a 'natural Tory vehicle'.[6] Following Carnell, this paper will argue that *The Unfortunate Bride: or, the Blind Lady a Beauty* is a Varronian satire in which blindness plays a metaphorical role to make a political point, and does so by also playing a non-metaphorical role to make a point about the importance of women in medical careers at the time when medicine was changing to privilege surgical intervention over herbal lore.

I have recently argued[7] that Delarivier Manley's earliest prose works from 1696 were in the form of Varronian satire, and follow John Dryden's 1693 formulation:

> The Titles of many of them ... are generally double: From whence, at least, we may understand, how many various Subjects were treated by that Author. Tully, in his Academicks, introduced Varro himself giving us some light concerning the Scope and Design of these Works. Wherein, after he had shown his Reasons why he did not ex professo write of Philosophy, he adds what follows. Notwithstanding, says he, that those Pieces of mine, wherein I have imitated Menippus, though I have not Translated him, are sprinkled with mirth, and gayety: yet many things are there inserted which are drawn from the very intrails of Philosophy, and many things

6   Rachel Carnell, 'Slipping from Secret History to Novel', *Eighteenth-Century Fiction*, 28/1 (2015), 1–24.

7   See Chris Mounsey, 'A Manifesto for a Woman Writer: Letters Writen as Varronian Satire', in Aleksondra Hultquist and Elizabeth Matthews, eds, *New Perspectives on Delarivier Manley and Eighteenth Century Literature: Power, Sex, and Text* (London: Routledge, 2016), 171–187.

severely argu'd: which I have mingled with Pleasantries on purpose, that they may more easily go down with the Common sort of Unlearn'd Readers.[8]

The doubleness in the titles of this form of satire, as well as its hiding a serious message beneath a mirthful surface makes *The Unfortunate Bride: or, the Blind Lady a Beauty* very difficult to read and understand since it was originally read in two contexts: of writing (c.1668) and its posthumous publication (1698). Thus, the way in which it was first presented to the world is possibly quite far from the original moment of utterance. The complexity is further born out by the facts of Behn's working life, since she began to write plays in 1670 for the Whig Thomas Betterton's Duke's Company, while, as Janet Todd argues, 'In the late 1670s the Exclusion crisis and Popish Plot politicized dramatists, and Behn became a propagandist for the king and the emerging tory faction.'[9] If my reading is correct, we can conclude two things: that Behn was writing for the Tory cause earlier than Todd suggests, and that Varronian satire was used to signify a Tory attack earlier than Delarivier Manley.

The Context(s)

Samuel Briscoe, publisher of Charles St, Covent Garden, sent Behn's story out into the world with an epistle dedicatory to 'Richard Norton, of Southwick in Hantshire', who until 1699 was noted to be of the court party (a Whig) and who, according to the *History of Parliament*:

> In 1696 ... published a play called *Pausanias, The Betrayer of His Country*, in which two songs contributed by Anthony Henley were set to music by Purcell. The play was considered 'feeble' by some, but Samuel Garth, author of *The Dispensary*, praised its 'Athenian wit', to which Sir Richard Blackmore, alluding to Norton's wealth, replied:

---

8   John Dryden, *The Satires of Decimus Junius Juvenalis: Translated into English Verse. &c.* (London: Jacob Tonson, 1693), xxvii.

9   ODNB.

> Without his gold what generous Oran writ,
> Had ne'er been standard, sheer Athenian wit.[10]

Garth's support for Norton's play is here satirized by the Tory Blackmore as being due to their shared Whiggish politics (or perhaps by the idea that Norton paid Garth, who was a member of the Whig Kit Kat club, for the praise) rather than a judgement of the play's true merit.

But how might the appending of a letter of dedication to Norton have been understood by a 1698 readership of Behn's novel? Behn had become known as a mouthpiece of Tory satire, and, being dead, could not gain anything from the dedication. I would argue that readers understood that her hitherto unpublished novel *The Unfortunate Bride: or, the Blind Lady a Beauty* had something to say against a prominent Whig who used his wealth to have bad plays performed and get the best musicians to set his poor lyrics. It may or may not therefore be a coincidence that in 1698 Sir Robert Howard died. He was a wealthy and well-connected Whig politician who had used his wealth and influence to publish, in 1660, a play called *The Blind Lady, a Comedy*.[11]

Howard was no great writer, albeit he was a theatre enthusiast. Co-sponsor with Thomas Killigrew and a group of eight actors of the Theatre Royal, Bridges Street, where he was also set designer, he published a number of other plays *The Indian Queen, The Surprisal, The Committee, The Vestal Virgin*, and *The Great Favourite, or, The Duke of Lerma*. His sister married John Dryden, who quickly became his political opponent in the theatre, and John Evelyn summed Howard up as 'pretending to all manner of arts and sciences ... not ill-natured, but insufferably boasting.'[12] Evelyn's was not a lone voice of condemnation. Thomas Shadwell ridiculed Howard under the character of Sir Positive At-All in *The Sullen Lovers* and

10   <http://www.historyofparliamentonline.org/volume/1690-1715/member/norton-richard-ii-1666-1732>, accessed 15 September 2015.

11   Robert Howard, *Poems* (London: Henry Herringman, 1660), 28.

12   John Evelyn, *The Diary of John Evelyn*, 2 vols (New York and London: Walter Dunne, 1901), 2. 450.

Lady Vane in the same play was supposed to represent his mistress, who became his first wife.

Shadwell's play is important to this argument. It was his first, and performed by the Duke of York's Company two years before Behn's first *The Forc'd Marriage*.[13] Shadwell's *The Sullen Lovers* was dedicated to William Cavendish, Duke of Newcastle (husband of Margaret Cavendish), and claimed in its Preface:

> ... in this very Critical age, when every man pretend to Judge, and some that never read Three Playes in their lives, and never understood one, are as positive in their Judgment of Playes, as if they were all Johnsons. ... Or like some other of our Modern Fopps, that declare they are resolv'd to justify their Playes with their Swords (though perhaps their Courage is as little as their Wit) such as peep through their loop-holes in the Theatre, to see who looks grum upon their Playes: and if they spy a gentle Squire making Faces, he poor soul must be Hector'd till he likes 'em, while the more stubborn Bully-Rock damn's and is safe:[14]

In a manuscript note in a contemporary hand by the words 'Modern Fopps' is written 'Sir Robt. H', and the same hand claims in the *Dramatis Personae* that 'Sir Positive At-All' is also Howard. Shadwell's Preface also notes, unwillingly, his debt to Molière's *Les Fascheux*, and also, that

> Another Objection, that has been made by some, is, that there is the same thing over and over:[15]

What Shadwell means here is that there is no plot to his *Sullen Lovers*. Rather it is the working through of characters which represent the humours, something he believed was necessary for the theatre:

13   Aphra Behn, *The Forc'd Marriage* (London: Printed by H. L. and R. B. for James Magnus, 1671).
14   Thomas Shadwell, *The Sullen Lovers* (London: Henry Herringman, 1668), Preface, n.p.
15   Shadwell, *Sullen Lovers*, Preface, n.p.

> I have endeavour'd to represent a variety of Humours (most of the persons of the Play differing in their Characters from one another) which was the practice of Ben Johnson, whom I think all Dramatick Poets ought to imitate ... .[16]

Shadwell's attack on Robert Howard goes a little further than Jonson would, and Howard is further hinted at as a target for the satire in the Preface when he notes

> ... most other Authors that I have read either have wilde Romantick Tales, wherein they strain Love and Honour to that Ridiculous height, that it becomes Burlesque[17]

However, while Shadwell's *The Sullen Lovers* is a development of the Jonsonian comedy of humours into the restoration satire of recognizable characters, it does not go as far as Behn would two years later when she began to write for the Duke of York's Company with *The Forc'd Marriage*.

In *The Forc'd Marriage*, the heroine, Erminia, is forced by her father and the king to marry Alcippus, a young warrior whom she does not love. The man she truly loves, and who loves her, is Prince Philander, the king's son, while the king's daughter, Galatea, is in love with Alcippus. In time-honoured comic fashion, the web is eventually untangled and true love wins out in the end. This is almost the identical plot to Robert Howard's *The Blind Lady* in which the princess Mirramente has two suitors, Mironault, whom she prefers, and Phylanter, but for she too the choice of husband is forced on her by her father, the king, and Phylanter's father, Albertus. Mironault also has a sister Amione who falls in love with Phylanter, and the end of the plot is identical to Behn's. But where in Behn's play comedy is allowed to play out as a force of nature, in Howard's, as Shadwell told us, 'Love and Honour [are strain'd] to that Ridiculous height, that it becomes Burlesque'.

In Howard's play, Phylanter goes to war with Mironault for the hand of the woman he claims to love to distraction, and he besieges Mironault in the house of the eponymous Blind Lady, Coeca. While Mironault is thus imprisoned, Amione demands of Phylanter to see her brother, and

---

16 Shadwell, *Sullen Lovers*, Preface, n.p.
17 Shadwell, *Sullen Lovers*, Preface, n.p.

at this meeting Phylanter falls in love with her at first sight and forgets Mirramente, the cause of the war. After Amione has been given safe passage into Coeca's house she comes out to marry Phylanter, while Mironault is now free to marry Mirramente.

This requires quite some suspension of disbelief and some truly poor dialogue, an example of which is Phylanter's first meeting with Amione, when she asks him to see her besieged brother. Phylanter takes no time at all in declaring his love for her:

> To be short then, know Phylanter loves you,
> Your seeming kindness will have power
> To draw him where you please, for to my breast
> He has committed all his thoughts,
> And bid me judge when I should see you
> Whether he has not cause for all his passions,
> (Indeed he has) ...[18]

To which confusion of pronouns Amione replies:

> Man's like a barren ungrateful soil,
> That seldom pays the labour of manuring.[19]

The reference to manuring has a place in comedy, though more usually in the scenes between rude mechanicals (of which we shall hear more shortly) than at moments of high drama, or of love at first sight. There is no time to expand on the topic, but manuring was a political issue in the late seventeenth century, a Whig practice that was rejected by Tories, and this leaves Behn free to have a 'field' day with Howard.

But what is important for the present argument is that the story of *The Unfortunate Bride: or, the Blind Lady a Beauty* is also similar to Howard's *The Blind Lady* and Behn's own *The Forc'd Marriage*, and thus it is not out of the question to read the novel as an apprentice piece offered to the Duke's Company, which demonstrated what Behn could do. Published

---

18   Robert Howard, *Poems*, 129.
19   Robert Howard, *Poems*, 130.

after her death and when Howard was dead so could no longer be libelled, it was perhaps originally given in manuscript to Margaret Cavendish to show how Shadwell's attacks on the Court Party in their growing seat of political power could be made in a more entertaining way than a revamping of the Jonsonian comedy of humours: in a way that would come to be known as Varronian satire, and as Behn's hallmark form of Tory satire.

Two Blind Ladies

In order to explore Behn's *The Unfortunate Bride: or, the Blind Lady a Beauty* as an early Varronian satire, we must begin with its double title and then move on to the text 'sprinkled with mirth, and gayety: ...[where] many things are there inserted which are drawn from the very intrails of Philosophy, and many things severely argu'd:... 'And in order to read it as a satire of Howard, we need to read it closely against his play *The Blind Lady*.

The heroine this time is called Belvira and the two men in her life are close friends Wildvill, who was 'admired for outward qualifications, as strength and manly proportions',[20] and Frankwit who was known for 'much softer beauty, for his inward endowments, pleasing in his conversation, of a free and moving air, humble his behaviour and if he had any pride, it was but just enough to show that he did not affect humility ... '.[21] Frankwit wins Belvira's love from the beginning, but because of a lack of funds he retires to Cambridge to mortgage his last estate in order to marry her on the proceeds. While there he becomes ill and a black woman, Moorea, who is taking care of him intercepts his letters, tells Belvira of his death (in order that she can marry him instead) and although Belvira finds out this is not true, she does believe that Frankwit was unfaithful to her. So, on the rebound, Belvira marries Wildvill instead. Rather than a comic

20 Behn, *The Unfortunate Bride*, 3.
21 Behn, *The Unfortunate Bride*, 3–4.

happy ending, Frankwit returns to London on the wedding day, intercepts Belvira who swoons in his arms, whence Wildvill immediately thinks she is being unfaithful to him and runs Frankwit through his left arm, killing Belvira in the process.

But where is the 'blind lady' in all this complicated plotting? In Behn's story she is Belvira's cousin, Celesia, who is used throughout the novel to question the idea of falling in love at first sight (that is, of women being entranced by beautiful men), who is cured of her blindness, and who marries Frankwit at the end following Belvira's dying wish. It must be remembered that Frankwit was run through the left arm only, and kills Wildvill, who has until that moment been his best friend. All this pseudo-heroic flummery of Wildvill and Frankwit beginning the story in 'a very Inviolable Friendship',[22] and ending up fighting one another over a woman who seems able to love either one interchangeably is, of course, a satire of Robert Howard's piffling *Blind Lady*. But when we read it as a Varronian satire it becomes much more interesting.

The first half of Behn's double title *The Unfortunate Bride: or, the Blind Lady a Beauty* exposes the question at the heart of her own story: exactly who is the unfortunate bride? Belvira who dies, or Celesia who marries Frankwit who loves her dead friend? But it also exposes Howard's happy ending: who exactly is the unfortunate bride? Mirramente who marries the defeated Mironault? or Amione who marries Phylanter who seems able to change his mind about whom he loves at the drop of a hat? or Coeca, the 'blind lady' of Howard's title who, in a side plot, is forced to marry a fool who does not love her?

The second half of Behn's double title dramatizes the two blind women, and the way women are treated in each story. In Behn's novel the women must wait on the sidelines until the men have fought it out over who is going to have which woman, and blindly accept their decision. In Howard's play the men do the same, but the women have to act as though they really have fallen in love with the victor when he comes to claim his prize.

---

22   Behn, *The Unfortunate Bride*, 3.

Linking the two stories and making sense of them is the role of the blind woman in each. Howard's Coeca is eighty years old, and welcomes Mironault with his companions Hyppasus and Pysenor into her house after they are defeated by Phylanter and on the run. Howard's technique is comedy with Coeca as the butt of the jokes, but the process of welcome is carried on in the language of courtship of the 'blind lady' by the three defeated men:

> *Pys.* We are Gentlemen, and have been hurt by thieves
> You need not fear to help our hard misfortunes,
> Our Weak Conditions cannot threaten danger,
> You may believe, we would deserve your kindnesse,
> And our lives, which if you preserve,
> Shall wait upon your beauty
> *Hyp.* What a dissembling tongue this rogue has, [*aside.*
> *Pys.* We went as long, as we could gain a leave
> From Weaknesse, as unwilling – – –
> To be a burthen to any but our fates,
> Threw us on you for which we dare not chide them.
> *Hyp.* This rogue would court a bitch – – – [*aside.*
> *Pys.* Sirrah I'le fit you – – –
> *Coeca.* A fine well-spoken gentleman.
> *Pys.* For if we did, we should be too unjust,
> For you must needs be good, because the gods
> Let you so long to live to instruct the world,
> – – – Or else afraid of all your blind company – – – [*aside.*
> But at your feet – – –
> We throw our selves and all our miseries.
> And cancell fear, whilst we expect to hear
> Our doom from your fair lips.
> *Coeca.* Quiniver.
> *Quin.* Madam.
> *Coeca.* I'st a handsome Man?
> *Quin.* Yes, indeed as e'er I saw.
> *Coeca.* I feel just such a Qualm, as I had
> When I was still falling in love, he has a sweet tongue.[23]

23 Howard, *Blind Lady*, 64–65.

Here, we see that Coeca is not treated with the dignity we might expect for one of her age and blindness either by the author or the characters. She is regarded as a foolish old woman, who, being blind, can be duped by those who want to use her momentarily and therefore say they see her as attractive (using her blindness against her) in their desperate condition. But the play adds to Coeca's humiliation since at the end when Mironault marries Mirramente and Phylanter marries Amione, Mirramente demands that Pysenor marry Coeca though he claims 'A dog were as good a husband for her / To lead her up and down.'[24] Although this is done as comedy, its (I would argue) unintended effect is to highlight the way the other two marriages have required the women to be as blind and accepting as Coeca of their husbands: they are women and should accept the correct man. Thus Pysenor's final couplet of the play as he exits with Coeca suggests that all thee will be unfortunate brides:

> *Pys.* We Bridegrooms disagree, for every day
> Will oblige most that adds to your decay.[25]

Behn's alteration of Howard's story is to make her blind lady, Celesia, indirectly the woman over whom her two men fight. Initially blindness puts Celesia out of the running as a prize in the marriage market (even though she is wealthy to the tune of £50,000), and she is only interesting as a foil for Belvira in her wooing of Frankwit. We hear that Frankwit 'basked in the bright lustre of [Belvira's] Eyes', and 'only valued the smiling Babies in Belvira's Eyes',[26] which dazzling makes him blind to the fact that his wealth is not unlimited and so he falls into debt, which brings the story to its denouement. At the same time Frankwit is dazzled, Belvira learns from Celesia to temper her love, who being blind, cannot be so dazzled by a beloved into acting precipitately. On her cousin's advice, Belvira suggests to Frankwit that they do not need to get married at once, wondering 'if it not be better

24   Howard, *Blind Lady*, 129.
25   Howard, *Blind Lady*, 140.
26   Behn, *The Unfortunate Bride*, 6.

to live still in mutual love, without the last Enjoyment.'[27] Celesia tells the love-sick pair that non-physical love is best, arguing that 'it is but a sickly soul which cannot nourish its Off-spring of desires without preying upon the body.'[28] But Frankwit is adamant that if she could see Belvira through his eyes, Celesia would 'be blinder then, than now unhappily you are.'[29] What he means is that could she see Belvira, Celesia would be as dazzled as he is and would spend all her money on her beloved in order to have sex with her, just as he plans to do.

As if to test this theory, Behn has Celesia cured of her blindness while Frankwit is away in Cambridge repairing his fortune by mortgaging his last property. At which happenstance, Belvira sends a poem to Frankwit:

> My poor Celesia now would charm your soul,
> Her eyes once blind, do now divine'y rowl,
> An aged Matron has by charms unknown,
> Given her clear sight as perfect as thy own.
> And yet beyond her eyes, she values thee,
> 'Tis for thy sake alone she's glad to see.
> She begged me pray remember her to you,
> That is a task which now I gladly do.
> Gladly, since so I only recommend
> A dear relation, and a dearer friend,
> Ne're shall my love — [30]

The last lines of the unfinished note act as an introduction of the newly sighted Celesia to Frankwit, to whom she will end up married. The cure for blindness is apt to the story since at the end of the story, when Wildvill sees Belvira fainted away in Frankwit's arms on his wedding day to his apparently unfaithful wife, all three are blind to what they see. Wildvill does not know that his wife is not actually being unfaithful to him, Frankwit does not know that Moorea has tricked Belvira into believing him unfaithful to her, and Belvira does not know that her former beloved is still enamoured

27 Behn, *The Unfortunate Bride*, 7.
28 Behn, *The Unfortunate Bride*, 9.
29 Behn, *The Unfortunate Bride*, 9.
30 Behn, *The Unfortunate Bride*, 13.

of her. But where these three people suffer from metaphorical blindness, Celesia's cure is real.

We know this because of Behn's lines about the cure:

> An aged Matron has by charms unknown,
> Given her clear sight as perfect as thy own.

I can find only one advertisement for an eye cure in the 1660s, in *Kingdome's Intelligencer* of 3–10 June 1661, which speaks of 'Rare Pills against ... deflux-ions of the eyes.' In the next surviving advertisement, dating from 7 June 1695 in *Collection for Improvement in Husbandry and Trade* we find 'The Chinese Eye-water, being the best in the World, which has done more Cures than any, and many of those extraordinary, is sold by Mrs *Hope*.' Two things are important here, first, for this 'Eye-water' to be the best in the world there must have been others, and it is sold by a woman. Twenty years later Mary Cater advertised just the type of remarkably speedy cure that Celesia underwent at the Hand and Eye in Castle Court (now Bengal Court, off Birchin lane). Cater continued to advertise until 1741, noting in her first advertisement that she already had over one hundred certificates for cures, which means she had been in practice long before she began to advertise.

Working from evidence I explore elsewhere,[31] we find in eye treatments in the Restoration period, that in the face of male doctors taking over the care of eyes with surgery, and in particular the couching operation, Cater's advertisements tell of a parallel female practice encompassing over 600 cures with her 'Medicines' for the removal of films over the eyes. Likewise, without going into details of the battle the male medicos had with each other in the seventeenth and eighteenth centuries over who could use instruments and who medicines to perform similar cures, what we find is that women practitioners got on with it and used traditional remedies with startling success rates.

---

31   See Chris Mounsey, *The Birth of a Clinic* (Lewisburg, PA: Bucknell University Press, 2016).

Furthermore, we can be certain that either Behn herself or someone she knew was treated in the same way for blindness from the description of Celesia's first experience of vision, when she has read the note quoted above:

> ... so eagerly ... [Celesia] perus'd ... [Belvira's unfinished note], that her tender eyes beginning to water, she cry'd out, (fancying she saw the words dance before her view) Ah! Cousin, Cousin, your Letter is running away, sure it can't go itself to Frankwit? A great deal of other pleasing innocent things she said, but still her eyes flow'd more bright with lustrous beams, as if they were to shine out, now all that glancing radiancy which had been so long kept secret, and as if, as soon as the cloud of blindness once was broken, nothing but lightning were to flash for ever after.[32]

In this passage, Celesia's misunderstanding of how her newly cured eyes work is typical of what was known in the Restoration period about people cured of blindness. Her tears blurring her vision leads her to suggest that the letter is 'running away ... to Frankwit', that is, it is moving of its own accord. This sort of 'pleasing innocent things she said' was recorded of others cured of being blind from birth, for example a boy couched by William Cheselden, who couldn't tell his cat from his dog unless he touched them,[33] or William Taylor, who was found climbing onto the roof of No.6 Hatton Garden trying to touch the moon.[34] The bizarre ways that people first saw after such procedures was theorized upon in the developing philosophy of empiricism, and John Locke mentioned it in his *Essay Concerning Humane Understanding*, second edition (1694), as did George Berkeley in his *Essay towards a New Theory of Vision* (1709). But as always theorization follows on to explain the well-known fact, and Behn's Celesia is an early example of the well-known fact that blindness could be cured, and after the cure people did not see correctly.

32   Behn, *The Unfortunate Bride*, 14.

33   William Cheselden, *Appendix to the Fourth Edition of the Anatomy of the Human Body* (London: William Bowyer, 1730), 19. There are many versions of Cheselden's story, of which this is the earliest.

34   William Oldys, *Observations on the Cure of William Taylor ... by John Taylor, junr. Oculist in Hatton Garden* (London: E. Owen, 1753), 5.

Varronian Satire

And this is where Behn's satire becomes truly Varronian. Restoration of
sight through the cure of blindness was not only possible in the real world,
it was also being used metaphorically of the English nation and its relation
to its newly restored monarch. *Three Royal Cedars* by Edward Sanders uses
the metaphor in a very interesting way. In describing the exile and return of
King Charles II, James, Duke of York and Henry, Duke of Gloucester, he
must account for their defeat and Cromwell's popularity with the people,
which is done in terms of the people's blindness and cure, followed by a
moment of 'pleasing innocent' misunderstanding:

> [King Charles] laments more his Subjects slavery then his own Exile, he grieves
> that they have been so long blind, yet rejoices for their sakes that they have now a
> Glimmering; he constantly prays for the restoring of their sight, not so much because
> they should restore his, as their own Rights and Priviledges.[35]

The English people have 'a Glimmering' of sight but must still learn to
love their monarch properly. We can now find also a reason for the role of
Moorea intercepting the lovers' letters and leading Frankwit astray, which
Wildvill interprets to Belvira:

> 'tis Witchcraft indeed that could make him false to you,[36]

35   *The three royall cedars or Great Brittains glorious diamonds, being a royal court narra-
     tive of the proceedings … of … Charles by the grace of God, King of Great Brittain, France
     and Ireland, His Highness Prince James Duke of York, and the most illustrious Prince.
     Henry Duke of Glocester. With a brief history of their memorable transactions … since
     their too-much-lamented Exile [sic] in Flanders, and the Lord Chancellour Hide, the
     Marquess of Ormond, the Earl of Norwich, the Lord Wentworth, the Lord Digby, and
     many other nobles and gentlemen, created lords of his Majesties privie-council. Also,
     the resplendent vertues appearing in these princely pearles, to the great joy of all loyal
     subjects … By E. Sanders Esq; a lover of his countries liberty, and a loyal subject and
     servant to his Sacred Majesty* (London: printed for G. Horton, living near the three
     Crowns in Barbican, 1660). 5.
36   Behn, *The Unfortunate Bride*, 14.

Moorea's witchcraft, which symbolizes Cromwell's attraction to the English people, is countered by the cure King Charles hopes for them, that Behn provides through the 'aged Matron' and her 'charms unknown', to make them and Celesia see again. Wildvill goes on to describe Moorea's magic in sexual terms as well

> ... what delight could ... [Frankwit] take in a Blackmoor Lady, though she received him at once with a soul as open as her longing arms, and with her Petticoat put off in modesty. Gods! How could he change a whole *Field argent* into down-right *Sables*.[37]

Celesia's addition to this aspect of Wildvill's opinion of Moorea, suggests a very un-Puritan motive within the black robes of Cromwell's followers:

> 'Twas done, returned *Celesia*, with no small blot, I fancy to the Female Scutcheon.[38]

The idea of the sexual attraction of Cromwell agrees with Celesia's argument at the beginning of the novel that non-physical love is better than sexual love. And this requires careful glossing as the imputation of sexuality to the puritans is odd indeed. It will be remembered that Celesia's words on the subject were 'it is but a sickly soul which cannot nourish its Off-spring of desires without preying upon the body',[39] and I would suggest that what she is saying is that while one might have ideas, they do not need to be acted upon. In the context of Moorea and the Puritans, it would seem that Behn is arguing that she is happy that they have their own peculiar ideas, so long as they do not impose them on anyone else.

This interpretation is also born out in Sanders' *Three Royal Cedars* where he describes Charles in very alien terms as 'the perfect pattern of Piety but more of Patience'[40] and compares him to Job. But whatever the truth, real or metaphorical about the relative sexual activity of Cromwell and Charles II, the blindness and cure of the English people is celebrated in Behn's character Celesia in a way which would be readily understandable

---

37   Behn, *The Unfortunate Bride*, 14.
38   Behn, *The Unfortunate Bride*, 14.
39   Behn, *The Unfortunate Bride*, 9.
40   Sanders, *Three Royal Cedars*, 5.

by her contemporary audience, and Frankwit, with his less than sexy body, and Celesia are married against all odds.

Conclusions

What I have argued would therefore suggest that neither the feminist nor the Foucauldian disability studies arguments with which we began are not wholly wrong in themselves, but that they are incorrect because they owe a simply application of theory and did not look back to the contexts which produced the texts. Behn's women are not feminist because they challenge patriarchal specularity, rather they privilege women's activities in taking the cure from the 'aged Matron' rather than from the increasingly fashionable process of couching cataracts. Nor is Celesia available to marry Frankwit at the end of the novel simply because she now fits the demand of compulsory able-bodiedness, rather it is because in Behn's Varronian satire she stands for the English people newly able to see the value of having a king.

SIMON JARRETT

Laughing about and Talking about the Idiot in the Eighteenth Century

ABSTRACT

The position of the 'idiot' in eighteenth-century public discourse cannot be dismissed as marginalized and liminal. Idiots lived before the eyes and in the minds of their communities. They were often the butt of jokes and mocked in slang language, but in an age where raillery and 'rattle' (mockery) were valued and universally applied to all sectors of society, this was more a signal of community visibility than an indicator of objectification. In this period, to be seen as lacking in mental faculty was not an inevitable precursor to social exclusion, as it would become in the nineteenth century.

Introduction

When the Prussian military man, historian and social commentator Johann von Archenholz visited England in the 1780s, he was impressed with London's street lighting, the affluence of the poorer classes and the growing industrial power of the country. However, he was particularly struck with something more ephemeral: the good humoured tolerance shown towards those who 'stood out' in appearance or behaviour. He commented, 'There, [in England] as everywhere else, they laugh at a ridiculous person, but they treat him with a great deal of indulgence; and they do not esteem a gentleman less on account of his oddity, provided he hurts no one.'[1]

---

[1]   Johann Wilhelm von Archenholz, *A Picture of England: Containing a description of the laws, customs, and manners of England* (London: Edward Jefferey, 1789), 3.

It was an insightful point. In Britain, which saw itself as the epicentre of a golden age of ridicule and satire, the citizens seemed at times to value and practice above all others the art of laughing at those whose appearance or behaviour amused them. They included the short, the fat, the thin, the tall, the stupid, the deformed, the blind, the deaf, the pompous, the overly clever, and anyone else who veered from some 'common sense' notion of what qualified as normative. Yet within this potential snake pit of vituperative banter, ridicule was not in fact synonymous with cruelty. It mediated a far more complex set of relations, between those who saw themselves as insiders and those at risk of being deemed an out-group. This ridiculing dialogue highlighted difference, often in disturbingly direct and unadorned language (to modern ears), yet simultaneously, by paying attention to potential outsiders in this form, signalled them as people who belonged.

This was particularly the case, I will argue, with those designated as 'idiots', the class of persons seen as lacking in mental faculties, 'simple' from birth, unable to understand, or indeed control, either their minds or their bodies. The nineteenth century would see a process of mass institutionalization of this group, first in workhouses and later in asylums, deemed pitiable, unable to fend for themselves or, in some cases, out of control and dangerous. Yet in the eighteenth century they lived, worked and took their chance in their communities; any sort of institutionalization was so minimal as to be negligible. To be a part of an eighteenth-century community in England was to be within the sphere of ridicule, and jokes and slang about idiocy and stupidity about those born slow and dull, abounded. Roger Lund's argument, however, that the 'deformed' of brain and body were ridiculed through 'an ideology of form which necessarily dismissed the deformed or the disabled as foreign, transgressive, ugly, and inherently worthy of contempt',[2] over-simplifies the case. To be laughed at, to be seen as fair game for ridicule, was more complex than that. It meant that a person was noticed, and accepted as part of the social fabric. Laughter and ridicule could of course be cruel and uncomfortable, and nobody escaped its barbs. As Simon Dickie has pointed out, the jest books featured 'blind men led

2   Roger Lund, 'Laughing at cripples: Ridicule, deformity and the argument from design', *Eighteenth-Century Studies*, 39 (2005), 111.

into walls, dwarfs thrown out of windows, lame matrons tumbled into ditches.'[3] However this was not inherently objectifying. In David Turner's words, 'humour shaped meanings of embodied difference ... the ludicrous possibilities of joking give humour the potential to interrogate conventional wisdom about bodily norms.'[4] Moreover, hunchbacks were laughed at, but then so were 'mackerel backs', people who walked with over-straightened backs. Idiots were ridiculed, but so were intellectuals divorced from the real world, clergy, schoolteachers, politicians, and doctors. Mrs Arlebury, in Frances Burney's *Camilla*, defended herself and all other wits from the accusation of unfeeling cruelty:

> Never judge the heart of a wit by the tongue. We have often as good hearts, and as much good nature as the careful persons who utter nothing but what is right, or the heavy thinkers who have too little fancy to say anything that is wrong. But we have a pleasure in our rattle that cruelly runs away with our discretion.[5]

Beneath the 'rattle' lay good hearts and good nature. The idiot could be accepted, indulged, and sometimes even admired and desired by those good hearts and good natures, just as much as they were laughed at and 'jeered'. In the age of ridicule and laughter, to be ignored, seen as beyond both, was the cruellest, most marginalizing fate. The 'rattle', as well as signalling inclusion and acceptance, also signalled much about the complex constellation of attitudes and opinions that shaped the concept of the idiot in the eighteenth century; their status in relation to other people, and in the chain of being that linked the higher forms of human life through the gradations of human capacity to the hierarchy of the animal world. As the century progressed, while idiots remained a part of communities, a growing concern was discernible in cultural discourse about their transgressive

---

3   Simon Dickie, *Cruelty and Laughter: Forgotten comic literature and the unsentimental eighteenth century* (Chicago: University of Chicago press, 2011) 18.

4   David Turner, 'Disability humour and the meanings of impairment in early modern England', in A. Hobgood and D. Houston Wood, eds, *Recovering disability in early modern England* (Columbus, OH: Ohio State University Press, 2013), 58.

5   Frances Burney, *Camilla, or a picture of youth* (Oxford: Oxford University Press, 1972), 780.

nature, mirrored in their position at the intersection in the chain of being between the lower forms of human and higher forms of animal. It was here that idiots would find their human status.

Laughing about Idiots

In 1760 a jest book included a lengthy joke (typically lacking in a punch line) featuring an idiot and a monkey:

> A great Lady that lived in a market town in the North, was pleased to give a fool, that was kept at the Town Charge, his Diet every Day; and one day coming at about eleven of the Clock, two of the Lady's gentlemen were playing a Tables in the Hall they on one side of the table and a Jackanapes on the other, looking on them as they played ... the gentlemen left their Game to carry up the Dinner. Then the Ape took up the Dice in his Paw ... Says the Fool to the Ape, Come i' Faith, I'd play with thee for a Pot and a Pipe; and went to take the Dice out of his Paw. Then the Ape grinn'd and chatter'd at him, and still kept the Dice in his Paw, and would not throw. Then, says the Fool, Throw, if thou be'st a Man, throw, and offered to take the Dice away from him, which so incensed the Ape, that he flew upon him, and had certainly killed him, had not some of the gentlemen that privately looked on, come to his Rescue; and from that time to this, the Fool could never be got to come in the House, would still go on the other side of the Street, looking fearfully on one side, fearing the Ape would see him, which it seems he did out of the Window, and had he not been chained, had certainly leaped down and fell upon him, which the fool seeing ran away crying, as fast as he could, and left his cap behind him for Haste, and could never be got to come through that Street again.[6]

What can this joke tell us about the status of the idiot, their place in the great chain of being in the eighteenth century? Does it reveal anything about the cultural mentality which framed common assumptions about idiocy, its characteristics and its meaning? Monkey jokes were common in the one

---

6   William Hickes, *Coffee house jests, being a merry companion* (London: S. Crowder, 1760), 33–34.

shilling 'joak' or 'jest' books that proliferated throughout the century. In these jokes, old ladies mistook monkeys for foreigners, pageboys or the Indian ambassador.[7] Welshmen went into shops and handed their money to the pet monkey, thinking it was the owner's father.[8] A country fellow delivered a letter to a monkey at a gentleman's door because, as he explained later, 'Truly sir ... I thought it was your son, it was so like you.'[9] Another, encountering two dandies in London, offered to buy them, because 'I keept a Monkey at home, but I never see one so big as them before.'[10] Yet the joke about the idiot and the monkey is qualitatively different and goes much further. Like the old lady, the country bumpkin or the Welshman, the fool mistakes an ape for a human. He then, however, continues to engage with the ape as a perceived equal, perplexed by its apparent unwillingness to engage with him. He is then attacked and violently mastered, only saved by the intervention of the gentlemen in the gambling hall. Yet it does not stop there. From that point he is dominated by the ape, which recognizes him and enforces his mastery by intimidating him from the window of the Lady's house. The monkey remains within, the idiot is pushed outside, not daring even to pass in the street where the house stands. This is no ordinary monkey joke. The idiot finds himself in a status battle, and loses out to the jackanapes.

There are other signals given by this joke concerning its idiot subject. First, he is an anachronism, wearing the cap of the traditional court jester, a phenomenon that had died out with the demise of Charles II's last fool.[11] This tells us that we are in the recurring world of the joke, a dream land-scape[12] where anachronism, dissonance and discontinuity are the norm,

---

7   *Coffee House Jests*, 109; J. S., *England's Merry Jester* (London: N. Boddington, 1694), 102.

8   *England's Merry Jester*, 102–103.

9   *Coffee house jests*, 11.

10   J. Cooke, *The Macaroni jester and pantheon of wit* (London: T. Shepherd 1773), 13.

11   Derek Brewer, 'Prose jest books, mainly in the sixteenth to eighteenth centuries in England', in J. Bremmer and H. Roodenburg, eds, *A Cultural History of Humour* (Cambridge: Polity Press, 1997), 105.

12   Sigmund Freud, *The joke and its relation to the unconscious* (Harmondsworth: Penguin, 2002), 22–23.

but also that we are in a changing world; the fool is sustained through a poor law dole, 'kept at the town's expense'. This was unusual throughout the eighteenth century, where parish funding for idiots was a last resort should familial care or independence break down.[13] This idiot is redundant, alone, an object of charity representing a dying feudal structure where lords kept fools for their entertainment and instruction, faintly echoed in the great lady's willingness to provide him with a meal each day. Second, he is both observer and observed. He watches the gentlemen play at cards, present but to the side, unable to participate until, like a child, he spots an opportunity when the gentlemen, the real players, leave the table. He is watched, as the gentlemen 'privately look ... on' amused, while he is wrestled by the ape. This is part of the power of the joke, the third parties who see and laugh at the situation for us,[14] intervening only once the humiliation has been sufficiently played out and before the ape 'would certainly have killed him'. However, he is most certainly *there*, a recognisable, known figure, roaming the streets, inside homes, amusing, exasperating, strange, not quite getting what is happening around him. He is protected, when necessary, from the consequences of his own misunderstandings: tolerated, his strangeness seen and understood, an eccentric bit-part player woven into the fabric of daily life. Was this, then, the idiot, or at least a type of idiot, recognized and understood by the people of the eighteenth century?

The idiot's slippery status and foothold in the chain of being took place under the amused gaze, at times malign and sometimes warm and engaged, of the 'cits'[15] of eighteenth century Britain. In the cultural imagination idiots loomed large. They were a stock feature of jokes, and populated them in many guises. They were also a pervasive and significant presence in the slang of the streets, eagerly collected by antiquarian gentlemen such as Francis

---

13   Peter Rushton, 'Idiocy, the family and the community in early modern north-east
      England', 59–60; Jonathan Andrews, 'Identifying and providing for the mentally
      disabled in early modern London', 66–67, both in Anne Digby and David Wright,
      eds, *From idiocy to mental deficiency* (London: Routledge, 1996).
14   Jacques Le Goff, 'Laughter in the Middle Ages', in Bremmer and Roodenburg, *A
      Cultural History of Humour*, 40; Freud, *The joke* , 97.
15   i.e. 'Citizens'

Grose.[16] Grose was simultaneously repelled and fascinated by the sharp argot of London's poor; the hawkers, labourers, prostitutes, and criminals who populated the alleys and ale houses of St Giles and Seven Dials, and who knew very well what in their opinion an idiot was. Thus they named the 'billy noodles' and 'bird wits', the 'empty fellows' and 'goose caps', the 'nizies' and 'nockys' who lived among them.[17] Idiots gazed back from the caricatures of daily life in this, the golden age of the satirical print; crowds from all classes swarmed around the print shop windows to laugh at these portrayals of themselves and their fellow citizens, the dim and the dull included. They were in the art of Hogarth, the novels of Cleland, Smollett and Burney, in popular but now forgotten cheap 'ramble' fiction such as *Tom Fool*,[18] plays, poems, epigrams and riddles. Much, but not all, of the characterization in these cultural productions involved humour. Idiots were everywhere and yet, at the same time, easy to miss, such a familiar yet unobtrusive presence that they could be both present and invisible. This is why when in the nineteenth century they began to slip from the public gaze and face new threats to any status claim they had of full humanity, it was a quiet, barely perceptible, and largely unnoticed process. As Corbyn Morris put it in 1744, 'the biggest challenge to ease in relationships is not Disrespect but Negligence and Disregard ... an inconvenience arising from the *Respect* which is paid to us may be easily excused; but ... *Neglect* ... gives a lasting offence.'[19] It was better to be seen and 'jeered' than to be seen yet ignored and, ultimately, forgotten. In 1783 Samuel Johnson echoed Morris: 'I hope the day will never come when I shall neither be the subject of calumny or ridicule, for then I shall be neglected and forgotten.'[20]

16   Francis Grose, *A classical dictionary of the vulgar tongue*, 2nd edn (London: S. Hooper, 1788).

17   All words for 'silly' or foolish people in Grose, *Classical dictionary*.

18   George Alexander Stevens, *The History of Tom Fool*, 2 vols (London: T. Waller, 1760).

19   Corbyn Morris, *An essay towards fixing the true standards of Wit, Humour, Raillery, Satire and Ridicule* (London: J. Roberts, 1744), 55.

20   Cited in John Brewer, *The pleasures of the imagination: English culture in the eighteenth century* (London Harper Collins, 1997), 48.

How reliable and useful are these cultural artefacts as indicators of popular assumptions about the place of the idiot in the human hierarchy, or indeed their liminal position in the human/animal continuum? Humour has come to be seen only relatively recently as a vehicle through which we can achieve historical understanding. Keith Thomas has noted that studying 'the laughter of our ancestors is to gain some insight into changing human sensibilities', a 'pointer to structural ambiguity' which brings us up against the fundamental values and innermost assumptions of past societies.[21] Jan Bremmer has called humour 'a key to the cultural codes of the past' because it is a culturally determined phenomenon, rather than an ahistorical ontology as argued by, amongst others,[22] Sigmund Freud.[23] Jokes in particular 'promote the humour and harmony of the group who share it', creating a 'collective psychological landscape' underpinned by implicit assumptions.[24] We cannot of course read jokes as 'unproblematic indicators of social reality'[25] – by their nature they simplify, subvert, fantasize and create absurdity. Their meanings change according to nuance and intention, who is telling, who is listening and why.[26] However, people 'joked about what they saw'[27] and the joke could only do its work if teller and listener, writer and reader, shared broad normative assumptions and social and cultural experiences. The joke, as Freud was to note, was an important social signifier:

---

21   Keith Thomas, 'The place of laughter in Tudor and Stuart England', *Times Literary Supplement* (21 January 1977), 77.

22   The 'universalist' theory of humour has often been expounded by anthropologists and sociologists. Jan Bremmer, 'Preface' and 'Introduction', in Bremmer and Roodenburg, *A Cultural History of Humour*, xi and 3.

23   Freud, *The joke*.

24   Brewer, 'Prose jest books' in John Brewer, *The pleasures of the imagination*, 90 and 96.

25   Anu Korhonen, 'Disability humour in English jestbooks of the sixteenth and seventeenth centuries', *Cultural History*, 3 (2014), 29.

26   Tom Shakespeare, 'Joking a part', *Body and Society*, 5/47 (1999), 52; Anu Korhonen, 'Disability humour in English jestbooks of the sixteenth and seventeenth centuries', *Cultural History*, 3/1 (2014), 29.

27   Korhonen, 'Disability humour', 28.

> ... we may ask whether the topic of jokes is worth such trouble? Let us ... bear in mind the peculiar, indeed fascinating, attraction jokes exercise in our society. A new joke has almost the same effect as an event of the widest interest; it is passed on from one to another like news of the latest victory.[28]

Slang, like jokes, built group identity, with its origins in the canting language of criminals, devised to deceive, defraud, and conceal.[29] The ability of slang to hide meanings from the unsuspecting meant that its main concerns were always matters that speakers wished to disguise, such as sexual relations, appearance and criminal activity, a principle aim therefore to identify the vulnerable,[30] easy prey, the empty-headed victim or the easily manipulated accomplice. This made it a rich source of popular opinion about how the idiotic, the dim and the dull looked and behaved. The poor of London recognized immediately those who, for some, signalled the opportunity to exploit, while for others they required protection and succour against those exploiters. They were the 'culls' and 'bubbles', silly, easy fellows who could be easily 'buttoned' or drawn in. Slang, like fashion, is used 'to define in groups and out groups'.[31] It is of course not uncomplicated as a source. The very moment in 1699 when the gentleman called 'B. E.' created his dictionary of *The terms ancient and modern of the canting crew* and when, in 1784, Francis Grose published his *Classical dictionary of the vulgar tongue*,[32] marked points at which this language began to pass from the private, concealed sphere to the public realm. It was appropriated by the gaze of the wealthier classes, frozen on the printed page and so denuded of its *raison d'être*. Yet prior to this de-authentication it was drawn from authentic sources. Grose toured the back slums and drinking dens of St Giles with

---

28   Freud, *The joke*, 9.

29   Julie Colman, *A history of cant and slang dictionaries, Vol. 1 1567–1784* (Oxford: Oxford University Press, 2004), 4.

30   Lee Beier, 'Anti-language or jargon? Canting in the English underworld in the sixteenth and seventeenth centuries', in P. Burke and R. Porter, eds, *Languages and jargons: Contributions to a social history of language* (Cambridge: Polity Press, 1995), 81.

31   Colman, *A history of cant and slang*, 1.

32   B. E., *A new dictionary of the terms ancient and modern of the canting crew* (London: T. Hawes, 1699).

his man, Batch, and from 'these nocturnal sallies, and the *slang* expressions which continually assaulted his ears'[33] he compiled his dictionary, laying before the world the secret codes of plebeian London.

Writers of fiction and caricaturists drew on the slang and the jokes and added their own versions of the idiot, which in turn fed back into the constellation of ideas that swirled in the minds of consumers and producers of culture, high and low. In Frances Burney's *Camilla* (1796) the intellectually challenged Sir Hugh, with his 'poor capacity' and 'poor weak head'[34] is referred to by his exploitative nephews as 'blockhead', 'old gull', 'ninny' and 'numps',[35] all terms which can be found in the slang dictionaries to denote an idiot, or vulnerable simpleton. Caricaturists drew the jokes they had read in the jest books, bringing visual form to their idiot characters; bamboozled idiot countrymen found themselves paying to walk in London sedan chairs which had had their floors removed, rustic simpletons misunderstood and were baffled by the questions of their intelligent visitors from London.[36] Idiot characters stared, eyes half-shut, from caricatures, displaying the low 'beetle brows' and sloping 'bullet heads' that Grose had gleaned from his vicarious fascination with London's low-life talk. The idiotic 'lowbrow' even became a term to define low culture. The idiot, and ideas about the idiot, unobtrusively permeated culture at all levels. As Patrick McDonagh has claimed about the nineteenth century, so it was in the eighteenth: 'cultural works foreground the symbolic functions of ... notions of idiocy ... [they] express culturally charged beliefs about [its] subtexts or connotations.'[37]

These notions of idiocy took many forms. There were first, of course, the perennial rustic idiots, the unintelligent country simpletons, ripe for the

---

33   Piers Egan, *Grose's classical dictionary of the vulgar tongue, revised and corrected* (London, 1823), xxxvi-xxxvii.

34   Burney, *Camilla*, 184, 534.

35   Burney, *Camilla*, 212, 225, 500, 505.

36   Isaac Cruikshank, *Paddy Whack's first ride in a sedan* (1800), based on Ferdinando Foot, *The nut-Cracker* (London: J. Newbery, 1751), 61; Isaac Cruikshank, *The buck and the goose* (1801), based on Joe Miller, *Joe Miller's Jests*, 4th edn (London: T. Read 1740), 28.

37   Patrick McDonagh, *Idiocy: a cultural history* (Liverpool: Liverpool University Press, 2008), 15.

picking on the streets of London, dull, slow and stupid. At the beginning of the century, this represented an entire idiot class, without distinction of rank or wealth. The 'rich bumpkin' and the county squire were just as stupid as the ditch-digger or ploughman, by virtue of not being smart city dwellers. In jest books countrymen see large ships in the London docks and on being told they are a year old, wonder how large they will be by the time they are adults;[38] they observe the new St Pauls being built and marvel that it must have cost even more than they spent on their new barn;[39] they are called 'loggerheads' by smart city boy apprentices.[40] 'Ignorant clowns' think they can read, but misread signs with comical effects and fall on their backsides on London's streets. They visit the theatre, wide-eyed, only to leave when the actors appear on stage, as they do not wish to disturb 'the gentlemen ... talking about business'.[41] The same jokes were plagiarized and recycled, sometimes from the previous century, throughout the eighteenth century.

An enormous array of slang terms and nicknames described the idiot countryman; booby, bumpkin, chaw-bacon, clodpate, country put, hick jop, clouted shoon, hobinail, milestone, and clown all captured his dull slowness of wit.[42] The rustic idiot was barely distinguishable from the animals and birds amongst which he dwelt. He was a bull calf, a donkey, a pea goose, and a sheep's head. Popular rural names became nouns to denote

38   John Taylor, *Wit and mirth* (London: J. Dawson, 1640).

39   J. S., *England's Merry Jester*, 31.

40   William Pinkethman, *Pinkethman's jests, or wit refined*, 2nd edn (London: T. Warner, 1721), 24.

41   Anonymous, *The merry medley, or, a Christmass-box, for gay gallants and good companions* (London: J. Robinson 1750), 30, 57; Anthony Copley, *Wits fits and fancies* (London: Edw. Allde, 1614).

42   These and subsequent slang references are taken, unless otherwise indicated, from the following slang dictionaries: B. E., *A new dictionary of the terms ancient and modern of the canting crew*; *New canting dictionary* (London: n.p., 1725); Robert Goadby, *An apology for the life of Mr Bampfylde-Moore Carew* (London: W. Owen, 1750); John Shirley, *The scoundrel's dictionary* (London: J. Brownell, 1754); Humphrey Tristram Potter, *A new dictionary of all the cant and flash languages* (London: J. Downes, 1787); Grose, *A classical dictionary of the vulgar tongue*; James Caulfield, *Blackguardiana, or a dictionary of rogues, pimps, whores etc.* (London 1795).

stupidity; an idiot figure was a Ben, Dick, Roger, Sam, Jack Adams, Johnny Raw, Simkin, Simon, or Donkey Dick. He was characterized by a thick, impenetrable skull and did not feel pain in the same way as others. Thus he was a puzzle pate or hulver-head, hulver being Norfolk dialect for a hard, solid wood, and Norfolk being the epicentre of rural stupidity.[43] In cheap popular drama aimed at mass audiences, characters called Hob and Dick became engaged in cudgel fights with their neighbours Puzzel Pate and Roger, with a prize for the first to break the skull of another. No matter how hard their skulls were hit, they came back, still alive, for more. As Puzzel Pate put it, 'I have had enough on 'en already, for he broke my Head but last week'.[44] There was clearly little brain to be damaged.

The country idiot was not simply a witty conceit but occupied a meaningful space in the consciousness of the eighteenth-century city dweller. Amused Old Bailey juries would acquit an accused felon on the grounds that 'he was a poor silly country fellow and might be easily drawn in'.[45] This reflects C. F. Goodey's argument that ideas of intellectual deficit in the early modern period were intimately tied up with ideas of class and poverty.[46] However, over the century there was an increasing recognition that idiocy was more nuanced than this. The countryman might appear idiotic due to lack of experience and education, but most had the capacity to learn and could demonstrate wit and intelligence to the surprise of the urban sophisticate. A mid-century anecdote/jest attributed to Beau Nash has him encountering an apparently gormless country porter, who is abused by Nash and told mockingly to find 'a greater fool than yourself'. When the porter returns with the mayor of the town, Nash appreciates the conceit and asks him *Being a poor Man, what Business have you with Wit?* He and the newly respected countryman agree that too much wit only brings misfortune to rich and poor, while both rich and poor fools

---

43   Home of the Norfolk dumpling, a particularly egregious yokel idiot.
44   Thomas Doggett, *Hob, or the country wake: A farce* (London: D. Brown, 1715), 26–27.
45   *Old Bailey proceedings* (<www.oldbaileyonline.org>, version 6.0), April 1690, trial of Edward Munden (t16900430-28).
46   C. F. Goodey, *A history of intelligence and 'intellectual disability': The shaping of psychology in early modern Europe* (Farnham: Ashgate, 2011).

prosper. Nash gives him a guinea and advises him to 'go Home, and study Stupidity'.[47] Empathy here is predicated on shared intelligence rather than class, idiocy a changeable and corrigible phenomenon. A clear distinction was developing between the 'real' idiot and those labelled as idiotic because of their foolish and exasperating behaviour. As the author of *Tom Fool*, three years before the Nash anecdote, put it: 'By Ideots I don't mean those unhappy objects, whose defective Organs makes them May-games to the sounder-formed part of the World. I mean ... that Society of men, who are nicknamed Ideots by their Wives, their Brothers, their Friends, their Partners, Masters and kept Mistresses.'[48] A divide was appearing between the incorrigible born idiot and the uneducated but improvable, or badly behaved fool, country or otherwise.

Who are the Idiots?

As, towards the mid-eighteenth century the idea of the natural-born idiot became distinct from the foolishly behaved ignorant person, there emerged a strongly held notion of the idiot as a human who is unable to learn. The low-born person might, with luck, progress from the ignorance into which they had unfortunately been born, but the idiot was perpetually marooned in a state of incomprehension, never moving on. Their problem lay in their thick, inflexible, impenetrable, unproductive, empty head, skull, or brain. As a typically scatological piece of graffiti from 1731 pronounced, 'Like Claret-Drinkers Stools, a Blockhead's Brain; / Hardly conceives what it brings forth in Pain.'[49] Thick-skulled idiots were, on the Galenic scale, the phlegmatic kind. However, there was also the thin-skulled 'vapourish'

---

47   Richard Nash, *The Jests of Beau Nash* (London: W. Bristowe, 1763), 40–42.
48   Stevens, *History of Tom Fool*, 72.
49   Hurlo Thrombo, *The merry thought: Or the glass-window and bog-house miscellany* (London: n.p. 1731), 69.

idiot:[50] they were corky brain'd fellows, crakt-brains, jingle brains or had their brains in their ballocks. Their skulls were soft, meaning that they were empty and unproductive. Thus they were paper skuls, num-skuls, sapsculls, empty skull'd , sap pates, and shallow pates. A silly fellow is like a feather bed, explained a riddle, 'because he is soft'.[51] Their heads, though, as a rule were generally hard, signalling that nothing, including a cudgel, could penetrate the blockhead, fat head, hulver head, loggerhead, or thick head.

In this rigidity and inflexibility, the inability to read situations or learn from them, lurked the humour of idiocy. Idiots refused to modernize, because they were incapable of learning how to do so. As the rest of society adopted increasingly complex modes of interaction and strived for polite forms of behaviour to signal social status, idiots persisted in doing the wrong thing. They did so because they were unable to abstract or apply knowledge flexibly, and the comic consequences of this incapacity permeated the jest books. An idiot on his death bed, assured by his friends that he will be carried to the graveyard, replies that he would prefer to make his own way there.[52] A crack-brain'd, soft-headed fellow is confronted by his wife: 'Come, says she, you are simple, and must go to school, to learn to read and write, and then you may get into a better employment.' He attends but, unable to learn even his Horn-book[53] is laughed out of the school by the children, and returns to ditch digging, attracting derision from London travellers when he tells them he has just started school.[54] In a more sinister vein, a fool, teased by a carpenter, gains his revenge by cutting off his head with an axe when he is asleep, and hiding it. Asked later why he is laughing he replies; 'Oh, the bravest funn that ever you heard of ... I laugh to think, when the carpenter wakes, how like a fool he'll look without a head, and lose his Afternoon's work, to find out where I have

50   Daniel Defoe, *Mere nature delineated, or a body without a soul* (London: T. Warner, 1726), 37.
51   *The complete London jester*, 10th edn (London: T. Lowndes, 1781), 139.
52   *Pinkethman's Jests*, 91.
53   A primer.
54   J. S., *England's Merry Jester*, 75–77.

hid it.'[55] Idiots were the ultimate comic bystander, obstinately failing to learn, a non-participant in the common human themes of life and death, startling others by the sheer level of their ignorance. As Frances Burney's Sir Hugh laments, however much he tries all this 'jingle jangle' (learning), 'I find myself turning out as sheer a blockhead as ever.'[56]

In the sexual sphere, the male idiot was an object of humour through two opposite and contradictory identities; easily deceived cuckold and well-endowed sexual performer. A 'nickum-poop' was not just a silly, soft, foolish fellow, but also one who 'never saw his wife's ****'.[57] Joke makers scorned the trusting, naïve, gullible idiot husband, who allowed the rules of chastity to be broken because he was unable to understand them. The husband explained innocently to his cousin that his wife was pregnant after eight childless years, although 'I protest I had no hand in it.' His cousin, the real father of course, accepts the invitation to be godfather, quipping that 'all the Neighbours will say you take God's name in vain there.'[58] In a satirical poem, the oblivious cuckold Simple Simon begs his friend Thomas to kiss his beautiful wife Susan:

> The Delight of my life
> Look at her again! Did you ever behold
> Such sweetness enshrined in so charming a Mold.

When the inevitable happens, the guileless and unsuspecting Simon helps things along by informing Thomas that he is out each day from 'Eleven til Two'. The only person to blame, the poem concludes, for Susan being subsequently 'visited', is Simple Simon himself.[59]

As well as these impotent idiot authors of their own matrimonial misfortune, there was a sharply different breed of sexual idiot. In John Cleland's 1749 pornographic work *Memoirs of a Woman of Pleasure*, the heroine Fanny Hill, seduces a servant named Will who is fresh from the

55   J. S., *England's Merry Jester*, 74–75.
56   Burney, *Camilla*, 39.
57   Grose, *Classical dictionary* (asterisks in original).
58   *Coffee House Jests*, 130.
59   *The muse in good humour* 2nd edn (London: J. Noble, 1745), 86–87.

country. As well as being a 'very handsome young lad ... fresh as a rose, well shaped and clean limbed' he is also a 'modest, innocent ... blushing simpleton ... in a strain of perfect nature.'[60] When Fanny unbuttons Will's breeches, his fore-flap flies open, and she sees:

> with wonder and surprise ... not the plaything of a boy, not the weapon of a man, but a maypole of so enormous a standard that, had proportions been observed, it must have belonged to a young giant.[61]

The simpleton Will is prodigiously endowed and an excellent lover. Cleland emphasizes the association of sexual endowment with idiocy, referring to the popular saying 'a fool's bauble is a Lady's play fellow',[62] bauble being, as Grose recorded, a slang word for testicle. The reason for the belief in an idiot's exceptionally sized genitalia was the trope of the compensatory faculty, where:

> nature ... made him amends, in her best bodily gifts, for her denial of the sublime intellectual ones ... in short had done so much for him in these parts that she perhaps held herself acquitted in doing so little for his head.[63]

The idea of the well-endowed idiot was encapsulated in the term 'lob cock', which meant both 'a heavy dull inanimate fellow' and 'a large relaxed penis.'[64] This was also the theme of the 'ramble' novel *Tom Fool* of 1760, where the proliferation of the Fool family is attributed to 'Nature making amends for the Deficiency of Head, by a Superabundancy in other parts.'[65] Like Fanny Hill's Will, Tom Fool is intellectually simple but physically handsome and attractive. As a lady's maid comments, after catching him 'unlaced' one day, 'he's such an ignoramus, and so bashful ... he looked so

60   John Cleland, *Fanny Hill: Or memoirs of a woman of pleasure*, [1748/49] (Harmondsworth: Penguin, 1994), 91–93.
61   Cleland, *Fanny Hill*, 94.
62   Cleland, *Fanny Hill*, 192.
63   Cleland, *Fanny Hill*, 191–192.
64   Grose, *Classical dictionary*.
65   Stevens, *The history of Tom Fool*, 3.

simple, and so innocent, that if I had been to be ravished by him, I must have forgiven him.'[66]

Fanny Hill later encounters a youth named Good Natured Dick.[67] He is a local ragged flower seller, 'a perfect changeling or idiot', stammering out 'the sounds that his half-dozen animal ideas prompted him to utter.' Though ragged, he is 'well made, stout, clean limbed'.[68] Fanny and her friend seduce him and find him 'rich in personal treasures ... of so tremendous a size that, prepared as we were to see something extraordinary, it still, out of measure, surpassed our expectation and astonished even me, who had not been used to trade in trifles.'[69] Dick's mental faculties are considerably more impaired than Will's, so his physical compensation is proportionately greater. The idea of the handsome, well-endowed and somewhat unrestrained idiot was not simply a literary trope applied for titillation by male authors. When Peter the Wild Boy was brought to the Hanoverian Court in 1726, courtiers were reported to have been disappointed by his indifference to women, after holding high expectations of the idiot youth's 'wild virility'.[70] Along with the savage man, the idiot could hold irresistible sexual appeal.[71] Notably absent from this discourse was any sense of danger, disgust, or loathing directed towards the idiot body, and nor was the thought of sexual liaison with a certain type of idiot, taboo. The humour lay not so much in the transgression of sexual encounters involving well-endowed idiots and highly sexed women, as in their predictability. Each behaved as expected. The idiot, not knowing the rules of sexual encounter, had to be seduced by the woman. The woman, who according to the eighteenth-century trope is sexually rapacious after the loss of her virginity, is driven to take the lead by the promise of the idiot's

---

66   Stevens, *The history of Tom Fool*, 26.
67   Tom Fool is also nicknamed 'Good-natur'd Tom'. Its meaning in this sense is naturally well-endowed, as well as easy and pliable.
68   Cleland, *Fanny Hill*, 190.
69   Cleland, *Fanny Hill*, 192.
70   Julia V. Douthwaite, *The wild girl, natural man and the monster: Dangerous experiments in the age of Enlightenment* (Chicago: University of Chicago Press, 2002), 21.
71   Douthwaite, *The wild girl*, 68.

physical endowment. Each behaves as expected, but in doing so creates a highly comical juxtaposition of opposites.

While the notion of the transgressive idiot was notably absent from jokes about sexual encounters, a transgressive discourse took form in the public imagination, as the century progressed, of the idiot as incontinent, in the broadest senses of the word; physically, emotionally, verbally, and morally. These multiple incontinences derived from a lack of control and restraint, which in turn was caused by an inability or unwillingness to self-control or self-restrain. Slang reflected this. Stupidity and the inability to control language were conflated. Thus a 'blab' was a prating stupid fellow, who tells all he knows. Foolish, nonsensical ramblers were spoonys, rattle pates, or blubbers. A blubber was defined as a thick headed 'mouth', a 'mouth' being a stupid easy fellow. Their words had no meaning, but were simply a function of an ever-productive, gaping mouth. There was no connection between idiots' facial expressions and the inner emotions they were supposed to reveal. They would grin for no reason. A 'grinagog' was a foolish grinning fellow, 'who grins without reason', 'flearing fools' were grinning, silly fellows. Idiots were slow, clumsy, barely able to move their own dull, blockish bodies, they were clumpish, lumps, and slubbers, all terms used to denote heavy, stupid fellows. A 'drumbelo' was a dull, stupid slug of a man.[72]

This lack of control over the body and mind clashed with growing public expectations of control of bodily functions and emotional restraint. As Thomas put it, 'bodily control became a symbol of social hierarchy.'[73] It was from this disparity between aspiration and individual behaviour that humour flowed. Conduct and rule books tried to instil new standards of restrained and hygienic behaviour underpinned by a sense of shame, delicacy and mutual obligation. In 1729 La Salle, the French rule-setter on manners, advised, 'it is very impolite to emit wind from your body when in company, either from above or below, even if it is done without noise ... it

---

72   Grose, *Classical Dictionary*.
73   Thomas, 'Place of laughter', 80.

is shameful and indecent to do it in a way that can be heard by others.'[74]
Thirty years later oblivious, idiot, jest book characters were doing just that,
and subsequently bragging about it. 'A simple fellow, before some Women
did let a Crack behind, and then he said that he had a very good Rapport
behind his back.' The punch line underscores the connection between the
uncontrolled body and unrestrained mind, as an observer tells the simple
man 'thy Tail [arse] can talk much better; for that has more wisdom in telling a Tale than thy Tongue.'[75] La Salle also enjoined that 'it is never proper
to speak of ... certain bodily necessities to which nature has subjected us,
or even to mention them.'[76] The enjoinment not to talk about such natural functions mingled with requirements, that had been developing since
the medieval period, to improve hygiene, to use separate hands for clean
and dirty tasks, and to wash them when necessary.[77] Thus the jest about a
fool's use of the wrong hand for greeting, and his explanation of why he
had done it, was doubly shocking:

> A natural fool was commanded to give such a Lord his Hand, which he presently
> did, but gave him his left Hand, for which his master chid him, and told him he
> should have given his Lord his Right hand. O fye, Master, says the Fool, I think you
> are more Fool than I, for that's an unseemly Thing indeed, to give to a great Lord
> that Hand which I wipe my Breech withal every day.[78]

There is a sense in these humorous discourses and vernaculars of a gap opening between the expectations and criteria that society was setting down
for membership and what the idiot could achieve. Their unawareness of
this and the resultant constant social *faux pas* were laughable matters, and
also alienating for the increasingly clearly defined idiot group. Alongside
this, however, there existed a certain relish in the idiot's stubborn refusal

---

74   Jean Baptiste de La Salle, *Les règles de la bienséance et de la civilité chrétienne*, [Rouen,
       1729] , 44, cited in Norbert Elias, *The civilizing process* (Oxford: Blackwell, 2000),
       112–113.
75   *Coffee House Jests*, 109–110.
76   Baptiste de La Salle, *Règles*, 24, in Elias, *Civilizing process*, 113.
77   Elias, *Civilizing process*, 50, 57.
78   *Coffee house jests*, 65.

to 'modernize'. The imprecations of La Salle and others, the exhortations to politeness and manners, were just that: imprecations and exhortations. Eighteenth-century society was not becoming an oasis of good manners and excellent personal hygiene simply because writers suggested that it should. As Dickie has argued there was a gulf, often humorously observed, between precept and practice. Ideals and exhortations to politeness were expressed precisely because it was not being attained, in an impolite world that talked about politeness.[79] People strained desperately to make themselves polite, to regulate their passions.[80] In 1740 *An essay on polite behaviour* demanded, 'A Man must be Master of Himself, and his Words, Gestures and his Passions, that nothing offensive may escape him'.[81] 'One must conform', wrote the diarist Anna Larpent, 'to the World ... I will do everything with the intention of doing right ... I must learn to dissimulate in this world.'[82] Thus the jesting satire was directed not only against the uncontrolled bodies and unmannerly behaviour of their idiot protagonists, it was also directed against those who were trying so hard not to be like them. In 1743, William Whitehead had written in verse, an *Essay on Ridicule*. Everybody, without exception, was subject to ridicule he noted, there was no escape, and no mercy. All stood at 'Mirth's tribunal, where Mercy sleeps, and Nature pleads in vain.'[83] Politeness opened two distinct conduits for humorous and ridiculing discourse on idiocy. There was the eternal and lifelong idiot, resolutely unchanging and unchangeable, not following the new rules because he simply had no grasp of them. Then there was the aspiring non-idiot, behaving like an idiot as they tried to conform to the new rules but fell short due to lack of skill, knowledge or ability.

This disparity between the humorous incontinence of the idiot body and mind and the demands of polite and civilized behaviour was spectacularly expressed in a deeply scatological mock-heroic poem, *The County*

79   Dickie, *Cruelty and Laughter*, 3, 6.
80   Brewer, *Pleasures of the imagination*, 102
81   Anonymous, *An essay on polite behaviour*, 1740, cited in Brewer, *Pleasures of the imagination*, 110.
82   *An essay on polite behaviour*, 1740, cited in Brewer, *Pleasures of the imagination*, 110.
83   William Whitehead, *An essay on ridicule* (London: R. Dodsley, 1743), 6 (lines 69–70).

Squire: a tale, which appeared in a 1757 jest book.[84] The 'hero' Humphrey, nicknamed Numps,[85] is the blockhead son of a despairing worthy squire, who hopes that he can 'mend the breed' by marrying his son to a 'prudent' young woman of good stock. Before sending him to be introduced to the intended bride and her family his father implores him:

> Humphrey says he, whate'er you do,
> Take heed your words be very few
> For you'll be quoted wise so long
> As you have wit to hold your tongue.[86]

He is keen not only to restrain Humphrey's verbal incontinence, but also the bodily incontinence arising from his insatiable appetite for sweet pudding:

> And never feed too greedily
> On custard, Pudding or sweet pye
> Lest your ungoverned appetite
> Bring shame and sorrow in the night.[87]

As always the inevitable happens and despite having learned by heart the appropriate verbal greetings and pleasantries and delivered them passably well, Humphrey cannot control his appetites and gorges on apple pie and cream, ignoring the pleadings of his servant. That night he fouls his bed as a result, and despite his servant's efforts to take the blame himself, gives away the secret and is sent back to his father in disgrace. The squire's desire to 'mend the breed' of his family, the ritual of courtship, the perpetuation of bloodline, the restrained formalities and polite manners of elite life, all are deeply subverted and mocked by the arrival of the amiable Numps with his uncontrolled appetites, words, and body.

---

84   'The County Squire: A tale', in Luke Lively, *The merry fellow, or jovial companion*, vol. 1 (Dublin: James Hoey, 1757), 113–116.

85   Humphrey's nickname, Numps, denotes a silly or stupid person (OED). *cf.* Frances Burney, *Camilla*, 523, where Lionel refers to his simpleton Uncle Hugh as 'Numps'

86   Lively, *The Merry Fellow*, 113–116.

87   Lively, *The Merry Fellow*, 113–116.

The most extreme and enduring image of the idiot body and its incontinence was the gaping, drivelling mouth. Idiots were imagined with mouth permanently open, the drooping lower lip pulled down like a hinge by the protruding lower jaw. The open mouth signified not only poor control over facial features and expression but a dull puzzlement at what was going on around the uncomprehending idiotic figure. They roamed the streets 'mouth half cockt', as the slang dictionaries put it, 'gaping and staring at everything they see.'[88] Their slack jaws earned them the epithet 'gab.'[89] In the jest books bemused country idiots wandering London's streets would address each other 'mouth at half cock',[90] while idiot country lads being asked the catechism 'stood gaping' as if they 'had heard Dutch spoken.'[91]

The open, uncontrolled mouth resulted in drivel, the idiot's internal fluids leaking from their bodies through this unguarded point of exit. Robert Nixon, the protagonist of the immensely popular 1715 almanac *Nixon's Cheshire Prophecy*[92] was a 'sort of an idiot' from the reign of Charles II, widely believed to have the power to foresee momentous political events 'as well attested as any of Nostradamus's or Merlin's.'[93] Nixon was able to deliver prophecy with 'gravity and solemnity ... speaking plainly and sensibly', despite being a 'Drivler [who] could not speak common sense when he was uninspired.'[94] Like Humphrey, Nixon displayed greedy, uncontrolled appetite, locked in a cupboard by the King's cooks because he 'grew so troublesome in licking

---

88   *New canting dictionary.*

89   John Bee, *Sportsman's slang* (London, 1825).

90   J. S., *England's Merry Jester*, 31.

91   J. S., *England's Merry Jester*, 84–85.

92   A popular feature among the hundreds of thousands of chapbooks in circulation through the seventeenth and eighteenth centuries, Nixon's prophecies were among the small number of books possessed by the illiterate labouring parents of John Clare,. See Margaret Spufford, *Small books and pleasant histories: Popular fiction and its readership in seventeenth-century England* (Cambridge: Cambridge University Press, 1981), 3.

93   Robert Nixon, *A true copy of Nixon's Cheshire Prophecy* (London: J. Roberts, 1715), 3, 5.

94   Nixon, *Cheshire Prophecy*, 3.

and picking the meat' in the royal kitchens.[95] His body both consumed and produced, with no controls. The head-lopping fool of the carpenter joke laughed uncontrollably at what he had done, 'till he drivel'd again'.[96]

Unrestrained and meaningless verbosity, combined with uncontrolled physical drooling, were signifiers of idiocy even if deceptively framed within a handsome beauty. In Frances Burney's *Camilla*, in the final years of the century, the idea of the drooling idiot took its place as a disturbing, primitive, presence at the heart of the polite and progressive world, gazing mindlessly at Camilla's deformed but intelligent sister Eugenia. Eugenia's father arranges for her to encounter 'accidentally' a young woman, who is 'a beautiful creature ... fair, of a tall and striking figure, with features delicately regular.'[97] Eugenia, who is devastated by what she perceives as her own ugliness and physical deformity, is then astonished to see the beautiful stranger break into nonsensical chatter. On being asked if she is well, she responds 'Give me a shilling!' while 'the slaver dribbled unrestrained from her mouth, rendering utterly disgusting a chin that a statuary might have wished to model.'[98] Eugenia understands immediately the moral message her father has arranged: 'beauty, without mind, is more dreadful than any deformity.'[99] Idiocy could be deceptive, but it would always become apparent, breaking out from any bodily disguise, the body unable to hold back its fluids, the mind unable to control its thoughtlessness. This trope appeared in a distinctly unmerry poem in the *Merry Fellow*, a jest book of 1757, called 'The Handsome Idiot'. The poet's heart is taken the moment he casts his eye on the young woman 'so heavenly fair, with eyes so bright', but:

> ... soon as e'er the beauteous idiot spoke,
> Forth from her coral lips such folly broke;
> Like balm the trickling nonsense heal'd my wound,
> And what her *eyes* enthralled, her *tongue* unbound.[100]

95   Nixon, *Cheshire Prophecy*, 14–15.
96   *England's merry jester*, 74–75.
97   Burney, *Camilla*, 306, 308.
98   Burney, *Camilla*, 309.
99   Burney, *Camilla*, 311.
100 'The handsome Idiot' in Lively, *The Merry Fellow*, 29.

The thick, solid head and body of the idiot concealed and unsuccessfully tried to contain the airy lightness and liquidity of the idiot mind. Idiocy oozed, trickled and dribbled into the sunlight and there, displayed on the chin, and evident in meaningless babble, turned the Handsome Idiot into something disgusting. Spittle, La Salle implored, must be concealed:

> ... you should take great care never to spit on your clothes, or those of others ... if you notice saliva on the ground, you should immediately put your foot adroitly on it. If you notice any on someone's coat, it is not polite to make it known; you should instruct a servant to remove it ... for good breeding consists in not bringing to anyone's attention anything that might offend or confuse them.[101]

While clearly not all, particularly those of the lower orders, conformed to La Salle's precepts (otherwise why would he have made them?), most did have the capacity to conform to polite standards if they wished. However, there was a certain type of idiot, with their involuntary slavering, who simply lacked the capacity to respond to this clarion call for acceptable, mannerly behaviour.

Conclusion

The idiot was then an undeniable and pervasive presence in the consciousness of eighteenth-century society. They appeared in the jokes people told, the slang they used, the novels and plays they read and saw and the caricatures they laughed at. They could often be peripheral, but they were always present. They appeared in a number of different guises, frequently as someone who lacked control in some way, in opposition to the exhortations to politeness, manners and self-restraint that permeated the age: a conservative figure in the face of the drive for social and personal improvement. This deficit could vary in extent, from the completely uncontrolled drooling

---

101   Baptiste de La Salle, *Règles*, 35, in Elias, *Civilizing process*, 131.

idiot to the amiable but dull 'stupid fellow', to the potentially mischievous and sly simpleton. However more than anything the idiot, in their cultural formation, was an object of humour. They made people laugh.

The eighteenth century was, as Gattrell has described, a period in which 'laughter flowed around other people's appearances, mishaps and affectation', when London was the 'city of laughter.'[102] Commentators and theorists tried to define just what it was that made people laugh, and why they laughed, in this town of 'absurdities ... smutty jests, loud Laughter.'[103] Humour came from observation; Corbyn Morris argued in 1744 that it was 'any whimsical oddity or foible appearing in the temper or conduct of a person in real life.'[104] Matters became even more amusing if similar or opposite subjects were unexpectedly juxtaposed with the main object of the laughter.[105] Thus an idiot invited into the house of a lady was humorous because of his inherent oddity and whimsicality; however he became hilarious when placed in opposition to an ape, mistaking it for his own sort. The level of laughter that humour elicited was graduated. It ranged from the gentle amusement of raillery, which was 'a genteel, poignant Attack of a Person upon any slight Foible, Oddities or Embarrassments of his' to the hilarity of ridicule, which 'is justly employ'd, not upon the Vices, but the *Foibles* and *Meanness* of Persons'.[106] However, even ridicule did not imply hatred or loathing for its object. It was 'directed not to raise your *Detestation*, but your *Derision* and *Contempt*.'[107] Contempt had a very specific meaning at this time: it was an action, the direction of derisive laughter against someone because of something about them, rather than the degrading mental attitude or feeling by which it is exclusively defined

---

102   Vic Gattrell, *City of laughter: Sex and satire in eighteenth-century London* (London: Atlantic Books, 2006), 6.

103   Anonymous, *Hell upon earth: Or the town in an uproar* (London, 1729), Frontispiece and 5.

104   Morris, *An essay towards fixing the true Standards of Wit*, 12.

105   Morris, *An essay towards fixing the true Standards of Wit*, 1.

106   Morris, *An essay towards fixing the true Standards of Wit*, 53.

107   Morris, *An essay towards fixing the true Standards of Wit*, 53.

today.[108] When an idiot was ridiculed or laughed at they were not being hated or loathed; their oddity and strangeness were being observed, noted and categorized as an object for amusement.

There was some concern that to laugh at people simply because of their natural state was wrong. Blackmore counselled heartless wits that 'to make a man contemptible ... by deriding him for his ... low degree of Understanding, is a great abuse of ingenious faculties.'[109] The German philosopher George Friedrich Meier echoed this, insisting that 'when a droll and ridiculous form is merely a natural defect, it claims our compassion and forbearance.'[110] However the threshold was set very high for the point at which ridicule should give way to compassion. Meier himself argued that 'many Failings and Miscarriages deserve a slight Ridicule' and that for the humour to work 'the ridiculous, which is exposed by the jest, must be actually in the object.'[111] William Hay, a man of letters and politician who was also a 'hunchback dwarf'[112] wrote in his *Deformity: An essay* (1755) that while he was mercilessly shown ridicule and contempt whenever he came anywhere near the mob, this being a 'certain consequence of deformity', he did not suffer affronts from gentlemen.[113] However he then revealed, amused, that his gentlemen friends would compare him to an eclipse when his small frame appeared from behind a bowl of punch as he sat at dinner.[114] To comment humorously on a person's defects, to ridicule and mock, was not regarded as necessarily pitiless or objectifying, unless it attained a particularly high level of violent abusiveness.

108   'Contempt, n.' *OED Online* (Oxford: Oxford University Press), December 2014. Web: 25 February 2015.

109   Richard Blackmore, *An essay upon wit*, [1716] (London: Augustan Reprint Society, 1946), 211.

110   George Freidrich Meier, *The Merry Philosopher: Or thoughts on jesting* (London: J. Newbery, 1764), 189–190.

111   Meier, *Merry Philosopher*, 111–112.

112   Stephen Taylor, 'Hay, William (1695–1755)', *Oxford Dictionary of National Biography* (Oxford: Oxford University Press, 2004); online edn (January 2008), <http://www.oxforddnb.com/view/article/12739>, accessed 25 February 2015.

113   William Hay, *Deformity: An essay* (London: R. and J. Dodsley 1755), 9, 59.

114   Hay, *Deformity*, 9.

James Beattie explored the paradox of laughter and sought to define the limits of ridicule in his *Essay on ludicrous composition* [1764]. Laughter was the outward sign of that 'agreeable emotion' we feel when we encounter 'irregularity and unsuitableness', and the 'unexpected discovery of resemblance between ideas supposed dissimilar ... that comic exhibition of singular characters'.[115] To laugh at such incongruous juxtapositions, Beattie argued, was both natural and agreeable. However, he echoed Blackmore's concern about the risibility of natural defects, proposing that no one should laugh at 'that person who has neither sense nor spirit to defend himself'.[116] How then could a person know the borderline of ridicule, when they should stop laughing and start pitying? How would they know if they were laughing at the incongruity which defects or absence of faculty gave rise to, or at the unfortunate person who lacked the faculty? Could 'pity, abhorrence and risibility be excited by the same object and at the same time?'[117] In the battle between laughter and pity, Beattie concluded, it was impossible to maintain contradictory emotions; the weaker would always give way to the stronger. Moral disapprobation would therefore always win out over the ludicrous sentiment when necessary.[118] The border between the two was self-policing and therefore that 'agreeable emotion', excited by a mixture of 'relative and contrariety ... in the same assemblage ... will always ... excite the risible emotion, unless when the perception of it is attended with some other emotion of greater authority.'[119] One knew when to laugh, and when not to laugh: the borderland was defined by the moment when pity arose. The act of laughter switched off the feeling emotions, until those emotions won through over unacceptable heartlessness.

So we may conclude that laughter and jokes about the idiot, the slang that quipped about the 'bottle heads' and 'nick ninneys', the caricatures of the slack-jawed but ever present simpletons, the jabbering characters in

115 James Beattie, 'Essay on laughter and ludicrous composition', in *Essays* (Edinburgh: William Creech, 1776), 323–325.
116 Beattie, 'Essay on laughter', 335.
117 Beattie, 'Essay on laughter', 424.
118 Beattie, 'Essay on laughter', 424.
119 Beattie, 'Essay on laughter', 454.

fiction and theatre, were not straightforward signifiers of objectification and marginalization. In the eighteenth century idiots lived before the eyes and in the minds of their communities. They were instantly recognisable, clumsy, awkward, often uncomprehending. They served in the houses of the great and the not-so-great, joined the crowds in the streets, participated in the events of daily life, worked and lived in families. They amused people, sometimes to the point of derision and cruelty, but also won their affection and protection. The exploitative identified and named them in order to take advantage, but others rallied to support and defend them. They were generally not perceived as dangerous, never a threat, unless perhaps to themselves. In the second half of the century a faint but strengthening discourse of transgressive anxiety began to appear in the language and phraseology of idiocy. This would gather pace in the early nineteenth century, but as the eighteenth century came to an end idiots remained neither loathed, nor pitied. They were, however, very much present.

STAN BOOTH

LESS is More: The Mysterious Case of the Invisible Countess of Derby

ABSTRACT

Lady Elizabeth Smith-Stanley, the first wife of the 12th Earl of Derby, has been eclipsed by her replacement, the actress Eliza Farren. This essay attempts to construct some sort of an account of this elusive woman – unfaithful wife, excluded mother, and paralytic – from the few facts that can be found out about her. As there is so little to go on, the contribution to this collection lies more in its methodological significance than in giving a full account of a woman's life.

Introduction

There is a major gap in our knowledge of the life of Lady Elizabeth Smith-Stanley, nee Hamilton (herein known as LESS), the first wife of Edward Smith-Stanley, 12th Earl of Derby, probably because she was succeeded in that role by an actress, Eliza Farren, who upstaged her in both contemporary and historical interest. What we know of LESS from recent critics and historians is that she played cricket:

> ... the match reported by the modish Countess of Derby at The Oaks in 1777, between two parties of ladies of distinction ... signalizes the rebellion of upper class women, ...[1]

---

[1]   Reported in the *Morning Post* (26 June 1777). See Betty Rizzo, 'Equivocations of Gender and Rank: Eighteenth-Century Sporting Women', *Eighteenth-Century Life*, 26/1 (Winter 2002), 70–118, 85.

Rizzo is unclear what the rebellion was. The Oaks, Lord Derby's house in Surrey, Daniel O'Quinn explains had been host to elaborate and expensive marriage celebrations:

> On Thursday the 9th of June 1774, General John Burgoyne of Saratoga fame, arranged an elaborate *Fête Champêtre* at the Oaks, in Surrey, to celebrate the wedding of his nephew Lord Edward Stanley and Lady Elizabeth Hamilton. The guests included the foremost men and women of the kingdom and this seemingly trivial gathering of fashionable society was the subject of extensive reporting in the newspapers.[2]

O'Quinn tells us further that the decorations for the masques performed in the Pavilion that was built specially for the occasion were at once political and allegorical:

> Patrician military rule, conjugal fidelity and mythic figures for the longevity and endurance of the British constitution are all conjoined into a distinct fantasy of national election which is explicitly pitched as a counter-performance to the fantasy of aristocratic sociability articulated in the first masque. It is this declaration of the guests' capacity–or should we say, in light of the tactical maneuvers of the second masque, their necessity to recognize and celebrate this conjunction, that constitutes Burgoyne's articulation of an aristocratic performance suited to the historical moment. It is why this diversion is but the flip side of the coercion he was seeking to enact in the realm of policy.[3]

But at the same time, O'Quinn notes

> The irony here is almost too much to bear. In October of 1777 Burgoyne surrendered at Saratoga and British rule in the American colonies would look anything but providentially secure. In 1779, Lady Elizabeth Hamilton left Lord Stanley, now Lord Derby, for John Frederick Sackville, the most notorious rake of the day. Derby eventually took up with the actress Elizabeth Farren. In short, the conjoined fantasy of military supremacy and conjugal fidelity would be in tatters shortly after its articulation on this particular evening.[4]

---

2   Daniel O'Quinn, 'Diversionary Tactics and Coercive Acts: John Burgoyne's Fete Champetre', *Studies in Eighteenth-Century Culture*, 40 (2011), 133–155, 133.
3   O'Quinn, 'Diversionary Tactics', 149–150.
4   O'Quinn, 'Diversionary tactics', 155.

Filling in the story of the infidelity is Hannah Greig, who explores the way in which 'Lady Betty' was treated by The Beau Monde, which first believed Derby would divorce her and continued to welcome a countess who might become a duchess, who forced her into exile when it became obvious Derby would never divorce her, and who finally accepted her back with open arms when Derby was making a public fool of himself chasing Eliza Farren, who equally publicly refused his sexual advances until she could marry him.[5]

In other accounts, LESS is sidelined, and typical of many women in history is reduced to a mere adjunct of accounts of the lives of the men who used and abused her. The ODNB entry for John Frederick Sackville gives a reason for the Countess organizing cricket matches – as a way innocently to meet with her cricket-mad Duke of Dorset. That for Edward Smith-Stanley tells us that 'Derby's steadfast refusal to divorce his wife and to grant her access to their children not only added to the sensation but also ruined the rest of her life.' But the account does not point out that by remaining married to her he, the richest man in England, stood to inherit the Hamilton fortune, the largest in Scotland. Nor does it tell us how her life was ruined, in a way which probably had nothing to do with him – she was paralyzed.

The only account of LESS's impairment comes to us in an historical fiction, *Life Mask* by Emma Donoghue. The novel uses fiction to explore the reason for Eliza Farren's resisting Derby's advances for so long, and suggests that Farren was engaged in a lesbian relationship with the sculptor, Anne Damer. Along the way, Donoghue surmises that:

> The Countess's descent into invalidism had caused him [Derby] a secret gratification.[6]

Using this fictitious animosity as a way to develop her characters, Donoghue imagines Farren visiting LESS just before she died, where the actress finds:

---

5   Hannah Greig, *The Beau Monde: Fashionable Society in Georgian* London (Oxford: Oxford University Press, 2013), 203–211.
6   Emma Donoghue, *Life Mask* (London: Hachette Digital, 2004), Kindle edition, Loc 286.

> The Countess was a most alarming yellowish-brownish colour about the eyes. ... She looked more like sixty than forty; one could tell that she's been ill for many years.[7]

Fiction also gives space for suggestions of a diagnosis, whence LESS explains:

> 'In the same month as the fall of the Bastille I lost the use of my legs. Now, whether the consumption brought on the paralysis or the paralysis had some separate origin is a fascinating question on which I dwell in my many leisure hours.'[8]

But Donoghue's fiction misses the opportunity to recount the probable meeting between Derby himself and his errant wife when she returned from exile to The Beau Monde while he was chasing his actress. If it did happen it was at a ball at Carleton House on 14 January 1790 where it was reported:

> Lady Derby, though much affected by an illness, said to be of the paralytic kind, was present, but was obliged to be conveyed through the rooms, in a chair upon wheels – she was, however, in high spirits.[9]

The chair, probably a Merlin Chair, was the first wheeled chair marketed specifically to enable paralyzed people to move about inside houses.

Medical Biography and Beyond

It was my original intention to write a medical biography of LESS and her paralysis, to question whether it was an early example of amyotrophic lateral sclerosis (ALS), a disease that was first described by Charles Bell in 1824. However, a lack of information, doctors' notes, newspaper reports, letters, diaries and contemporary text books on this form of paralysis proved a major impediment to telling the story of LESS's eighteenth-century impairment.

7   Donoghue, *Life Mask*, Loc 8313.
8   Donoghue, *Life Mask*, Loc 8320.
9   *London Chronicle* (London), Issue 5220 (14–16 January 1790).

Another reason this is not a medical biography of LESS becomes clear with the question of retro-diagnosis, a process that is the staple of medical humanities, which applies twentieth-century diagnoses to eighteenth-century people. For a scholar with a science background, I was surprised that not much work has been done to evaluate retro-diagnosis and that William Ober's famous *Boswell's Clap and other essays*, published some twenty-five years ago still holds sway in the field.[10] A doctor of his period born in the 1930's, Ober was accomplished as a medical men but he remains in our minds because of his remarkable retro-diagnosing. Christopher Smart, the poet, is diagnosed as a religious maniac because, we are told: 'From Jubilate Agno we know that he created public disturbances by praying in St James's Park and Pall Mall ... [and] Smart also committed the solecism of praying naked in the rain ... .'[11] The retro-diagnosis takes no account of Smarts ultra-Anglicanism, shown by his attendance at St George the Martyr, Queen Square, whose vicar, William Stukeley, exhorted his parishioners to pray continually. Nor does it notice that in Potter's madhouse where he prayed in the rain, it was the custom to put the inmates outside unclothed when it rained to get them clean and in lieu of a bath.

It is not his retro-diagnosing *per se* which I call into question, for his conclusions may sometimes be valid, but the validity of his methodology. For if one of his patients had gone to him with such woolly explanations would he really have accepted what they were suggesting about themselves? Even if a fellow doctor had approached him with the sort of vague evidence on which he makes his diagnoses would he have accepted it? I would argue 'no' for as we all know when we visit our doctors, suspicions remain suspicions until the qualitative data is backed up by quantitative testing. Ober, as a Doctor would have readily dismissed the speculative, only recognizing the truth with the evidence of test results. As to why he believed it was acceptable for him to use such wide indicators for specific diagnosis is open to speculation. But perhaps this was a case of do as I say and not as I do.

10   William B. Ober, *Boswell's Clap and and Other Essays: Medical Analyses of Literary Men's Afflictions*. (Carbondale, IL: Southern Illinois University Press, 1979).

11   Ober, *Boswell's Clap*, 182–182.

The main problem with retro-diagnosing is the indelible links it forges between patients and diseases even when the patient could not possibly have had the disease. Pope had Pott's disease, or so say all the accounts of his life. No he did not. Pope died in 1743 and Percivall Pott did not publish his account of the symptoms of spinal tuberculosis to which disease he gave his name until 1779. Pope could not, and nor could his doctor have known what Percivall Pott was going to name as a specific disease. And in the case of LESS's paralysis we do not even know for sure the name of her doctor.

But we do know a number of facts about her life, and there are more than have appeared in the previous accounts noted above. But we need to marshal these facts in an effective way, and it is the question of how to make MORE of the few facts we have that will be the argument of the rest of the paper.

Towards a Cultural Studies Approach to Historical Impairment

Facts about bodies have a habit of leading us astray, and it is important to remember the unaccountable influence the body can bring to writing. As Chris Mounsey points out in the Introduction to *The Idea of Disability in the Eighteenth Century*, we treat all bodies as the 'same only different'[12] from our own, that is, we project ourselves to some extent into other people's bodies in order to understand them albeit we are distanced from them in experience or in history. It is this added dimension of intimacy that makes biography interesting even if we may not know much about the person, and by which we can extend the story to bring an added dimension to what we are trying to tell. But if we get too intimate, too imaginative, we can get carried away and write about something for which there is no evidence. Working in eighteenth-century studies it is important to explore

---

12   Chris Mounsey, Introduction in *The Idea of Disability in the Eighteenth Century* (Lewisburg, PA: Bucknell University Press, 2014), 2.

the available evidence in its historical context and try not to bring in anachronistic ideas with which to justify a particular position. Therefore, I want to propose a model for a cultural studies approach to historical impairment which uses the information available, interpreting it according to the strictures of what could be known, and based on the evidence available.

I have already noted that a lack of information, newspaper reports, letters, diaries and books are a major impediment to providing what we think should be necessary for telling the whole story of an eighteenth-century subject. Even with access to databases such as Eighteenth-Century Collections Online and the online Burney Collection, the OCRing[13] is a maximum of 80 per cent accurate, so searches show no more than four out of five hits, and probably many fewer. And what should the search term be for 'Lady Elizabeth Smith-Stanley', who was born 'Lady Elizabeth Hamilton' and became the 'Countess of Derby'? All of these, of course, and also, perhaps not surprisingly, 'Lady Betty', although 'Lady Betty' was also the name of a horse owned by her husband. And is *this* a significant fact?[14]

Even with all these searches now available, the information derived may still be fragmentary. In the long article about the ball at Carleton House we read – or at least try to read (see Figure 7.1):

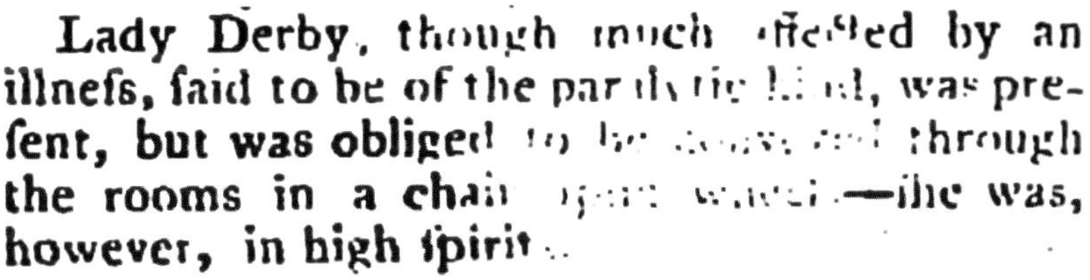

Lady Derby, though much affected by an illness, said to be of the par... ... was present, but was obliged ... ... through the rooms in a cha... ... ... —she was, however, in high spirit...

Figure 7.1: *London Chronicle* (London, England), Issue 5220 (14–16 January 1790).

13   Optical Character Recognition, the method of harvesting data, which recognises and modernises hand-carved fonts into modern fonts, and in the process loses a large quantity of the information.
14   It is significant that in my searches on the Burney collection, I did not find the references Greig did for LESS's travels in Switzerland, Austria and Italy, noted in *Morning Post and Daily Advertiser* (London; 3 June 1780); *Public Advertiser* (London; 14 February 1782); *Morning Herald and Daily Advertiser* (London; 8 May 1782); *Whitehall Evening Post* (London; 7 January 1783).

We can reconstruct this, as above, as 'Lady Derby, though much affected by an illness, said to be of the paral[ytic kind], was present, but was obliged [to be conveyed] through the rooms in a chai[r upon wheels] – she was, however in high spirits.'[15] But there is a possibility that the illegible words have been misread, although the imagined whole seems to make sense of the parts.

Due to all the discrepancies and missing pieces of information, no single narrative can be constructed that might be called a 'total picture.' Rather, I would suggest that if we sort the evidence into parts I shall call 'Information Streams' we can make a 'whole' out of a group of linked analyses which together will be more convincing by referring to a number of different contexts, and a picture of an impairment can emerge somewhere in between. I would like to suggest in this paper that these Information Streams might include:

- The Patient
- The Social/Familial Context
- The Physician
- Medical Education And Practice
- Treatments And Prosthetics

Each of these streams has an internal logic, a 'self-checkability', because of the related nature of the information. A wedding date is a wedding date, and if there is a discrepancy a reason needs to be worked out with reference to other information related to that marriage: its own context. Where there is no information about the medical practitioner who attended LESS, what might the practitioner who would have attended her, from his education, have diagnosed. Where there is information that LESS used a prosthetic, what does that say about the character of that person using it? A wheelchair says something different about a countess than a wheelbarrow about a legless beggar.

---

15   In this case, the reading is confirmed by the *Whitehall Evening Post (1770)* (London), Issue 6467 (14–16 January 1790).

What holds the methodology together and gives it something like a sense of a biography is the chronology. Information Streams separate out different narratives that tell different stories. But each is an aspect of one person, sometimes shared with other people (like a medical practitioner), sometimes unique (like a delayed wedding celebration).

Following this methodology, what this paper will try to do is to locate the person that was Lady Elizabeth Smith Stanley, to unearth the life of this most tragic of heroines and reconnect the words written about her to her paralyzed body.

The Patient

LESS was not ill all her life, she becomes a patient only when she is ill. We first hear of her, or at least a Lady Betty, coughing in 1787, in a scandalous letter 'To the printer of the St James Chronicle' disguised as a comment about card playing:

> Whist in most Families is become quite a TALKING Game, and the Cards now, instead of banishing Conversation, serve only to fill up a little Interface while Sir George is blowing his Nose, or Lady Betty coughing. Hence Characters and Cards are thrown down together, and of all Topicks, Men and Things, Cards alone are fairly dealt by.[16]

It would have seemed strange that a person should be associated with a cough, had I not known someone with a particular cough as I grew up in North East Manchester. There was a man, one of those characters which every area has: affable, pleasant and totally un-troublesome, whom everyone knew by his cough, and who every minute would give that most distinctive cough. Short, throaty with a tinge of a bark. It would be hard

---

16   *St. James's Chronicle or the British Evening Post* (London), Issue 4184 (29 November-1 December 1787).

for anyone to replicate; it was very distinctive. So when I saw the report in the newspaper of Lady Betty and her cough it brought her closer to me and my experience. As to what Sir George (Sackville?) was suffering from with his nose, one could only speculate and think of John Wilmot, Earl of Rochester and wonder if the reporter was trying to imply a sexual link through shared illness, between Sir George and Lady Betty.

Three years later, the newspapers of the 14th of January 1790 reported the attendance of LESS in her wheel chair at the ball at Carleton House given by the Prince of Wales. But what the article also shows is how information can fail to give us the most important information: was the Earl of Derby in attendance? or for the present paper – a diagnosis. The non-attendance of any members of the Royal Family except for the Prince of Wales and the Duke of Cumberland is reported, as is LESS's conveyance in a wheel chair, noted above. However, though even the type of chair is named, and the reason for the non-attendance of other members of the Royal Family explained in a corrective report of the same event a fortnight later, neither the presence of Lord Derby, nor the illness is glossed further:

> The conduct of Lady Derby, in appearing at the Prince's Fete in a Merlin Chair, has been improperly censured in the Papers, and improperly represented. The Prince, with his usual condescention, requested Mrs Fitzherbert to invite Lady Derby; and to induce her to come, it was represented as to be a select party of friends, all of whom she knew. On this Lady D. went, and, to her surprise, found a numerous assemblage of persons of distinction.[17]

Whether or not the 'numerous assemblage of persons of distinction' included Lord Derby is only hinted at, but LESS's place as the cast off countess at a ball hosted by the mistress of the Prince of Wales is thus explained, but the same report gave her condition only in general terms: 'Lady Derby's health is very indifferent – her spirits in general worse',[18] which might suggest she was cast down by meeting her husband with his new mistress on his arm, or it might mean that she was depressed.

17   *Public Advertiser* (London), Issue 17326 (29 January 1790).
18   *Public Advertiser* (London), Issue 17326 (29 January 1790).

Soon after, and again the next year, newspaper reports claimed that her health was declining and she needed extra support from her family: first from her mother, then from her Uncle, General Gunning.[19] The implication would seem to be that she had been coping with her ailments by herself – and she had been able to attend the event at Carleton House even though reliant on a chair, but that now she needs to be helped by her family. Again, there is no suggestion as to what her ailments might have been.

In 1793 newspapers asked further questions as to the health of 'The lovely Lady Derby',[20] though it is interesting that the report is not clear as to whether her condition was a result of her poor mental health or her poor mental health was a result of her paralytic condition: we read only that 'Her health is much injured by the reflections of her mind, on her undeserved situation.'

On 7 December 1796, Lady Derby was reported 'very dangerously ill',[21] and on 14 March 1797, she left this mortal coil 'at twelve o'clock.'[22] As for the cause of her demise we are not told. But she was forty-four years of age, very young for an aristocrat to die, and for any woman not in a perinatal state.

As noted above Emma Donoghue's *Life Mask* suggests she died from Tuberculosis, that is from the cough. As she was impaired by a 'paralysing kind' of disease, it may follow that she really did have Pott's disease (the tuberculosis of the spine may have spread to her lungs). However, the disease having been formalized by Percival Pott in 1779, it may well have been the latest fashionable diagnosis by physicians. But again this is pure speculation as we do not have the quantitative analysis to back up the supposition.

LESS may equally well have had tuberculosis but not to the debilitating extent that Donoghue suggests. I would argue it is also not beyond fantasy to suggest, as does the report about her mental health, that LESS may even have suffered from a motor neurone disease or multiple sclerosis,

19   *Gazetteer and New Daily Advertiser* (London), Issue 19 (19 March 1790); Issue 19
     121; *Argus* (London; 5 November 1791).
20   *Star* (London), Issue 1510 (1 March 1793).
21   *Morning Post and Fashionable World* (London), Issue 7718 (7 December 1796).
22   *Telegraph* (London; 17 March 1797).

something which could not have been diagnosed in the eighteenth century, but that would be to retrodiagnose.

Socio-Familial Context

'The Dutchess of Hamilton, was brought to bed of a Daughter on the 26th'[23] of January, 1753 at Holyrood House in Edinburgh. Both the Duke of Hamilton, her father, and her mother, Elizabeth Gunning, who later became the Duchess of Argyll, gave her a noted lineage, and her ancestors were prominent in Scottish society. Whether this lineage should alert us to some family history of illness would require a great deal further research,[24] but being born in an upper-class family would have given her the best chance for survival – as it does now.

Several weeks later, on 20 February, she was baptized with the name of Elizabeth.[25] The lateness of her baptism also gives us an indication that she was a healthy baby as she was not baptized hurriedly in case she died.

Then she grew up, and other than being a noted beauty she lived a typical genteel life until she was engaged to and then married the Earl of Derby – Edward Smith-Stanley. By the time of the wedding her mother was already re-married after the death of her father, so the wedding was held at 'Argyle-House', by 'the Rev. Mr Church'.[26] Whether this was Argyle-House in London or in Scotland is unclear, but the announcement states that they set off to Derby's new house at The Oaks. A special license was required for the marriage on 23 June 1774, perhaps because they were different denominations, or because they were marrying in Scotland, or because they were both of the peerage. The special license may also be a reminder

---

23   *London Daily Advertiser* (London), Issue 541 (5 February 1753).
24   Her father died of a cold caught while out hunting, her mother pre-deceased her aged sixty-seven in 1790.
25   *London Evening Post* (London), Issue 3952 (24–27 February 1753).
26   *General Evening Post* (London), Issue 6347 (23–25 June 1774).

that LESS's parents had married in haste at the Mayfair Chapel which did not require one.

However, the run up to the marriage was not as smooth as it might have been. The wedding seems to have been delayed and the Fete Champetre organized by General John Burgoyne, which we might have thought would have been part of the celebrations took place two weeks before the wedding, on 'Theusday' (7 (?) or 9 (?) June) rather than after.[27] The newspaper report adds to the confusion by stating that the Fete that it 'is said to be the marriage of that young nobleman with Lady Betty Hamilton.'

Further confusing the start of a supposed happy life, a couple of days after the wedding, Lady Elizabeth Smith-Stanley as she now was, appears still to be firmly in the grip of her mother as she was giving gifts to the Duchess of Argyll's servants.[28] Where the announcement for the wedding suggested that the happy couple left Argyle-House directly for The Oaks, though she remained at Argyle-House, we must pause for question. Was the wedding delayed due to LESS's indisposition? Whereas the 'near three hundred persons of distinction' attending the Fete Champetre could not be put off?

Nevertheless, as a dutiful wife, ten months after the wedding she gave birth to Lord Derby's heir, Edward on 21 April 1775. This would suggest that LESS was at least healthy at that time, but it was some eighteenth months after Edward was born, that LESS gave birth to her second child, a daughter Charlotte. Considering how quickly she became with child when first married, there is a distinct time lag if there was any urgency in ensuring the addition of the spare. Was she ill, did she have a miscarriage? Or was she beginning the affair with Dorset (who is noted to have attended the Fete Champetre)?

The next surviving newspaper report of LESS is that she is in Bath. Styled as an '*Extract of a Letter from Bath, Dec.7*', the statement is brief and scandalous:

27   *General Evening Post* (London), Issue 6341 (9–11 June 1774).
28   *Middlesex Journal and Evening Advertiser* (London), Issue 819 (25–28 June 1774).

Lord Camden, Lord George Germain, Lord Nugent and Alderman Wilkes are here. Lady Betty takes large draughts of hot water, a thing to be wondered at, as it is probable she will find herself near hotter water by the 20th January.[29]

Lord George Germain (Sir George of the nose?), a relative of the John Sackville, Duke of Dorset, the hot water, along with the absence of her husband might suggest she was pregnant with her lover's child. Elizabeth Henrietta was born on 29 April 1778. That they were accompanied by two ex-politicians Camden, known as a lazy gourmand, and Nugent, known for his coarse and licentious wit, as well as John Wilkes, the author of the most famous piece of eighteenth-century pornographic poetry furnishes the rest of the scenario of an illegitimate birth.

After the birth, rumours began spreading that she had been having an affair with John Sackville, 3rd Duke of Dorset, and Hannah Greig fills in her life among the Beau Monde: accepted, rejected, exiled and returned. Nevertheless, despite the suggestion of illegitimacy, the Earl of Derby claimed the child after his wife left him:[30] was he claiming that he could NOT have been cuckolded? What is important here is that in Bath, LESS would have been away from her family support systems, and we have no idea what help she would have had during the birth of her child.

The next family information we have comes in 1796, just before she died, when a dispute over inheritance of the Hamilton estates of the deceased Duke of Hamilton and Brandon surfaced in the newspapers.[31] The reports suggest that after the death of LESS's brother, 'The more substantial inheritance, the Estate, if not the Scots Titles, may probably descend to the Countess of Derby, ...' What this could indicate is a reason why Lord Derby did not divorced her. However, there are ramifications to the idea. Had he known she was chronically ill earlier he might have expected a premature death, divorced her and saved himself the wait to marry Eliza Farren. Knowing she was healthy, his remaining her husband then becomes

29   *Morning Post and Daily Advertiser* (London), Issue 1621 (31 December 1777).
30   See Peter Thomson's article on Lady Elizabeth Henrietta Cole, *Oxford Dictionary of National Biography* (online edn; Oxford: Oxford University Press). doi:10.1093/ref: odnb/9191.
31   *Sun* (London), Issue 1078 (10 March 1796).

a calculated act of control to become heir to her fortune, perhaps satisfying his greed or ensuring that her illegitimate child was paid for? Is this why the Hamilton's disputed the succession? Again we cannot be certain but it is important to note the role played by those around the patient who help add extra detail to the narrative of her condition.

But the information does not lead to conclusive statements. Given that no further records exist as to her state of health, can we conclude she was in good health after she had left her husband and extend this view when the relationship with the Earl of Dorset faltered? Possibly, but we cannot exclude that she may have had a chronic or developing condition which had delayed her marriage, that may have affected her later on. In fact we know very little about her medical records as it is difficult to identify who the doctors were during her lifetime.

Physician

In exploring her paralysis, we do not know who LESS's doctors were so we cannot say whether she was treated by Percival Pott and whether it was Pott's disease that caused her paralysis. Another possibility is that her condition was associated with the birth of her third child away from the help of her family physician who had brought her safely through the first two births, and this opens up three new possibilities.

Medical Education and Practice

The newspapers of the time show many examples of anonymous doctors offering services for all sorts of conditions. Since LESS was noted to be alone in Bath, or at least surrounded by a number of unreliable people, raises the question of whether her doctor(s) were adequately trained.

To Pregnant Ladies
A Physician and Man-Midwife, of established Practice and Respectability, continues
to accommodate those Ladies, who may wish to LYE-IN privately, with the utmost
Tenderness, Honour, and Secrecy, agreeable to their respective Circumstances and
Consequence in Life.
Letters (Post-paid) addressed to X. Y. to be left at Mr Woodham's, No. 52, High
Holborn, will be duly attended to.

The anonymity of the contact details suggests that the service was being
offered to unmarried women, and the capitalization of the words 'LYE-IN'
suggest that this might even be an advert from a back street abortionist.

Another possibility for LESS's paralysis could derive from the field of
man-midwifery, which is an attempt to medicalize childbirth sometimes
utilizing the latest developments in childbirth such as forceps. We can see
examples of this practice in man-midwives such as William Smellie who
became a great advocate of the method. If there are problems with the
advancement of the head, Smellie advised:

... the Fingers are to be introduced as before, and one of the Blades of the Forceps
(lubricated with lard) is then to be applied along the inside of the Hand or Fingers,
and left Ear of the child ... [32]

Smellie's views however, were not universal and there were others who do
not advocate their use due to the potential damage they may cause. Richard
Manningham was more cautious, he advocated the use of Lying-In beds
for pregnant women and would not use forceps even in difficult births.

... those Operators who are fondest of it, don't pretend to use it, but when the Head
is FAR ADVANC'D IN THE PASAGE; and even then they acknowledge, the
Mother is always liable to be bruised and much hurt and oftentimes the Infant too: ... [33]

32   William Smellie, *A set of anatomical tables, with explanations, and an abridgment of
      the practice of midwifery; with a view to illustrate a treatise on that subject, and collec-
      tion of cases* (Edinburgh: Charles Elliot 1780), 31.
33   Sir Richard Manningham, *An abstract of midwifry, for the use of the lying-in infirmary:
      which with due explanations by anatomical preparations, &c. the repeated Performances
      of all Kinds of Deliveries, on our great Machine, with the Ocular Demonstration of the
      Reason and Justness of the Rules to be observed in all genuine and true Labours, in the*

It is hard not to agree with Manningham, When we view such implements we begin to grasp the physicality and interaction on the body that such devices have. We can be left in no doubt that damage must have occasionally occurred and in untrained hands such damage would have been more severe as to make paralysis of the patient a very possible reality.

When a mother is damaged in childbirth the impact of the physician can be one of those transition points which have long lasting consequences. The lack of proper responses to a condition can be detrimental, even when made with the best intentions, mistakes can be made and the effects manifest themselves years later, and be misinterpreted giving the medical biography a plausible but inaccurate account.

Treatments and Physical Aids

However, whatever the consequence of treatment there may be a need for adaptions to help cope with any new circumstances in a subject's life. These can be as simple as grinding up food so as to maintain nutrition but for LESS her needs required a more substantial response to help her move around. Treatment may provide a cure but for others the illness leaves a need, and this need can be insurmountable in its physicality. Implements have been used since people stood upright when they used a branch to support their weight as they moved about with something as simple as a sprained ankle. This is not medicine, this is prosthetics and is part of the wider narrative that adaptions can hold when telling the stories of those trying to adjust to a major transition point in their lives.

Paralysis has obvious issues for the sufferer, the most obvious one being the difficulties in getting about. Paralysis as a condition of the body

---

Lying-in Infirmary, on our Glass Machine, makes a complete method of teaching midwifry; by giving the Pupils the most exact Knowledge of the Art, and perfectly forming their Hands, at the same time, for the safe and ready practice of midwifry. (London: T. Gardner, 1744), vii.

has probably existed since time immemorial and aids to help in moving people have always been available. The one that was prominent in LESS's life was the Merlin Chair. Many forms of wheelchair had existed throughout various civilizations from antiquity,[34] but John Joseph Merlin, a Belgian, brought a refinement to them using his mechanical genius to improve the design which I would argue developed into the modern day wheelchair. However, they were still bulky and required assistance if any translocation was to be addressed.

LESS could well have purchased one of these models from Merlin's Mechanical Museum which was established in 1788 though he may well have been developing and selling merlin chairs for some years before.

The Merlin chair as an aid allowed LESS to move beyond the confines of her own residence and interact with wider society. For one so young the chair must have aided in maintaining her mental stability through what must have been a difficult period of her life. And it is the recognition of other contributing factors which give us some intimacy with the way she coped whilst suffering from the paralysis. The freedom to get out and about and be a part of society must have helped satisfy Lady Derby's urge to be sociable, an element of her life that had been so important to her while she was married to the Earl of Derby. We can draw on other paralytics to fill the missing information.

Mary, Countess of Chatham, suffered a series of debilitating paralytic episodes which, when they occurred, meant long periods of being house bound. Lady Harriot Pitt wrote to the Countess of Chatham that:

> [Mary] has not I think been quite well lately. Some how or other she has got a Lameness in her Hip. It is better now and perhaps nothing of any Consequence but I think it makes her look Languid and pale.[35]

---

34   See Irina Metzler's paper in this collection.
35   Lady Harriot Pitt to the Countess of Chatham, 19 May 1783, John Rylands Library Manchester University, Eng MS 1272.f.38

However, Lord Grantham reporting that she had been using a Merlin Chair noted that Mary's 'health is now very good'.[36]

And it is the other factors that go with the patient, their illness and their suffering that again brings us added dimension to the story we are trying to tell. We can well imagine LESS, benefitting from a change of scenery, taking in fresh air and her recovering as Lady Mary did. But she would not have taken fresh air in the Merlin chair given the complexity of its operation.

The chair itself was bulky, it has tiny wheels with which the occupant controls the direction of travel. Only people who had movement in both arms could be in control. This would have precluded a lot of people who had strokes and other hemiplegic paralyses from using the Merlin Chair. As LESS is reported to have use one can we then conclude that her paralysis only affected one or both of her legs? Can we conclude she did not have a stroke?

Conclusion

What our exploration of Lady Elizabeth Smith-Stanley has shown, is that the medical element often forms a smaller part of the overall story in the general biography of the subject. The available resources are prone to gaps in the information streams and these reflect the problems of ascertaining information from eras past but also of the nature of record collecting at the time. Many services especially those which may have caused controversy were performed with a degree of anonymity and will never reveal

---

36   Lord Grantham to Frederick Robinson, 3 January 1785, Bedford Archives Wrest Park (Lucas) Mss L30/15/54/238; Lord Grantham to Frederick Robinson, 14 January 1785, Bedford Archives Wrest Park (Lucas) Mss L30/15/54/246; Lord Grantham to Frederick Robinson, 17 January 1785, Bedford Archives Wrest Park (Lucas) Mss L30/15/54/249.

their secrets. Likewise, a patient may not have wanted certain details of incidents in their lives recorded.

However, what we can do is reassess biography in other terms. Modern biography utilises many of the methodologies applied to the disciplines of history and literature but modern cultural studies allows us a wider range of analyses from which interpretations can be explored using related subjects like family, morality and law to provide a frame work to explore the gaps in the chronologies of the information streams.

Chronology is what gives sense to the process, and this is why it is important it should be remembered when utilizing information streams. Of course information streams may cross but the individual streams still continue. Ultimately the analysis of the evidence is that Lady Derby was in relatively good health for the first twenty-four years of her life. We could speculate that perhaps not all was right when the wedding was delayed for a week. But she then went on to have three children which as we all know was a precarious affair for all women during the eighteenth century. Whether childbirth had any detrimental effect on her health is speculation. The use of forceps had become commonplace and if used in any of her births could have caused damage to her even though her children appear to have been in good health.

She returned from her exile with what could be questionable health as noted by her distinctive cough, but this is in parallel to what could be a discreet mention of a sufferer of a infectious disease picked up from 'Sir George'. The downward spiral is indicated in the decline in her mental health, and the use of a Merlin chair and ultimately her dying young. In an era when medical cure was not really an option and medical care was less than well defined, medical biography is not always clear cut.

MIRIAM L. WALLACE

Improper Conjunctions: Scandalous Images and Dangerous Bodies in 'Crim. Con. Temptations with Prices Affix'd'

ABSTRACT

The essay examines variations of a satirical print, 'Crim. Con. Temptations with Prices Affix'd', to a late century debate about legal treatment of adulterous liaisons, one that depends upon the legal fiction (a 'queer' conjunction between law and the fictive) that a wife is the property of her husband rather than a desiring body. Women are innately troubling because as both subjects of law (covered by their husbands and fathers) *and* as property that can be contested at law, they drag the object-physical status of the body into courts of law. This image exemplifies the value of visual imagery for exploring how human variability made visible and significant. However difficult to engage, caricature, *because* it discovers what is unique about someone's face, posture, or physique and exaggerating it to produce a recognizable and mocking image, attends carefully to (and perhaps even *creates*) signifying cultural markers that undercut *both* a classical ideal *and* a modern 'normal'.

Improper Conjunctions

In *The Power of Images* David Freedberg reminds readers of something about images that academics (or at least art historians) often prefer to elide:

> People are sexually aroused by pictures and sculptures; they break pictures and sculptures; they mutilate them, kiss them, cry before them, and go on journeys to see them; they are calmed by them, stirred by them, and incited to revolt. They give thanks by

means of them, expect to be elevated by them, and are moved to the highest levels of empathy and fear. They have always responded in these ways; they still do.[1]

Freedberg's concern was 'with those responses that are subject to repression because they are too embarrassing, to blatant, too rude, and too uncultured ...'.[2] I open with Freedberg's words because they are pertinent to the image examined in this essay – an image that intended to be titillating, shocking, and that retains something of its shock value across the centuries. Additionally, as a scholar used to working primarily with textual materials, working with visual images raises related but perhaps more visceral questions.

There is a reason that images – particularly figural imagery – are more likely to raise demands for 'trigger warnings' from my students or to elicit physiological responses among viewers.[3] Freedberg, steeped in classical art history's carefully intellectualized response to sacred or profane imagery, is particularly sensitive to what is elided when we approach images of the human body as a cognitively managed aesthetic experience. Citing Nelson Goodman, he reminds us that 'the cognitive ... does not exclude the sensory or the emotive,[4] ... what we know through art is felt in our bones and

1   David Freedberg, *The Power of Image: Studies in the History and Theory of Response* (Chicago, IL: University of Chicago Press, 1989) 1.

2   Freedberg, *The Power of Image*, 1.

3   One thinks of scandals in which someone attacks a revered work of art like the 1972 vandalism of Michelangelo's *Pièta* or alternatively, of protests over shows of work considered blasphemous like Andreas Serrano's 'Piss Christ' and Chris Ofili's 'Holy Virgin Mary' encrusted with elephant dung, or pornographic like some of Robert Mapplethorpe's more explicit works. Serrano's 1987 'Piss Christ' was controversial from the beginning, but as recently as 2012 the photograph was attacked and damaged by Christian protestors while on display in Avignon.

4   'The staring encounter arouses us as well. Our heart rate increases when we are stared at; being subjected to a stare even registers on a cortical EEG. So viscerally potent is the staring encounter that we can even feel stares directed at us. In fact, humans from infancy can detect unseen stares. We not only believe that we can tell when we are being stared at, but repeated experiments dating as early as the late nineteenth century suggest that in fact we do'. See Rosemarie Garland-Thomson, *Staring: How We Look* (New York: Oxford University Press, 2009), 17.

nerves and muscles as well as grasped with our minds.'[5] In a late eighteenth-century context, the resonance of the viewer's body to the image-body is often figured as 'sympathy' – an almost magnetic feeling with another that corresponds to contemporary concepts of empathy (a term that enters English from German at a later date).[6]

Turning to another site of embodied theorizing, Leo Bersani's seminal 1987 essay, 'Is the Rectum a Grave?' traced a connection between attitudes toward receptive gay male sex and female prostitution. Writing in the late 1980s Reagan-Thatcher era of AIDS policies, Bersani suggested that in the public imagination, both were understood as improperly open and sexually voracious. Historical conceptions of women's (i.e. prostitutes') sexuality were mapped, Bersani suggests, onto fantasies about receptive sexual appetite and capacity. Part of Bersani's point was in the face of AIDS panic to embrace homophobic charges of immodesty and insatiability (linking them to fears of female prostitution and sexual desire) in order to resist the demand for a particular kind of heterosexual, self-contained, masculinity. This masculinity is phallic certainly, but also 'able-ist', in the sense of imagining an impenetrable and self-contained, self-controlled body that penetrates other 'leaky' bodies as the ideal or 'norm.'

In a fairly scandalous passage, Bersani writes that the threats in the nineteenth century of syphilis and in his own time of AIDS,

> 'legitimate' a fantasy of female sexuality as intrinsically diseased; and promiscuity in this fantasy, far from merely increasing the risk of infection, is the *sign of infection*. Women and gay men spread their legs with an unquenchable appetite for destruction. This is an image with extraordinary power; and if the good citizens of Arcadia, Florida, could chase from their midst an average, law-abiding family, it is [...] because in looking at three hemophiliac children they may have seen [...] the infinitely more seductive and intolerable image of a grown man, legs high in the air, unable to refuse the suicidal ecstasy of being a woman.[7]

5   Nelson Goodman, *Languages of Art*, cited in Freedberg, *The Power of Image*, 25.
6   See for example S. D. Preson and F. B. M. de Waal, 'Empathy: Its Ultimate and Proximate Bases', *Behavioral Brain Science*, 25/1 (2002), 1–20.
7   Leo Bersani, 'Is the Rectum a Grave?', *October* Special Issue: AIDS: Cultural Analysis/ Cultural Activism, 43 (1987), 197–222, 215.

Bersani refers here to a notorious case of anti-AIDS hysteria that took place in the central Florida town of Arcadia between 1986 and 1987: the Ray family's three haemophiliac HIV-positive sons were banned from attending a local school. After the ban was overturned by a court order, the Rays' home was burned and the family left Arcadia.[8] The point of Bersani's argument is to highlight the power of a body open to, begging for its own penetration, even ecstatically so – and to suggest *that* is the image that comes to stand for danger to an ideal self-contained subject.[9]

These two quite different critical approaches from Freedberg and Bersani each have something to say about the scandal of the desiring/desired body – and about embodiment as a form of knowledge that is part of something we might call embodied affect. Linking Bersani's image of a queerly open, receptive body and Freedberg's careful attention to the visual image's power to mobilize response usefully brings bodily variation – and its challenges – into view.

Conjoining Freedberg's welcome reminder of the sensory call of images with Bersani's shamelessly receptive body frames this essay's approach to an image first published in 1796, entitled 'Crim. Con. Temptations with Prices Affix'd' (see Figure 8.1).

8   See for a good quick overview Stephen Buckley, 'Slow Change of Heart', *St Petersburg Times* (2 September 2001) <http://www.sptimes.com/News/090201/State/Slow_change_of_heart.shtml>, accessed 26 September 2015.

9   Although useful critiques have been launched against a resistant model of 'gay shame' that I think is rooted to some degree in work like Bersani's, particularly by gay men of color, there is still something about Bersani's classic essay that seems useful for thinking with and perhaps friendly to some of the points made by gay men of color writers like Lawrence La Fontaine-Stokes. La Fontaine-Stokes promotes a conception of Latino *sinverguencia* or 'shamelessness' that I would argue is actually another way to name what Bersani finds so compelling about the image of the open, available body (male or female) – its legs in the air. See Lawrence La Fountain-Stokes, 'Gay Shame, Latina- and Latino Style: A Critique of White Queer Performativity', in Michael Hames-García and Ernesto J. Martínez, eds, *Gay Latino Studies: A Critical Reader* (Durham, NC: Duke University Press, 2011), 55–80. See also Lynne Huffer's overview of this debate in *Are the Lips a Grave?* (New York: Columbia University Press, 2013), 17.

Figure 8.1: Isaac Cruikshank, "Crim. Con. Temptations with the Prices Affixed". 4 April 1796, by S. W. Fores. Print on wove paper, etching, hand-colored, platemark 35.1 × 48.2 cm on sheet 37 × 49 cm. Courtesy of The Lewis Walpole Library, Yale University.

It was published by the print shop of S.W. Fores, designed by the artist George 'Moutard' Woodward, known for his comic social-commentary images, and perhaps etched and drawn by Isaac Cruikshank.[10] This image engages anxiety about female bodies and illicit sexual activity in the context of an on-going period debate about legal treatment of adulterous liaisons.[11] The print refers to the civil charge of 'criminal conversation' or adultery, in which a husband could bring

10 Isaac Cruikshank the elder (b. 1756?-d. 1811). Isaac was father to Isaac Robert (b. 1789) and George Cruikshank (b. 1792). George Moutard Woodward (b. 1760) published *Eccentric Excursions* with his own illustrations in 1796, the same year this print appeared. He designed social caricatures that were often etched and realized by Rowlandson and Isaac Cruikshank.

11 Another version of this print may be found at the British Museum website at: <http://www.britishmuseum.org/research/collection_online/collection_object_details/collection_image_gallery.aspx?partid=1&assetid=308045001&objectid=3016510>.

suit against the wife's lover for damages. While 'crim. con.' charges had been brought since the late seventeenth century as the ecclesiastical courts lost standing, they became more prevalent following the case of Grosvenor v Cumberland in 1769, a case in which the King's brother, the Duke of Cumberland, was sued successfully by Lord Grosvenor for damages stemming from the Duke's adulterous liaison with Grosvenor's wife, Harriet. In addition to the scandal and titillation of the details of royal misbehaviour, the enormous amount of damages awarded to the husband, £10,000, caught the public's imagination.

From this point, so-called 'crim. con.' cases became popular entertainment in the second half of the eighteenth century; [12] trials were followed by a broad audience and widely publicized in print, ranging from official documentation (sessions papers, *Journal of the House of Lords*) to newspapers, to periodicals.[13] *Town and Country Magazine* featured a popular tête-a-tête section depicting famous illicit couples in cameos with pseudonyms. It was succeeded by the even more salacious *Bon Ton*, which recounted details of actual cases to a wide readership. Another short-lived publication, *Trials for Adultery; or the History of Divorces* (1779–1780), included selected trial evidence from cases at Doctor's Commons, and shades over into overt erotica with images that range from suggestive to explicit, as in 'The Earl of Kerry and Mrs Daly in the Dining Room.'[14] The title fails to

12   Susan Staves, 'Money for Honor: Damages for Criminal Conversation', *Studies in Eighteenth-Century Culture*, 11 (1982), 279–297, 280.

13   Other scholars have noted that 'by the 1780s and '90s the courts were virtually flooded with crim con cases' See Lawrence Stone, *Road to Divorce* (Oxford, Oxford University Press, 1990), 399. See also J. E. Loftis, 'Congreve "Way Of The World" And Popular Criminal Literature', *Studies in English literature, 1500–1900*, 36/3 (1996), 561–578. Loftis notes that 'cases and thus printed accounts of the trials were rare' in the late seventeenth century. He and Stone agree that there were few cases between 1692 and 1730, and 'the truly dramatic flood of cases only after 1740, peaking in the 1780s and '90s.' Loftis, 563.

14   The picture can be found at: 'Charles Daly against Anastatia Daly, Libel Given in the 27th of June, 1769', in *Trials for Adultery, Or, The History of Divorces: Being Select Trials at Doctors Commons for Adultery, Fornication, Cruelty, Impotence, &c. from the Year 1760 to the Present Time. Taken in shorthand by a Civilian.* vol. 1 (London, 1779), <https://books.google.com/books?id=cZk-AQAAMAAJ&lpg=RA2-PA33&ots=Irtf7v8Osq&dq=The%20Earl%20of%20Kerry%20and%20Mrs.%20

prepare the reader for the image itself, which appears to show the couple *in flagrante*, with Mrs Daly prone on a settee with her legs languorously extended, the Earl leaning over her on one standing leg, the other raised with a bent knee, and raising her voluminous skirts – all placed beneath a classical style painting of a draped nude (perhaps a Venus) similarly mounted by a small cupid. The image is framed by a box-like model of the dining room that positions the viewer as privy to the scene through the missing fourth wall, the whole surrounded by drapery, oak branches, and a head that may be a theatrical satyr at the top centre. Such accounts frequently depended upon the testimony of servants or inn workers, and the illustrations often depict their evidence and privileged view for the delectation of more elite readers.

Legal Fictions

Despite the term 'criminal' conversation, this was a civil legal charge of property damage that read adultery as property theft on the part of the wife's lover. It also constitutes a 'legal fiction.' Conjoining two categories that are conventionally held apart or even imagined as opposed – the fictive and the legal – one could argue that legal fictions are in themselves 'queer' in the sense that they belong at the same time to two usually mutually exclusive fields. They do not fully adhere to the principle of non-contradiction.

Legal fictions are certainly embarrassing to the body of law. William Blackstone tried to explain them away as ancient and harmless conventions that 'prevent a mischief, or remedy an inconvenience', while Jeremy Bentham vehemently rejected them as 'to law what fraud is to trade.'[15] Legal

Daly%20in%20the%20Dining%20Room&pg=PA44#v=onepage&q=The%20 Earl%20of%20Kerry%20and%20Mrs.%20Daly%20in%20the%20Dining%20 Room&f=false>, accessed 1 April 2016.

15   In *Commentaries on the Laws of England*, 'Of private wrongs'; cited in Moglen; Raymond Wacks. Eben Moglen cites Bentham as mocking '[f]iction of use to justice?

fictions are short cuts – a way to recognize that while something is not *really* so, law may treat it as the case in order to move forward. A period example would be the concept of 'Constructive Treason' – a charge that treated a call for parliamentary reform, 'as if' it were calling for the king's overthrow or death.[16] A contemporary example is the convention in the United States that understands corporations as persons that was at issue in the Citizens United v Federal Election Commission 2010 campaign finance reform case, which held that corporate donations must be protected under the First Amendment to the constitution as 'speech'.

It was a legal fiction that held that a husband and wife are one person under the law. The limits of this fictional 'person' become quite apparent in the case of adultery. Arguably the civil charge of 'criminal conversation' itself participates in legal fiction by equating the sexually active woman with inert property such as her clothing or jewels, theft of which could be included under the suit and considered in the damages awarded.[17] Trial accounts

Exactly as swindling is to trade', {n3} and 'that each of the law's fictions 'affords presumptive and conclusive evidence of moral turpitude in those by whom it was invented and first employed'' {n4}(7 Jeremy Bentham, *Works* 283, Bowring ed. 1843 and 9 *id*. 77. Cited in Eben Moglen, 'Legal Fiction and Common Law Legal Theory: Some Historical Reflections' Originally prepared for publication Tel-Aviv University Studies in Law, 14 August 1989, <http://emoglen.law.columbia.edu/publications/fict.html>, accessed 2 July 2015.

16   See Nancy Knauer, 'Legal Fictions and Juristic truth', *St Thomas Law Review*, 23, 1–51, 2. Knauer explains that the idea comes from Roman law 'where the *praetor* would endorse a false procedural statement, known as a *fictio*, in order to extend a right of action beyond its intended scope'. See also Miriam Wallace, 'Constructing Treason, Narrating Truth: The 1794 Treason Trial of Thomas Holcroft and the Fate of English Jacobinism', *Romanticism on the Net* (2007).

17   Here I would disagree with Laura Hanft Korobkin's otherwise strong study *Criminal Conversations: Sentimentality and Nineteenth-Century Legal Stories of Adultery* (New York: Columbia University Press, 1998) – at least in the trials I have read from this period, the emphasis on the loss of the wife's labor and sexual use is often augmented by accounts of emotional anguish explored by attorneys. Attention to emotional suffering then is not just a trope of novels. It is also worth noting that this kind of trial is a relatively early example of a case in British practice that is argued entirely by professional jurists. Charges of Treason were the other earlier case in which a representative and guiding attorney was considered necessary because of the power and

from this period stress the damage done in terms of loss of companionship and marital satisfaction, but specifically, the legal trial for monetary damages followed from the wife's status as chattel or property.

Another aspect of fictionalizing found in 'crim. con.' trials if not strictly a 'legal fiction' is that the trial for 'criminal conversation' breaks with the long tradition that founded criminal common law of pitting plaintiffs and defendants against each other in open court. 'Crim. con.' cases invited dramatic and rhetorically complex narratives from each counsel, yet neither party (nor the wife) was permitted to speak in this kind of civil damages case. Rather, their stories are ventriloquized by jurists – one of the earlier legal settings in which this became standard. Eloquent and theatrically effective representation of the parties' arguments made these popular entertainment for viewers and also helped propel several jurists into prominent and successful careers (including Thomas Erskine and William Garrow).[18] The cases that proliferate in popular literature and salacious magazines from about 1770 to 1815 are mostly cases involving elite and prominent couples. By the later nineteenth century, a suit for 'criminal conversation' had become, a necessary preliminary to applying for a legal separation (which did not allow remarriage) or a parliamentary divorce (which did).

'Crim. Con.' in the 1790s

'Crim. con.' cases set two narratives in competition. The prosecution portrayed the husband as a blameless victim whose good nature and trust in his wife's self-regulation was taken advantage of by a male seducer. The defendant's counsel might suggest that mistreatment, a lack of sexual

---

weight of the Crown's prosecution. However, while Treason was a criminal charge, Criminal Conversation was a civil charge.

18   See for details of this shift, John H. Langbein, *The Origins of Adversary Criminal Trial* (Oxford: Oxford University Press, 2003).

interest or impotence, or that the husband's own sexual activities outside of marriage and neglect of his wife left her vulnerable to another man's overtures. Judges and juries were particularly concerned that the 'seduction' might have been a kind of collusion between husband and wife to entrap a wealthy man, or that a scheming husband might set up his own wife's seduction in order to get a financial windfall. As cases of 'criminal conversation' proliferated, a heated debate emerged about how treating such charges as civil suits in which a husband won damages might be incentivizing wives' prostitution. This treatment of adultery among the gentry alarmed educated men (and Mary Wollstonecraft) with its structural similarity to women selling sex.

Directly addressing the peculiar intersections between the law's fictions and bodily variation is 'Crim. Con. Temptations with the Prices Affix'd.' The image presents twelve female figures with widely varying body-types in two rows of sex. Each figure names the damages a prospective lover might expect to pay in court were he to be sued by the husband:

Row 1:

1) I am but a servant of all work / and you may rest secure on no more than one shilling damages.
2) I think the brilliancy of my / charms – cannot be estimated at / less than fifteen pounds tho my / husband thinks so slightly of them
3) One pound and / not a shilling more
4) Six hundred at least.
5) Those that win me must / not be afraid of their purses
6) It's as broad as it's long every / thing must be paid for

Row 2:

1) Four hundred if you touch / but the hem of my garment!!
2) Surely one Thousand cannot / be called excessive damages.
3) My husband is a very old Man / which will have a great weight / with a Jury
4) I dont see why my husband may / not make his fortune as well as / other people
5) The price rests with the Jury
6) Only Twenty Thousand! for a mornings ride on the circular road.

The print was reissued several times into the early 1800s, and there are three versions shown here, from Yale University's Lewis Walpole Library, and Mount Holyoke College's special collections. Two are coloured prints, measuring about 34×45 cm (depending on various trims and margins). There is an additional pencil drawing version held at Holyoke that differs in some key respects from the finished engraving/etching. Woodward might have drawn the model, and then Cruikshank would have designed the engraved and etched version for printing based upon, but redrawn based upon Woodward's design. The Holyoke drawing, I speculate, lacks the engraver's modifications and sends a somewhat varied message.

The Lewis Walpole library's copy (see Figure 8.1) has different coloration from the earlier images (see Figure 8.2 and 8.3) and is marked as a later reprint, perhaps from 1818, which suggests some staying power if the print was reissued across two decades (less likely to be the case with highly topical political prints).

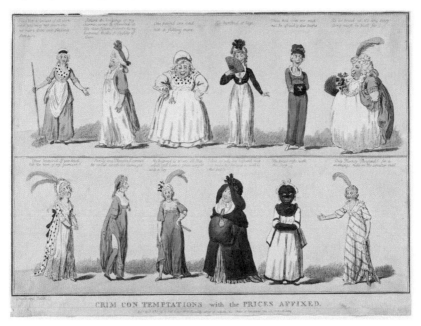

Figure 8.2: "Crim. Con. Temptations with the Prices Affixed!," George Moutard Woodward, 4 April 1796. Engraving, hand-coloured. 13 3/8 in × 18 1/16 in; 34 cm × 45.9 cm. Courtesy of Mount Holyoke College Art Museum, South Hadley, Massachusetts.

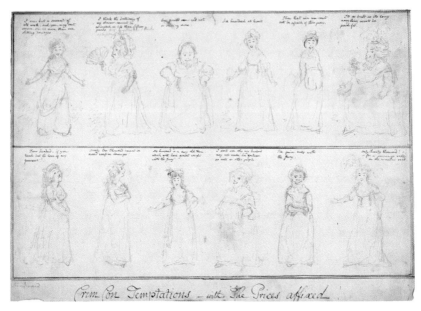

Figure 8.3: "Crim. Con. Temptations with the Prices Affixed!," George Moutard
Woodward, 1796. Pencil. 13 in × 18 5/8 in; 33.02 cm × 47.3075 cm. Courtesy of Mount
Holyoke College Art Museum, South Hadley, Massachusetts.

Satirical images are complex objects to work with. By their nature, they
have an overt message for the right viewer, and by their nature they also
traffic in bodily exaggeration and mockery. Additionally *pace* Freedburg,
they may evoke feelings of disgust and distress even in modern viewers
whose sensitivities are quite different from their original audience. In their
own day they often shocked visitors to Great Britain from other European
countries with their explicit imagery and their lack of respect for institutions and social elites. Yet they are also complex in themselves as composite
products with multiple authors – print dealer; designer; etcher and drawer;
colourist; author of text. Viewers and audiences are not necessarily limited to the ideal reader – the well-off gentleman who might buy prints for
hanging, collecting, an album, or sending as gifts. Although there is heated
debate about just how public they were, most critics agree that they were
to some degree visible to a broad audience because they were displayed
both in showrooms and in print shop windows.

This particular print capitalizes on the fear that 'crim. con.' was a form of legal prostitution; it implies that women are complicit in turning themselves into commodities. One could read it as a comment then on the on-going debate about 'criminal conversation' charges, because they led to monetary damages, as in essence not only legalizing prostitution, but perhaps creating an incentive for husbands and wives to seek to entrap wealthy men for financial benefit. It also demonstrates conventional anxiety about 'crim. con.' as popular entertainment that minimized the social harm of adultery and worse, invited common audiences to laugh at their betters. The print overtly invites the viewer to laugh at women who optimistically advertise themselves as 'temptations' with price tags – particularly such unappealing figures as these.

To some degree, this may be considered as a kind of 'fantasy' image. While there are some cases of 'crim. con.' prosecutions that appear to involve men of small property (the 1789 trial of William Atkinson, a linen-draper, for 'criminal conversation' with Mrs Connor whose husband kept a pub, The Mitre, is one such example),[19] most that received attention involved wealthy or titled defendants. It seems initially unlikely that several of the women presented here *could* have been the objects of a 'criminal conversation' suit in the first place since bringing a suit was costly and damages were generally limited to those with more elevated social standing and an interest in the legitimacy of their heirs. Moreover, some of the women portrayed here would have had little recourse even to a charge of sexual assault.[20] I have found no cases in which a servant-woman's master sued for 'criminal conversation', under which the accused is charged with depriving the husband of the rightful society and companionship of his wife. This print is

---

19   Conner, Mr, *Adultery. The trial of Mr. William Atkinson, linen-draper, of Cheapside, for criminal conversation with Mrs. Conner, wife of Mr. Conner, ... which was tried in Hilary term, 1789, in the Court of King's Bench, before Lord Kenyon.* (London, [1789]).

20   See Anna Clark *The struggle for the breeches: gender and the making of the British working class.* (Berkeley: University of California Press, 1997); Randolph Trumbach, *Sex And The Gender Revolution. Volume 1: Heterosexuality And The Third Gender In Enlightenment London.* vol. 1 (Chicago: University of Chicago Press, 1998); A. D. Harvey, *Sex in Georgian England: Attitudes and Prejudices from the 1720s to the 1820s* (London: Gerald Duckworth, 1994).

more interested in addressing a larger cultural anxiety about the complex status of the legal charge of 'criminal conversation' and the popularity of such trials – and containing it with humour.

It is quite possible that some of these figures would have been recognizable persons to a London audience, but they are perhaps even more interesting as types. Woodward's prints are more often caricatured 'types', as compared to Gillray's caricatures of prominent and recognizable persons. But even as types, some of these figures blur the line between respectable or even appealing female body-types and figures recognizable as likely prostitutes. Cindy McCreery points out that some prints of well-dressed types (the 'demirep' or socially elite woman with a damaged reputation, or the 'milliner') could serve a double function as a type of the attractive London prostitute and also as a fashion plate for more rural audiences.[21] Some such images were even reproduced on crockery as pretty decoration, obscuring their double-message. McCreery argues that 'we need to broaden our understanding of why people bought satirical prints. At least some customers bought prints of prostitutes for the beauty of the women and/ or their fashionable dress. In these cases the women's identity as prostitutes was incidental, rather than integral, to the purchaser's enjoyment of the prints. Such examples indicate that customers bought satirical prints for a variety of reasons, including their aesthetic appeal'.[22]

McCreery offers an extended discussion of a mezzotint entitled 'All Sorts' designed by J. R. Smith and published circa 1776 by Carrington Bowles, known for their 'drolls' or comic prints (rather than more biting satire). Mezzotints too were used more often for sociable scenes, reproductions of historical paintings or portraits, and far less associated with political and strong social satire. The Bowles print shows four women of varied ages and dressed according to different social spheres, identifying them as the 'Tid Bit' (a young, delicate looking woman in fichu, wide skirts, and long gloves), and the 'Bunter' (posed with her fists on her hips, arms akimbo), confronting a more elitely dressed older woman wearing a high hairpiece

21   Cindy McCreery, *The Satirical Gaze: Prints of Women in Late Eighteenth-Century England* (Oxford: Clarendon Press, 2004).
22   McCreery, *The Satirical Gaze*, 59–60.

with powder and ornate overskirts tied up in panniers, identified as the 'Pompadore'. Finally in front, three-quarter profile but looking directly at the observer, stands the 'Bouncing Jack Whore', a mid-range prostitute, who except for her direct gaze and apparently unescorted status looks like a respectable middling-sort of woman with a long decorative apron, petticoat with an over-gown and a mantle wrapped neatly about her shoulders. The *Catalogue of Prints and Drawings in the British Museum* calls this figure 'a very plump woman ... leering to the front'.[23] While the modern viewer can easily identify the 'bunter' as both a woman of the laboring classes and perhaps one who might be propositioned, the young 'Tid Bit' brings to mind the confusions about Evelina's status in Frances Burney's eponymous novel, and the 'Bouncing Jack Whore' if isolated, could certainly double as a modest fashion plate beyond London.

Woodward's print is more obviously comic than Carrington Bowles' drolls, and it seems unlikely that any of these figures could be taken out of context as fashion plates. Yet they too seem to echo the earlier print of 'All Sorts' – expanding the number beyond four figures and ranging across a wider range of social classes, but preserving the sense of a menu from which to choose. Despite the joke – that all women perhaps are to be bought, are even eager to strike a bargain, these images insist additionally that women are not simply inert property. They have desires, they act, and they are mobile – perhaps dangerously so.

Freedberg's salvo helps us consider that buyers might have had *multiple* reasons for purchasing or viewing an image, not excluding a combination of political affirmation *and* sexual titillation. Elizabeth Fay explains that transcriptions of 'criminal conversation' trials, like satirical prints, serve multiple functions: 'the historical fact of legal transcriptions is self-interested: narratively framed as the exposure of private acts for public good, the title titillates even as it screens authorial scandal mongering. The same dynamic was at work in political cartoons of the day, whose immense popularity

---

23   Frederic George Stephens, *Catalogue of Prints and Drawings in the British Museum, Division I. Political and Personal Satires. Vol. IV: A.D. 1761 to circa A. D. 1770, Prepared by, and containing may descriptions by Edward Hawkins* (London, 1883), 723.

and often daily publication spread reputed or reported scandal faster than any verbal text could do.'[24]

These images clarify the anxiety about the conjunction of physical embodiment and the abstract claims of the rule of law. Women are innately troubling because as both subjects of law (as parts of their husbands or fathers) *and* as property that can be contested at law, they drag the object-physical status of the body into courts of law. They make explicit the senses and embodiment of humankind – and so reflect back upon those who enact, determine, and uphold the law themselves.

Perhaps, thinking of Bersani, we also should not dismiss the possibilities of the image serving as a kind of erotic enhancer – one that appears to dismiss, but really lingers on variable bodies and their pleasures. The print invites us to laugh at these women who imagine that they have a ready market for their 'charms', but it also invites us to consider whether perhaps indeed, we might not consider a 'ride on the circular road', what pleasures could be found with one who states 'it's as broad as it's long', or whose price is 'but a shilling'. If these figures engage a legal anxiety – that the law itself is a pimp – they also figure market promiscuity. Their 'infinite variety' unlike that of Shakespeare's Cleopatra, is that of consumer capitalism – and their language of bargains and haggling ties sexual promiscuity (openness) to market promiscuity (creating desires through excessive options), even to class promiscuity (ranging beyond one's proper realm).

It is instructive to examine a few images more closely. The figure in Row 1, Number 1, bears the superscript: 'I am but a servant of all work / and you may rest secure on no more than one shilling damages' is paired with figure holding a broom, arms out to her side, palms open and up.[25] (This gesture, but not the iconic broom, is also found in the pencil sketch.) Her gesture suggests invitation or welcome, and it resonates oddly with high art images of saints and holy figures. She is among the most conventionally

---

24   Elizabeth Fay, 'Mary Robinson: On Trial in Public Court', *Studies in Romanticism*, 45/3 (2006), 397–423.

25   The Holyoke drawing does not include the broom – suggesting that the engraver may have added it to clarify her status; the broom is an emblem, but also perhaps a fetish.)

attractive of the figures – slender, well proportioned, young – her standing as a servant of all work seems to be the key focus for a viewer's contemplation and desire.[26] Caroline Steedman, documenting the case of a servant woman's solution to a pregnancy outside of marriage, discusses the association of servant women's laboring bodies with erotic charm.[27] Put simply, certain kinds of labour were held to present a woman as particularly attractive.

The tag line of the woman in Row 1, Number 3, is 'One pound one and / not a shilling more' is paired with a figure whose body type is less conventionally desirable: she has a wide frame and the cut of her bodice suggests that she is buxom and aging, as well as wide-hipped and big bellied. Her dress is that of a working woman, though the keys hanging at her waist suggest some position of authority – a housekeeper, a cook, or perhaps an innkeeper. (This in turn suggests the bawd, seeking to make a little extra on her own experience.)

Her language too suggests that she is used to bargaining and getting her way – in another context it could be *she* who is offering to pay 'one pound one and not a shilling more'. Her stance, direct frontal with fists on her hips is assertive rather than pleading, is associated in other prints with the aggressive insistence of London fishwives, as in James Gillray's print 'Billingsgate Eloquence'.[28]

---

26 See Caroline Steedman's *Master and Servant* on the attractions of particular kinds of women's labor. See also work on Hannah Cullwick and Arthur Munby.

27 See Carolyn Steedman, *Master and servant: Love and labour in the English industrial age* (Cambridge: Cambridge University Press, 2007) for a specific discussion of kinds of labor held to make the woman worker attractive. There is an example in George Eliot's *Adam Bede* in which Hetty's gestures and plump arms making butter are part of her erotic charm. See also Kristina Straub's *Domestic affairs: intimacy, eroticism, and violence between servants and masters in eighteenth-century Britain* (Baltimore: Johns Hopkins University Press, 2009).

28 One of a set of eight illustrations of professional 'eloquences', this image of a fishwife snapping her fingers at her opponent while cursing, the other hand on her hip, is also intended as a caricature of Lady Henrietta Cecilia Johnston, according to M. D. George's *Catalogue of Prints and Drawings in the British Museum*, vol. 7, 1793–1801 (London: Trustees of the British Museum by British Museum Publications, 1954. Reprint, 1978), Print No. 8604, <http://images.library.yale.edu/walpoleweb/oneitem.asp?imageId=lwlpr08470>.

She has an unconventional look around the eyes that is exacerbated in the Walpole library copy by the colourist's work. One could read this simply as an error in the print's execution, but given that smaller details in the rest of the print are handled better, I suggest that we are invited to read her as having a cast to her eyes, or perhaps a glass eye. (In the Holyoke image, the colourist has left her hair white, which in her case suggests age rather than powder – one might not need be concerned about an unexpected pregnancy.)

The superscript for Row 1 Number 6, is: 'It's as broad as it's long every / thing must be paid for' suggestively accompanies a better-dressed and even rounder figure. If the third figure is well-fleshed, this is a large figure is egg-shaped with a head balanced on top. Her profile is reminiscent of caricatures of the Hanovers, with a short but hooked nose, heavy protruding lips and a double but weak chin. (It is not unknown in such prints to represent a well-known and recognizable caricature of a Duchess as fishwife, or members of parliament and even the monarch as Black men.)[29] She stands in profile but casts her eye towards the viewer, and coquettishly pulls her overdress back with her hand on her hip. (Stronger colours make this gesture more noticeable in some prints.) The expression conventionally implies two equally good choices, but here it takes on a salacious, even obscene tone perhaps referencing not only the figure's body but the shape and size of her genitalia or even other orifices.

The black women figured as Row 2, Number 5 is certainly the most shocking for a modern audience, particularly as she states 'the price rests with the Jury'. The figure's face and head are heavily caricatured in a mode of blackface that carries into our own time – which perhaps accounts for the

---

29   See James Gillray, 'Billingsgate Eloquence' (London, 1795), <http://images.library. yale.edu/walpoleweb/oneitem.asp?imageId=lwlpr08470>, which represents a Duchess as a London fishwife (and using the same language), and an anonymous print 'The Poor Blacks Going to Their Settlement' (London, 1787, publisher listed as E. Macklew, but identified by M. D. George as William Dent), <http://images. library.yale.edu/walpoleweb/oneitem.asp?imageId=lwlpr06137>. The image represents George IV, Edmund Burke, Lord George Gordon, and other prominent Britons as black men being sent abroad.

contemporary shock value. This image still signifies for us in its ugliness and power some of the ways Freedberg highlights. Her head seems simply stuck onto a fairly conventional body. Lest we think eighteenth-century satirists were incapable of delineating varied features for black figures, images such as James Gillray's 'Wouski' (which idealizes the beautiful black woman) and the 'Caricature Shop' from 1801 (which includes a much milder caricature of a Black man; see Figure 8.4), as well as portraits of well-known Black Britons such as Olaudah Equiano and Ottabah Cugoano suggest more range than is apparent here. The black-face doll-like round head and exaggerated facial features are clearly intentional in the final engraving, as is her young and attractive figure.

Because color has been applied on top of fairly heavy etching, her features are actually quite difficult to see in the colorized images – but they include a wide and round head, large lips (though not so pouty as figure Number 2's), and prominent ears with tightly curled hair close to the edges of her cap. She wears earrings, as do several of the others, but hers have the effect of making her ears more prominent, evoking the earring-wearing exotic black figure found in decorative objects and historical paintings. (The Holyoke colourist has taken this to an extreme, colouring her *ears* yellow along with the earrings.) Her form is conventionally attractive – but her dress is cut lower than the others, her rounded breasts pressing up out of her bodice suggesting perhaps a link to the animal-function of female mammals. She wears no shoes in the Walpole or British Museum image, but the colourist of the Holyoke version has kindly coloured her feet to match the trim on her dress so that she wears slippers.

Her 'modest' refusal to set a price, leaving it to the gentlemen of the jury, may be ironic in this context, suggesting that in fact her exoticism may bring a higher price, or even that she is in collusion with her employer or her husband to earn for them both (an English viewer would be invited to imagine both that being in England she was a free woman, but also to imagine her origins in a West Indian slave-holding colony). Such a reading – that her exoticism may make her self-marketing particularly profitable is augmented by James Gillray's 1788 print 'Wouski' – which references a black character in George Colman's comic opera 'Inkle and Yarico' to depict a recognizable Prince William, Duke of Clarence, curled around a black woman in a hammock. The image plays on a rumour that he had purchased a Creole woman in Jamaica and brought her home.[30]

Conclusions

Visual imagery is an important site for exploring how human variability – both queer and differently dis/abled – was made visible and significant. If we look carefully enough, cartoons and caricature tell us something about what kinds of embodiment and difference signified at particular places and times. Precisely because caricature specializes in finding what is unique about someone's face or posture or physique and exaggerating it to produce a recognizable and mocking image, it attends carefully to and perhaps even creates signifying cultural markers: protruding lips, squinting eyes, large hips and bellies, bare feet, pendulous ears, dark skin, signs of labour like brooms and keys. What if we think of this kind of material as documenting a process of denormalizing that undercuts both a classical ideal and a modern 'normal'? Yes, caricatures are often biting and even mean-spirited, but they also do present bodily variation and highlight the range of variation that is possible – as we see in an 1801 print entitled 'Caricature Shop' by an unknown artist (see Figure 8.4). Here the prints in the caricaturist's shop window are mirrored in the flesh by the viewers who come to gawk. They represent a full range of caricature types drawn from Hogarth and others – hooked noses and straight ones, elderly and young figures, conventionally attractive ones (like the young woman in the right corner who bears a passing resemblance to the final figure in Woodward's 'Crim. Con. Temptations') and those considered unappealing (the bent man in the spectacles on the left behind the dog to the plump matron just behind him, or the figure propelling himself

---

30   <http://www.britishmuseum.org/collectionimages/AN00132/AN00132471_001_l.
      jpg>, accessed 26 September 2015.

on a kind of sled who seems to have both legs amputated at the knees). There is even a black figure, mouth open in admiration like many of the others, to the far right. Standing in the doorway is a figure we might take as the artist – pen in hand, but also rather full-fleshed and complacent looking, who observes the living crowd before the more comic images in the window.

Figure 8.4:   Anonymous, 'Caricature Shop', London, 1801. Publisher: Piercy Roberts. Courtesy of the Lewis Walpole Library, Yale University.

Warren L. Oakley writes of this image that it 'presents the pleasure of a diverse crowd', continuing 'Roberts' image ... presents visual erotica as a commodity that was publicly relished and not simply reviled.'[31] Turning

31   Warren L. Oakley, *A Culture of Mimicry: Laurence Sterne, His Readers and the Art of Bodysnatching* (Modern Humanities Research Association), vol. 73 (London: Maney Publishing, 2010), 89.

back then to 'Crim. Con. Temptations', I have argued that the print participates in an on-going fear that the legal charge of 'criminal conversation' was encouraging lax attitudes towards marital chastity and tempting husbands and wives to use the courts to 'make [their] fortunes' as figure Number 10 suggests. But, working against the popular periodicals' association of 'crim. con.' with the aristocracy, this print also associates collusion and temptation with women of middling to labouring status – particularly servants.

It was primarily women servants – who changed bedding, washed undergarments, emptied chamber pots, entered and exited rooms without notice – who were key witnesses at such trials. Is the print perhaps also a kind of *revenge* fantasy on the part of middling and landed gentry? If the proper market was gentlemen who wanted a titillating print under the cover of social critique and humour, was the print innately aggressive towards the very 'inferiors' who might become quite powerful indeed in their potential role as witnesses?

The print trades on anxiety about women's voracious appetites not for proper reproductive sex, but for money. But the print *also* implies viewers' capacity to desire body-types conventionally considered repellent. Class-status, physical 'deformity', racialization, and body-size suggest variation common to consumer goods. These figures' pleas play on different sorts of attraction: bargain goods versus luxury goods, easily accessible commodities versus those that are rare or even exotic.

To bring this full circle back to Freedberg's point that images have more resonances than we often recognize, and Bersani's celebration of shameless and voracious desire, one might read this image against the grain as interested in variable desire(s). Presented as concupiscence – a desire for money – the images link erotic desire to consumerism quite explicitly. A legal debate about treating women as material objects that can be stolen or sold is rendered into a familiar critique of female promiscuity and male danger. Yet, at the same time it seems to celebrate the very desire that is created by commodification and its peculiar variability. The range of choices is supposed to whet our appetites – but perhaps it also creates the very desire it both documents and mocks. In offering themselves these figures take charge of both desires, shamelessly inviting penetration – and resisting recontainment in romantic sensibility.[32]

To end, I want to turn to Lynne Huffer's effort in her surprising series of essays in *Are the Lips a Grave?*, itself an open reference both to the thought of Francophone feminist philosopher Luce Irigaray's essay on feminist resistance to commodification under the sign of difference, 'When Our Lips Speak Together' ('Quand nos levres se parlent') and Bersani's essay 'Is the Rectum a Grave?'. Huffer's complex argument tracks across feminist and queer theories, using particular readings of Foucault among others to draw together the insights of difference feminism and Queer Theory (both she argues essentially anti-foundationalist). She ends by interrogating the contemporary call for 'work-life balance' – a call both pressing and easily associated with neo-liberal pop feminism, noting that the 'life' in such an account is a particular kind of life, one connected with a view of family and species continuity that might not be what we would choose to celebrate as a final goal:

> Isn't even the phrase *work-life balance* a manifestation of what Foucault describes, in biopower, as an 'attention to the processes of life – characterized by a power whose highest function is perhaps no longer to kill, but to invest through and through.' (HS1 139)? When viewed through this lens, 'life' loses some of the dreamy qualities it takes on ... where 'life' as family means healthy relationships, parental intimacy and well-behaved children, warm soup on cold nights, the quiet pleasures captured by the phrase 'all in the family.'

> ... What I am suggesting is that work-life balance is still operating under an old logic that is gradually being supplanted: the old logice of the *dispositif* of alliance for its understanding of family and the old logic of deduction for its understandings of workers with systems of power. When we try, and fail, again and again, to 'take back' our time, to 'take back' the energies of our own vital bodies, we are still functioning within an understanding of power as what Foucault calls the sovereign, juridical 'right of seizure: of things, time, bodies, and ultimately life itself (HS1 136).[33]

---

32   See Lynne Huffer, *Are the Lips a Grave? A Queer Feminist on the Ethics of Sex* (New York: Columbia University Press, 2013).

33   Huffer, *Are the Lips a Grave?*, 183–184.

Although this print comes to us from a considerably earlier time period, the print's overt message appears to be to inscribe a desire for the safe and *Heimlich* family in which the husband can count on the 'mutual support and companionship' a wife ought to provide, in which 'the goods' do not get together on their own, to make their own market (pace Irigaray), and husbands do not pander their wives nor desire other flavours. But to a variable and queer reading, the print's own prolific nature, the range of body types, of pricing structures, of attitudes toward the viewer (direct frontal gaze, oblique and sidelong, apparently unavailable with a turned up nose) work against precisely this view of social and domestic family life and its legal fictional substructures.

KATHARINE KITTREDGE

The Blind Made Happy: Arcs of Reward and Redemption in Early Modern Children's Texts[1]

ABSTRACT

The children's literature of the late eighteenth and early nineteenth centuries (1780–1840) provides a fascinating lens for examining the perception of blindness in American and British culture. Didactic literature sought to give children a view of the real world and to teach them about the moral way to respond to that reality. The blind characters depicted in these texts include people of all ages and from a wide range of socio-economic classes. Comparisons of early to late texts and of British to American texts reveal significant differences in the perception of medical treatments and educational opportunities available to the blind.

Introduction

The children's literature of the late eighteenth and early nineteenth century provides a fascinating lens for examining many aspects of Anglo-British society. Connoisseurs of children's literature find works from this time period less readable than the texts that emerged in the mid-nineteenth

1   I would like to thank Laura E. Wasowicz, Curator of Children's Literature and the rest of the staff at the American Antiquarian Society for their help in navigating their extensive Children's Literature Collection, the source of most of my American materials for this essay. Thanks are also due to the very patient staff at the Bodleian Library's Duke Humfrey reading room, without whom the British part of this essay would have been greatly curtailed. And, of course, the warmest thanks go to Stan Booth and Chris Mounsey for not only organizing a wonderful conference, but for creating the technological infrastructure which made it truly inclusive.

century during the genre's 'Golden Age', due to the tendency of these texts to be highly didactic, lacking in imaginative touches, and filled with mundane description. These are precisely the qualities which make them an excellent source for information about the contemporary time period, since during this time period one of the primary mandates of children's literature was to depict the world for children, and the depictions tended to be so distilled or simplified that neither the youngest, most naive child – or a scholar from another century – could mistake their meanings.

Children's literature between 1780 and 1840 is an especially rich source of images of blindness. Although it is difficult to make a quantitative study of children's literature, since so many children's texts were classified as 'ephemera' and were rarely preserved, I can say that among the volumes which have made their way into research libraries and on-line databases, I have been able to locate over fifty sources which deal specifically with blind characters. The blind people depicted in these texts include those who lost their sight at birth, during childhood, as adults, and in their declining years. The texts also include characters from a wide range of socio-economic classes: from the iconic blind beggar through resourceful working-class individuals, to those on the highest rungs on the social ladder. This paper is devoted to an intriguing sub-set of this larger group: blind individuals whose status is changed over the course of the narrative, converting them from a pitiable and largely helpless state to one of happiness.

Looking at these narratives allows us to detect a remarkable shift over the course of these sixty years: while the early tales feature dramatic medical cures of the blind protagonists, the later part of the time period saw an emergence of texts presenting the acquisition of knowledge and specialized training as the route to self-sufficiency and happiness for the blind. The first of the tales advocating education appear around 1815 and they become stronger and more detailed as time progresses, attaining their strongest expression in *The Blind Made Happy*, an American text from 1837. It is also important to note that the rise of the 'education' texts did not eliminate the 'curing the blind' plot, which continue to be published during the same time period. However, the increasingly dramatic or unrealistic plots which the 'curing' texts featured and the contrast they provide to the complex and extensive depictions of blind education in a variety of formats show the ascendancy of the latter form.

According to Chris Mounsey, the primary medical procedure used to restore sight was popularized in England from 1695 by Sir William Read who raised the status of the profession to become a socially powerful 'royal oculist', and 'couching' became both more widely available and more visible after the 1740s with the advent of well-publicized itinerant practitioners like John 'Chevalier' Taylor. Heavy advertising during the mid-eighteenth century by both oculists and the less reputable (but more affordable) liminal and folk-healers offering a variety of eye-washes and treatments – many of which featured named testimonies and accounts of miraculous cures – gave the increasingly literate population of America and Great Britain the impression that blindness was a transient state which could be terminated at any time as long as the patient had access to the right physician – and was able to pay.[2]

As Andrew O'Malley has noted, children's literature in the late eighteenth century also underwent a significant shift away from the extended allegories which had dominated the field in earlier decades towards the use of individual case studies; O'Malley describes how these texts reflect a growing interest in 'the individual and the individual within society, [which] necessitated a new form of narrative that reflected this ideological change: the individual case study in both its medical and pedagogical forms.'[3] The earliest examples of this sub-genre of tales about blindness are frequently hybrids which include these two genres: medical in their fascination with the physical sensations of blindness and the mechanisms available for its cure, and pedagogical in their intent to inculcate appropriate morality in their young audience and to help them overcome the challenges and temptation which daily life presented.

2   Chris Mounsey, *The Birth of a Clinic* (Lewisburg, PA: Bucknell University Press, forthcoming).

3   Andrew O'Malley, *The Making of the Modern Child* (New York: Routledge, 2003), 13.

Virtue Revealed and Vision Restored

Madame de Genlis has the earliest children's tales about the curing of
the blind.[41] Although current academic practices tend to separate literature by country and language of origin, it is abundantly evident through a
variety of sources that Genlis should be considered a foremother of both
English and French children's literature, since so many English women of
the middle and upper classes spoke and read French, and translations of her
texts into English were readily available. Genlis' s 1784 *Veillées du Chateau*
(*Evenings at the Castle*) includes two tales of blind individuals who are
cured through the intervention of an aristocratic young person. The focal
point for the first story is Delphine, a spoiled rich girl convalescing in the
country in Dr Steinhaussen's home in the country, where she observes his
daughter Henrietta intercede to have her father cure an old blind woman.
The motive behind this is that the woman's young and beautiful granddaughter, Agatha refuses to marry Simon, a local rich farmer, because 'she
should then have a family to manage and could not take proper care of
her poor blind grandmother; she could not assist her, prattle to her and
lead her about; and that she would not consent to leave her to the care of a
servant'.[5] Henrietta's father removes the old woman's cataracts and Agatha
consents to marry Simon with the caveat that her grandmother will have
an apartment in their house.

All honour and credit for the blind woman's cure goes to Henrietta;
The old woman calls her 'my heavenly protectress', and says, 'But it is to
Miss Henrietta that I owe all! It was she that found me out! That brought
me hither! That had me kept in the house! She seeks out the wretched and

---

4   Stephanie de Genlis, *Tales of the Castle*, Thomas Holcroft, trans. (London: Scatcherd
     and Letterman, 1819), 148–151. An even earlier de Genlis text, her extremely influen-
     tial *Theatre à l'usage des Jeunes Personnes*, 4 vols (Paris, 1779–1780) also prominently
     featured a blind character: 'The Blind Woman of Spa' which describes the joy that a
     family of children take in aiding an older blind character. This text is not included
     in this consideration because it falls under the category of drama.
5   De Genlis, *Tales from the Castle*, 29.

the sick, she finds comfort for them, she makes them happy!'.[6] Perceiving the praise heaped upon Henrietta, Delphine vows to reform and become an agent of charity in the future. There are a number of distinctive features of this story, the first being that this is the only time in my research that I have come across an elderly person who is cured of blindness – and it is significant that she is not cured so that she will derive monetary benefit from her regaining her sight, but rather so that her granddaughter will go on to have a fuller life. This emphasizes that in spite of the increased availability of cataract operations during this period, there was still an equating of blindness and old age, and a sense that it was somehow natural and tolerable for an older person to be deprived of sight.

The second tale of restored sight features a more conventional subject. Genlis recounts how 'The Princess', the six-year-old daughter of the Duchess of Chartres, spends three months in the country every summer. While there she meets Nanette, a blind peasant girl with 'very fine eyes' whose mother doesn't have the money to take her to the surgeons in Paris. The Princess replies 'Well, then, I will take her to Paris myself, when I return thither; I will make room for her in the Coach by my side'.[7] Nanette goes to the house of an oculist, who keeps her there all summer and part of the winter. When the Princess returns to the country the next summer, she finds Nanette cured and glad because 'I can work now'.[8] However, when the Princess learns that the girl cannot read, and that her mother has no money for her schooling, she determines to teach the girl herself, and accomplishes the task during her three months in the country although 'Nanette, as had been predicted, was not very industrious'.[9] Nanette's progress is attributed entirely to the patience and persistence of the princess who gives her 'sweetmeats, clothes and books' as a reward, and promises to teach her 'something else' the next summer.[10] The presentation of Nanette as a charitable project of the young Princess rather than a character of interest herself, supports not only the

---

6   De Genlis, *Tales from the Castle*, 35.
7   De Genlis, *Tales from the Castle*, 149.
8   De Genlis, *Tales from the Castle*, 149.
9   De Genlis, *Tales from the Castle*, 151.
10   De Genlis, *Tales from the Castle*, 151.

dominant goal of encouraging charitable giving and care, but also emphasizes the distinction between the various classes.

This use of the blind within children's texts solely as objects of pity or
charity was largely overturned by one of the most successful texts of this
era, Elizabeth Pinchard's *The Blind Child, or Anecdotes of the Wyndham
Family*[11] a book which was immediately lauded by critics and pedagogical
writers (Edgeworth mentions her in company with Genlis)[12] and was com-
mercially successful, going through multiple printings in the eighteenth
century. Its history is also distinguished by its widespread and almost instant
pirating in the United States, a blatant plagiarism in the form of a French
version,[13] and steady re-publication throughout the nineteenth, twentieth
and twenty-first centuries.

Pinchard's book describes the life of the very privileged Wyndham
family, which features an idealized mother and her four children, the second
youngest of whom, nine-year-old Helen, is blind. The family's daily life with
Helen serves as a framing tale to allow the author to discuss the theoretical
and philosophical significance of blindness as well as the maturation and
moral growth of the eldest sister, Emily, whose tale is truly the heart of
the text. Pinchard employs the format of dramatic dialogue[14] – frequently
a discussion between mother and child – as a mechanism to discuss not

11   Elizabeth Pinchard, *The Blind Child, or Anecdotes of the Wyndham Family* (London:
      E. Newbury, 1791).
12   Maria Edgeworth, 'Blind Kate', in *Rosamond, A Sequel to Early Lessons* (Philadelphia,
      PA: J. Maxwell, 1821; London: J. Johnson, 1801), 45.
13   Isabelle Montolieu, *La Jeune Aveugle* (Paris: Bertrand, 1819). An imitation of, or
      pirating of *The Blind Child, Anecdotes of the Wyndham Family*.
14   Gary Kelly, writing about Hannah More's cheap repository tracts (the first of which
      was published the year after *The Blind Child*) argues that although dialogues are 'an
      ancient device in didactic writing' their particular use in late eighteenth-century
      texts was as ritual rather than interaction: 'one side is always already right, and so
      they resemble catechism, revival of which, by the way, was an important element in
      the Evangelical's literary-theological culture. Catechism is pseudo-talk, determined
      by a pretext ...' 'Revolution, Reaction, and the Expropriation of Popular Culture:
      Hannah More's Cheap Repository', *Man and Nature/L'homme et la nature*, 6 (1987),
      152.

only the nature of blindness, but also to make some cogent points about the emerging fashion of 'sensibility', to comment on correct parenting and to establish the importance of a firm moral code for all children. Much of Pinchard's book also discusses the daily life of the family, with the children acting in identifiably 'child-like' ways rather than merely serving as avatars for the author's philosophical treatises. The climax of the story is the entire family's pilgrimage to London to have Helen's blindness cured by a famous oculist.

The description of the operation focuses heavily on the family's participation:

> The day arrived, and the anxious family assembled to witness the event ... Mrs Wyndham, alike unable to see the operation , or to quit the room, retired to one end of it, trembling, pale, her hands and heart lifted up to God, but concealing her face on the shoulder of Arthur, whose arms were thrown round his mother, while his tears fell fast on her cheek. Emily, struggling with extreme agitation of her mind, but by a strong effort composed, knelt with her eyes fixed on Helen, and one of her arms round her waist, while the other hand held both the hands of Helen.[15]

We learn that their father felt 'in his heart every touch of the instrument which the skilful and tender oculist applied to the eyes of the patient, quiet Helen',[16] but we do not see the instrument or learn about the sensations which Helen experienced. We are told that 'In about ten minutes Helen gave a faint shriek, and exclaimed 'Ah, my god! What is this! *Do I see*!'; this is followed by an account of every family member's response, and the section is concluded with: '[t]he surgeon, having finished the operation, with the help of the servants, covered her eyes, and forbade them to remove the bandage, as everything depended on her not being suffered to use her eyes'.[17] Helen is banished from the narrative to lie in a dark room 'for some days' and then to be gradually introduced to the light.[18] In contrast, we next have four pages discussing Emily's response to the operation, and

---

15 Pinchard, *The Blind Child*, 169.
16 Pinchard, *The Blind Child*, 170.
17 Pinchard, *The Blind Child*, 171.
18 Pinchard, *The Blind Child*, 173.

the nature of 'true sensibility' (Pinchard uses the opportunity to opine: 'True sensibility is active and useful; false tenderness enervates the mind, and renders its best wishes unavailing').[19] Some notice is given to the progress of Helen's transition into the sighted world: 'By degrees she became familiar with the objects about her, which at first she knew not how to avoid in walking across the room',[20] but the final word we are given on the character is her gratitude: 'Attached with enthusiasm to her parents and sisters, she never forgot their cares in her helpless state. If they were sick, she devoted herself to them, saying frequently, 'Oh, can I ever repay your attention to me when *I was blind*".[21] This element highlights the extent to which blind characters – even eponymous ones – are rarely the focus of their own books. Within the didactic texts they function primarily to receive aid and to teach lessons to sighted characters; they are distinctive due to their relationships to others, not due to their different relationship to the world.

And yet, Helen does emerge through the text as a believable child: she pouts when deprived of an outing; she fails to understand visual referents, and her siblings are not always able to either understand her feelings or to respond correctly to her desires. Pinchard's creation of a blind character whose inner life is visible to the audience is the first time that a children's text about blindness has sought to invoke empathy rather than sympathy in its audience. This different perspective may have arisen from Pinchard's personal experience with blindness. Unlike the blind characters which proceeded this work – Genlis's blind in need of succour or relief or the stereotypical elderly blind beggars in children's texts by Barbauld and Thomas Day[22] – Helen is recognizable as a real child, and her tastes and concerns mirror those of the actual child readers. We know from the

19   Pinchard, *The Blind Child*, 175.
20   Pinchard, *The Blind Child*, 175.
21   Pinchard, *The Blind Child*, 177.
22   Anna Laetitia Barbauld, 'The Blind Fiddler', *Lessons for Children* (London: J. Johnson, 1781), 136–138; Thomas Day, 'The Good-natured Boy/The Ill-Natured Boy', in *The History of Sandford and Merton* (London: Stockdale, 1783), 43–52.

records of John Taylor's Clinic in Hatton Garden, London,[23] that there was a 'Windham' family of Fellbrigg Hall listed as patrons some forty years before the appearance of this book. We don't know exactly what Pinchard's relationship was to the family – a relative, friend, or even a domestic employee such as a governess? That she had an on-going relationship with the family is suggested by the etching which serves as the book's frontispiece; the picture's caption reads: 'Emily, Helen, Maria & Arthur Walking on the Garden Terrace', the two younger children, shown in the background are as youthful as the characters who appear in the text, but the figure of Helen featured in the foreground, is a mature young woman, not the nine-year-old featured in the text. This seems to indicate that Helen is an actual person whose portrait was taken a some date significantly after the performance of the surgery and yet prior to the writing of the book. It also suggests that Pinchard had an on-going relationship with the family that stretched back to the childhood of the protagonist – when the family was actively supporting Taylor's clinic as a way of assuring treatment for their daughter – but which also reaches forward to the current time when she is attempting to celebrate Mrs Wyndham's excellence, and the effect that it has on her children. It may be this personal connection which is the reason for the very different tone and focus of the work – her knowing Helen as a 'real' person rather than just as a plot device.

The success of Pinchard's tale seems to have stimulated a spate of didactic children's texts which featured the dramatic healing of a blind person, but most of those which followed reverted to the earlier texts' relentless focus on the lessons learned by sighted characters. One of the most egregiously sight-centred texts is Maria Edgeworth's story 'Blind Kate',[24] which expands on the theme explored by Genlis in placing primarily emphasis on Rosamond (the heroine of Edgeworth's most famous morality tale, 'The Purple Jar') rather than on the eponymous labouring-class character whom she helps.

23   William Oldys, *Observations on the Cure of William Taylor … Also, Some Address to the Publick, for a Contribution towards the Foundation of an Hospital for the Blind* (London: E. Owen, 1753), William Windham is mentioned in the Subscribers' List.

24   Maria Edgeworth, 'Blind Kate', in *Rosamond, A Sequel to Early Lessons.* (Philadelphia, PA: J. Maxwell, 1821; London: J. Johnson, 1801).

The book's focus is not on Blind Kate's arduous journey to London to subject herself to the surgeon's needle, but rather young Rosamond's offer to sell
her new horse in order to raise the money for the operation. Kate is a young
woman who is 'a sweet-tempered, cheerful, kind-hearted creature.'[25] She is,
first and foremost, the perfect object of charity. Kate is only twenty-four;
her blindness is the result of her forgetting to bring in one of the family's
sheep at age fifteen, and having her eyes irritated by the cold wind as she
searched for it all night.[26] At the time of the story (nine years later), she is
pious and attentive to God's will, grateful for every favour, her only regret
being that she cannot help others more – although she is already an integral part of her community, taking care of the local children and teaching
them to plait straw. She has to be talked into submitting to the operation
by Rosamond, at first arguing that she 'wants nothing' and that she would
prefer to stay 'as I am'.[27] Although initially reluctant to accept additional
charity, she quickly acquiesces to Rosamond's arrangements.

The process of restoring Kate's sight is presented from start to finish
as an educational opportunity for Rosamond. Her father agrees to sell the
horse and to contribute to the other expenses if Rosamond makes all the
arrangements, and so, over the course of the story she must 1) find a traveling companion for Kate, 2) arrange to have the companion's family cared
for in her absence 3) have Kate's clothes washed and packed, 4) calculate
all of the expenses of the journey and Kate's convalescence, 5) find lodging
in London for the two women, 6) arrange transportation (which she bun-
gles so that she must improvise an alternative conveyance), and 7) procure
a letter of introduction to the oculist. The strangeness of making a child
into a medical ombudsperson, caseworker and travel agent is explained
by Rosamond's father as a means of teaching her that 'it is not only necessary to wish to do good, but to know how to do it'.[28] It is clear that, as an

25   Edgeworth, 'Blind Kate', 294.
26   Although this form of blindness seems odd to modern readers, 'a great Cold' was
      given as the cause of blindness in most of those whom John Taylor of Hatton Garden
      cured. Queen Mary II was also treated for the condition while she was young.
27   Edgeworth, 'Blind Kate', 296.
28   Edgeworth, 'Blind Kate', 289.

aristocratic girl, Rosamond must take seriously her dominion over others and learn how to employ working-class people to make her own plans come true. In detailing the lessons learned by Rosamund, Edgeworth is also describing the practical and logistical obstacles which may stand in the way of a labouring-class person's attaining medical attention.

In contrast to the high drama of the preparations for Kate's operation, the medical event itself seems like an anti-climax; Kate describes the operation as: 'no more than a prick of a pin, and so quick I cannot well tell what it was like'.[29] She does though, describe the sensation of regaining her sight:

> [it was] most like a stretching and lifting up of a great weight,; and that being taken off, on a sudden, like a shot, came back my eyesight; and, for the first time these nine years, I saw the daylight, and could not believe at first but it was a clash and would go again from me ...[30]

When the oculist, who is 'very kind-spoken' although foreign, sees how 'happy and thankful' Kate is, he 'would not take half, nor a quarter [of what they were prepared to pay].[31] Kate offers to sell one of her sheep to repay Rosamond for the expense of the operation, but of course, Rosamond will not hear of it, 'yet she was not displeased by the scrupulous honesty and gratitude of Kate'.[32]

A similar image of labouring-class fortitude is presented in Barbara Hofland's *The Blind Farmer and his Family*[33] which features Farmer Norton, his wife and his six young children. Norton's blindness comes upon him in the course of a financially ruinous year in which his father suffers a costly illness, the crops fail, his cows die, and, finally, the family is evicted from their farm by the greedy local Baronet. It is clear that Norton had been a successful and morally responsible member of society before this run of bad luck, and the tale revolves largely around how his family pitches in

---

29 Edgeworth, 'Blind Kate', 298.
30 Edgeworth, 'Blind Kate', 298.
31 Edgeworth, 'Blind Kate', 299.
32 Edgeworth, 'Blind Kate', 300.
33 Barbara Hofland, *The Blind Farmer and His Children* (London: Harris and Son, 1819).

to support themselves in a new environment, and work together to save up the money for Norton's sight-restoring surgery. Mrs Norton sews for a tailor, the children do factory work, run errands, care for wealthy children, engage in urban husbandry, and one becomes an artist's assistant. Although most of the book is dedicated to the self-sufficiency of the family members, their hard work and ingenuity, the operation ultimately is achieved through the intercession of a rich man – in fact, the very squire who had callously evicted them – who supplies the money to pay for the operation, and uses his influence to compel the oculist to treat Farmer Norton. In the end, the oculist (like the one in Edgeworth's tale), refuses to take the full amount for his work, the farmer's sight is restored, and he is given a new farm. The dominant message seems to be rather discouraging to a modern audience: no matter how pious, hard-working and inventive the working-class family members might be, they are ultimately unable to rise out of poverty and disability themselves. It seems that the true goal of all of their hard work and the reward for their unremitting goodness is their ability to attract the attention of a wealthy person, rather than to advance their own cause; and, ultimately, after all of their hard work, the final reward is that they are restored to their original place within society.

In all five of these tales, children play roles which put them beyond the usual place of juveniles – the working-class children must become the protectors and providers for their blinded parents; the wealthy children must take the lead in providing charity. The restoration of sight for Nanette, Blind Kate and Farmer Norton return them to useful, class-appropriate lives, and leave the children in their lives (both wealthy and working class) to resume their child-positions, although they – like their juvenile readers – are made wiser by their experience of caring for a blind individual. The peripheral message conveyed about the state of blindness is that it is a condition which renders one a burden to one's family or community and that no matter how cheerfully one accepts their fate (and this acceptance is a moral necessity), the loss of sight is tragic.

In contrast, the working-class adult women in two tales intended for older readers share certain characteristics which place them into a different category. For these young women, blindness has interrupted their appropriate progression through maidenhood to marriage. Sophie, the heroine of 'Sophie Lefevre, or The Poor Blind Girl'[34] is a woman driven out of the upper class by a train of events which begins with her stepfather's imprudently investing her inheritance from her dead father. This leads to her being reduced to the role of nursemaid in a relative's house, but she leaves this post when he 'attempts her virtue'; she then works for a laundress until her health is ruined and her sight is lost, at which point she is put out to beg on the street. A wealthy young man passes her at her post, and notices that 'though in rags and barefooted, [she] presented a figure uncommonly interesting.'[35] He takes her in, her sight is restored by an oculist and then the two marry. In this context, blindness is just the most dramatic of a series of setbacks experienced by the young woman. Her ability to maintain enough of her class identity in the face of the ultimate misfortune (blindness) marks her as extraordinary and worthy of restoration into the upper class.

Susan, the heroine of 'The Hampshire Cottage'[36] is truly working class – her parents are described as 'English peasant[s] of the olden time' and her father, Nicholas Foster, had been a hedger before being disabled by old age and blindness (he lost his eyesight when almost sixty). When the story opens Susan is just twenty-one and engaged to be married to George Wells, an able young man who has promised that they will live in a cottage near her parents so that she can continue to care for them. She is initially presented as a 'normal' country girl – her blindness comes about through overheated dancing, exacerbated by the application of folk remedies, and

---

34 Anonymous, 'Sophie Lefevre, or The Poor Blind Girl' in *The Fatal Mistake* (Hartford, CT: John Babcock, 1801). Although the edition that I found was printed in Hartford CT, I hesitate to designate this as an 'American' text since there is no author, the story is set in Britain, and the printer John Babcock primarily published pirated editions of British and French works. In his essay, 'The Blind Authoress of New York: Helen De Kroyft and the Uses of Disability in Antebellum America', *American Quarterly*, 51/2 (1999), 385–418, James Emmett. Ryan accepts this as an American text, but since he misreports the tale's plot, he may not have had first-hand familiarity with the book itself.

35 'Sophie Lefevre', 25

36 Arabella Jane Sullivan 'The Hampshire Cottage' in *Tales of the Peerage and Peasantry*, Lady Dacre, ed. (New York: Harper & Brothers, 1835).

the lack of 'real' medical care. When her blindness proves to be permanent, she dissolves her engagement, and learns to knit so that she can continue to support her parents. We are led to believe that she benefits from her blindness in a moral and spiritual fashion, and is, as time passes, improved by her condition; the narrator opines: 'Of all the visitations with which human nature is afflicted, none assuredly has such a tendency to calm, to purify, and to refine the heart as blindness'.[37] The improvement in Susan's character attracts the attention of the daughter of the local gentry, whose husband's friend 'had the care of an eye-hospital'.[38] Susan agrees to subject herself to the treatment because it 'might possibly enable her to assist her parents more effectually'[39] and is sent away to the hospital in London for six weeks of treatment. Although she no longer has the vibrant beauty of youth, her experience has left her with a cheerful and 'sedate self-possession' which attracts a Mr Otley, a recent widower left with many children and a farm to tend. In their brief courtship we are told:

> Susan herself had no pride of romance about her. She esteemed Mr Otley, and she was aware that he became everyday more particular in his manner to her; she knew that the home he could offer her would be comfortable beyond what she had any right to expect; his plain manners appeared to her neither rough, nor homely, and she felt sorry for the little children ....[40]

Their marriage meets with the approval of the whole village, and Susan's parents feel that 'their task was ended, their duties fulfilled'.[41]

The strongest sense we gain from the tales of Sophie and Susan is the sense of social order restored. Blindness has taken them out of the normal arc of their lives, and the intervention of enlightened aristocrats allows them to resume their rightful place – Sophie in a life of luxury, and Susan in a life of comfort earned through hard work and loyalty. This is one of the strongest marks of the British tales – blindness is presented as a disruptor of

---

37   Sullivan 'The Hampshire Cottage', 218.
38   Sullivan 'The Hampshire Cottage', 255.
39   Sullivan 'The Hampshire Cottage', 256.
40   Sullivan 'The Hampshire Cottage', 265.
41   Sullivan 'The Hampshire Cottage', 266.

social order, and medical intervention is a double corrective. Having passed through the experience, the characters feel a profound sense of gratitude for their lot in life. The upper-class philanthropists whose intervention is essential in each of these stories both demonstrate their suitability to hold a higher place in society, and reinforce the idea that the existent social order benefits people of all classes.

As Gillian Avery has discussed in *Behold the Child: American Children and their Books, 1621–1922* most of the texts published in America during the first two decades of the nineteenth century were written overseas; Avery maintains that it was not until 1828 that a 'native literature' for American children appeared. However, even though these texts did not emerge until later than the British texts, blindness is still represented prominently; as James Emmett Ryan notes:

> Visual disability, considered within the context of nineteenth-century American sentimental themes and tropes, can thus serve a dual function: on the one hand, blindness works perfectly to represent the deserving recipient of charitable support, while on the other hand, blindness serves as a perfectly formed alteration of sensibility that can sustain cultivated interior perceptions and emotions of the sort favored by sentimental writers of the antebellum period.[42]

The final three texts of restored sight that I am going to be discussing highlight some of the subtle differences between American and British depictions of blindness and its cure. *Blind Susan, or the Affectionate Family*, is ascribed to 'M. of Lowell', but its prefatory material says that it was 'taken from *The Juvenile Miscellany*, a children's periodical founded by Lydia Maria Child in 1826. The plot is reminiscent of Pinchard's *The Blind Child*, featuring a family of multiple children (including a rowdy brother and a maternal elder sister) guided by an exemplary mother, all of whom demonstrate the correct way to interact with and support a blind child. As in Pinchard's story, most of the textual attention is devoted to the sighted siblings, describing their response to their sister and using their questions as a vehicle for conveying medical information.

42   Ryan, 'The Blind Authoress of New York', 400.

In the British stories the availability of a qualified surgeon is assumed – although the details of traveling for treatment, arranging recuperation, and (in the case of working-class patients) paying the fee is a topic of discussion. In the American versions, discovering a qualified surgeon is often the starting point for the story of the cure. In *Blind Susan*[43] it is Dr Carter who has 'returned from Europe, and performed successful operations on the eyes, having made himself well acquainted with this branch of his profession.'[44] The operation is performed in the family home (the younger children are sent away) and then Susan is 'removed to a dark room, and a close bandage placed over her eyes.'[45] When the children return, their mother describes the nature of cataracts 'A cataract is a hard substance which forms over the eye, so as to exclude the light ...'[46] and then she gives a medically inaccurate account of the operation, where instead of describing the cutting away of the cataract, she presents an entirely fantastical story about how 'a small delicate instrument is introduced, which pushes this hard substance from before the pupil of the eye, and after a time it dissolves.'[47] The larger point that she wants to make is that Dr Carter is 'a very humane man and skilful [sic] operator, and if your sister is restored, will never cease to feel grateful to him.'[48] The lionizing of the surgeon continues: only he and the mother are present when the bandages are removed, and after identifying and embracing her mother, Susan turns to Dr Carter and says 'and this the kind physician. What do I not owe you both!'[49] Susan's placing the doctor on the same plane as the mother who gave her birth indicates the role that he continues to play in her life – as the years pass, Dr Carter 'to whom she was most tenderly attached' watches over her and offers advice about her health.[50] The implication is that the doctor is, if not part of the family, at

---

43   M. of Lowell, *Blind Susan, or the Affectionate Family* (New York: Mahlon Day, 1832)
44   Lowell, *Blind Susan*, 6.
45   Lowell, *Blind Susan*, 8.
46   Lowell, *Blind Susan*, 9.
47   Lowell, *Blind Susan*, 17.
48   Lowell, *Blind Susan*, 9.
49   Lowell, *Blind Susan*, 12.
50   Susan, alone of the blind characters does not go on to live a 'normal' life; instead, she is said to suffer from an 'early decay' and gradually loses her strength: 'She faded,

least part of the family's community, and that his interest in Susan signals an emotional connection rather than a simple professional transaction.

A doctor plays a similar role in *Blind Little Lucy* one of 'Sister Mary's Stories' published in 1836.[51] This tale differs from all of the other examples since Lucy is blinded by her brother's careless use of fireworks. Significant time is spent on Lucy's physical and emotional pain as a result of the accident; she gradually learns to cope with her blindness and she gradually evolves into a blind child who is 'so patient, so gentle, so cheerful that every one loved her.'[52] Although the story seems to be very similar in tone to most of the other tales discussed, it is unusual in the extent to which the blind character is actually at the heart of the story – once he had blinded his sister, little Tommy fades into the background and the author devotes herself to describing the physical and emotional sensations that Lucy experiences, encouraging young readers to imagine themselves in her place and to develop empathy for her situation.

In terms of plot, the story follows the well-worn path to visual restoration. Some months after her loss of sight, Lucy's father is taking a ship back to America when he meets Dr Hutton, described as 'well known abroad, and famous for his skill in curing the blind. He is a very pleasant man, too.'[53] When Dr Hutton reads Lucy's letters and learns 'how her eyes were hurt, and how much she feels the loss of them, and how sweetly and gently she bore it all.'[54] He becomes determined to cure her. Once again, it is implied that she has earned her cure by demonstrating the appropriate attitude towards her disability. Of all of the tales I have considered, this one is the most medically inaccurate – not only is it impossible to cure blindness caused by a concussive explosion, but the vague methods prescribed are

---

and seemed still more lovely; she sickened and became still more dear; but no care or skill could free her from the spoiler. She was taken from this dark world to enjoy true felicity in the courts of God' (18). The final etching is of a young lady (her devoted sister Isobel?) looking out the window to watch her funeral procession.

51 'Sister Mary', *Blind Little Lucy* (Philadelphia: American Sunday-School Society, 1836).

52 'Sister Mary', 23.

53 'Sister Mary', 39.

54 'Sister Mary', 39–40.

clearly unsound. We are told that 'Lucy would have to take medicine, and to eat but little for some time ... he [Dr Hutton] would wish first to watch her, and to look at them [her eyes] often.' Lucy and her sister are housed in lodgings near the doctor's house and left entirely under his care; 'No one could be kinder than Dr Hutton is to Lucy. He speaks to her and touches her as gently as possible. Yet he has to hurt her a good deal.'[55] We are told that when he has 'done to Lucy's eyes all he was going to do' (there is not explicit mention of surgery) she must remain bandaged in a dark room and keep still, and then, when the healing is complete, he and his wife take the girls home to be reunited with their family.

The family is ecstatic to see Lucy cured, and their reception of Hutton is reverent: 'how the children kissed the doctor's hands, and thanked him again and again! And how fondly they led him to the house! And how they ran to get him fruit, and cake and milk, and everything they had!'[56] Interestingly, the author (who is writing for the Sunday School Union) ultimately pulls back from this idolatrous celebration, ending her tale with the lines: 'God has made you able to see, and that, too, without hurting you at all. He has made you all hear, too, and to smell, and taste, and move, to think, and feel. He is kinder to you than Dr Hutton was to Lucy.'[57] Still, in spite of her demurral, it is clear that the American doctor holds a status that is very nearly Divine.

The third American example from the 1830s of blindness cured is a sub-plot in the tale of the moral education of the self-centred wealthy title character of *Charles Liston, or Self-Denial* (1834).[58] Near the beginning of the story we meet Jane, a blind orphan whom Liston's family places with an educated spinster, Miss Atwood, who promises to teach her 'every thing that can render her misfortune less irksome, and perhaps she may in time recover her sight.'[59] Note here that in this narrative education can simply ameliorate the suffering of the blind; cure continues to be the only positive

---

55   'Sister Mary', 43–44.
56   'Sister Mary', 48.
57   'Sister Mary', 50.
58   Anonymous, *Charles Liston, or Self-Denial*. (Higham, MA: C & E. B., 1834).
59   *Charles Liston*, 14.

outcome. Although Jane's case had earlier been considered hopeless, years later the family becomes acquainted with 'Dr C.' and the male members of the family go to visit him:

> Dr C. was noted for his eccentricity and liberality. He was a man of learning and science, and Charles had often wished to see him. He took them over his grounds, which were laid out with taste and showed them several curious plants of rare medicinal virtues. A cabinet of curiosities was opened for their amusement and he gave Charles some fine specimens of ores.[60]

While Dr Carter and Dr Hutton are very specifically identified as having been trained by European surgeons, this description of Dr C. presents him as a more wide-ranging scholar, and it is not clear whether his skill is derived from foreign training or home-grown academic application. The specifics don't seem to matter very much due to the lack of detail conveyed about Jane's cure. Dr C. agrees to take on the case after hearing of Jane's misfortunes, and we are told he 'performs the operation with gentleness and skill'.[61] Like all the other blind patients returned to sight, 'at the last touch of the instrument she [Jane] exclaimed 'I see! And instantly fainted.'[62] Compared to the other American doctors, Dr C seems less involved with his patient and/or her family; he performs routine follow-up exams rather than adopting her or becoming part of the family. In the time-honoured way, Charles Liston marries his family's protégé (who is now lovely, as well as sighted) a few years later.

The tales of these three American girls reveal a number of things: first how deeply entrenched the trope of the blind cure has become by the 1830's, and, second, the extent to which the medical facts have become so insignificant or interchangeable that the authors now feel free to disregard them or to employ them in service of their personal goals (such as writing a cautionary tale about the dangers of playing with fireworks). The importance of moral fortitude and acceptance of one's fate is highlighted, as are the feminine virtues of 'gentleness' and 'patience', and in each case

---

60   *Charles Liston*, 26–27.
61   *Charles Liston*, 26.
62   *Charles Liston*, 27.

these virtues are directly linked to the victims' cure. The primary difference between these tales and those originating in Great Britain is that whereas the British tales feature aristocratic characters who determine which blind characters are worthy of cure, in America it is an individual doctor – distinguished by his unusual education or personal eccentricity – who decides the subject is worthy of visual restoration. Money is not mentioned at any point in the American narratives, nor does distance or access to care seem to be an issue. In the thirty years that have elapsed since Pinchard's tale, the healing of the blind has become a dramatic device to be employed in a moral tale instead of an opportunity to discuss anatomy, medicine, or the philosophical ramifications of attaining sight.

'Give thine alms – thou canst not heal': Blind Schools as Salvation

Throughout my research, I came across numerous poems from this time period featuring blind characters. Although the number of words devoted to blind characters is considerably fewer in poetry sources than in prose works, the role that poetry played in late eighteenth-century education makes the consideration of blind characters in poetry particularly significant. In his 1802 treatise, *Poetry Explained for the Use of Young People*, Richard Lovell Edgeworth decried the practice of having very young children learn poetry by rote memorization, which causes them to 'acquire the habit of repeating words to which they affix no distinct ideas'.[63] It is likely that while this practice may have done little to help form the 'poetic taste' which Edgeworth saw as the ultimate goal, the extensive anthologizing of poetry featuring blind characters, and its subsequent memorization and recitation by generations of school children must have enhanced the impact

---

63   Richard Lovell Edgeworth, *Poetry Explained for the Use of Young People* (London: J. Johnson, 1802), iii.

which these images had on young readers – even if they did not have the intellectual tools to engage with them in a critical fashion.

From 1723 to 1815, most of the poems create sentimental pictures of the blind character – often elderly blind beggars – to whom the child narrators or protagonists give pity and alms. The plot arc of these poems may feature the tale of the blind person's loss of sight, often includes their expressions of piety, and never extends beyond the relief of their immediate poverty. Starting in 1815, we begin to see poems which introduce a new theme: the celebration of blind schools or asylums as sources of shelter, education and occupation for the blind.

The earliest reference I have been able to find is Elizabeth Hill's poem 'Blind Asylum – Liverpool' which appeared in her *Sequel to the Poetical Monitor* in 1815. Hill's initial publication, *The Poetical Monitor* (1796) was a collection of 'Pieces Select and Original, for the Improvement of the Young in Virtue and Piety; Intended to Succeed Dr Watts' Divine and Moral Songs.' According to Sarah Trimmer writing in *The Guardian of Education*, the book was originally intended for use in London's charity schools,[64] but proved so successful among parents of all classes that it went through multiple editions and led to Hill's sequel in 1815.[65] She indicates that the sequel is intended for older children 'those approaching maturity' and she says that her goal is to 'exhibit lively and pointed descriptions of the deformity of folly and vice, and the beauty of wisdom and virtue.'[66] Towards this end, she includes a number of poems (most not attributed to any author, and most likely her own work) which deal with quotidian, highly sentimental subjects: charity schools, Opie's 'The Orphan Boy', 'Lines on an Infant Dying ...', 'A Young Soldier's Address to his Mother'. Her 'Blind Asylum – Liverpool' refers to the institution that had opened in Liverpool in 1792, the first institution of its kind in England. In this poem

64 Sarah Trimmer, *The Guardian of Education conducted by Mrs Trimmer* (London, 1802–1806), 130.

65 Ryoji Tsurumi, 'Between hymnbook and textbook: Elizabeth Hill's anthologies of devotional and moral verse for late charity schools', *Paradigm*, 2/1 (2000), n.p.

66 Elizabeth Hill, *A Sequel to the Poetical Monitor*, 2nd edn (London: Longman et. al, 1815).

Hill's narrator beseeches a 'stranger' to 'learn the sorrows of the blind'; after detailing the hardships of blindness: unable to appreciate natural beauty, appreciate art, or see their loved one's faces, she also invokes the image of the blind man negotiating the street with the help of a staff or a guiding child, but filled with fear until they arrive at the asylum where:

> Lonely blindness here can meet,
> Kindred woes and converse sweet,
> Torpid once, can learn to smile
> Proudly o'er its useful toil,[67]

It is interesting that although she ends this stanza with the word 'toil', no account is given of the kind of work that is to be done in the asylum – only the safety and companionship it offers. This vagueness can be seen as a kind of white-washing put on for the juvenile audience, since at this time the Liverpool Asylum was, in fact, little more than a workhouse, providing shelter and sustenance in exchange for constant, tedious employment.[68] The final stanza is an appeal to the reader to donate in support of the institution, indicating that blind people are also the work of God, and concluding with the line 'Give thine alms---thou canst not heal.'[69]

The anonymously authored *The Keepsake; or, Poems and Pictures for Childhood and Youth*,[70] focuses on homely, everyday images and moral tales; the spoiled child who complains about her breakfast, a brother who falls through the ice, a group of children digging in the garden. In keeping with this positive tone, 'The Blind Boy' opens with Emma's mother showing her a beautifully crafted new basket which was made by Jem, 'the blind boy on the green' who had been left 'in poverty, sickness and grief, / Without protector or guide'[71] until 'a kind rich lady' 'plac'd him secure in the house

---

67   Hill, *A Sequel to the Poetical Monitor*, 39.
68   Chris Mounsey, 'Edward Rushton and the First British Blind School', in *LA QUESTIONE ROMANTICA*, forthcoming 2016.
69   Hill, *A Sequel to the Poetical Monitor*, 40.
70   Anonymous, 'The Blind Boy', in *The Keepsake: or Poems and Pictures for Childhood and Youth* (London: Darton and Harvey, 1818).
71   'The Blind Boy', 19.

for the blind, / and all the expences defray'd.' There Jem is taught to make baskets and to do 'straw-work of every kind' so that 'now he's employ'd and his living can earn, / And is useful and happy, though blind.'[72] Emma and her mother subsequently visit the institution, now identified as 'the School for the Blind.' Calling the Liverpool institution a 'school' at this point is somewhat misleading. Although an anonymously authored pamphlet *An Address in the Favour of the School for the Blind* claims that since its founding, the Liverpool Asylum's managers have sought 'to improve the nature of the establishment' ... to render it less an ASYLUM, and more approaching a SCHOOL,' and claims the institution formally opened as 'The School' in 1800, its true nature is revealed in the pamphlet's discussion of how this 'school' is dedicated to instructing the blind in 'some useful art or trade',[73] as well as its stipulation that any blind people who 'in consequence of bodily or mental incapacity' were not capable of engaging in manufacture 'were under the necessity of returning to their friends.'[74] Fortunately, the 'Blind Boy', Jem, has the manual dexterity and strength to master the tedious task of basketry, and the poem depicts him in the midst of constructing another basket: 'he sung at his work, / and smil'd with contentment and joy.' The intended moral is one of the importance of well-chosen charity – Emma vows 'Neither gingerbread, comfit, nor nut will I buy' so that she can purchase one of Jem's baskets, but the larger story is of a blind child's finding a place where he can be a useful (and class-appropriate) member of society due to the intervention of the 'Blind School'.

In her discussion of Henry Sharpe Horsley, Patricia Demers notes his 'liberal use of maudlin, pathetic exempla to further his practical and pious design.'[75] Towards this end, many of the poems in Horsley's 1828 offering, *The Affectionate Parent's Gift and the Good Child's Reward*,[76] expose

---

72 'The Blind Boy', 20.

73 *An Address in the Favour of the School for the Blind* (Liverpool: G. F. Harris, 1817), 12.

74 *An Address in the Favour of the School for the Blind*, 13.

75 Patricia Demers. *From Instruction to Delight* (Oxford: Oxford University Press, 2004), 190.

76 Henry Sharpe Horsley, 'A Visit to the Blind Asylum', in *The Affectionate Parent's Gift and the Good Child's Reward* (London: T. Kelly, 1828), 168–174.

children to the grittier sights of London: 'A Visit to Newgate' and 'The Lunatic Asylum' as well as those most deserving of pity: 'The Cripple Girl', 'The Orphans', and 'The Blind Fiddler'. The message to be derived from each of these scenarios is much the same: 'prize the blessing you possess, / And prove the feeling you profess'.[77] It is not surprising, then to find a poem entitled 'A Visit to the Blind Asylum'. Horsley uses many of the same themes as Hill, but shifts the emphasis: the poem is prefaced by a page-long celebration of the delights of sight, encouraging the child reader o rejoice in their ability. The reader is then confronted by a wide array of blind people 'The healthy, young, and wrinkled old', all of whom are 'Shut up, poor souls, in gloomy night, / Walking without one ray of light' (169). The narrator reassures and comforts the reader: 'Come, child, I'll take you by the hand. / And lead you through the gloomy band'[78] and the child is subsequently comforted by the diligence of the inhabitants of the 'School for the Blind': basket-making, spinning, weaving, whip braiding. Although this poem celebrates the industry and abilities of the blind: 'All hands are busy in their rooms; / Some highly-gifted we shall find', these images are largely employed to make the child-auditor 'grateful that you have good eyes ... give God the praise, / He deals with you in milder ways'.[79] Here the asylum / school is presented as a mere repository for the blind; a convenient place for an impressionable child to see horrors which make them self-satisfied rather than promoting any sense of empathy or iden-tification with the blind. The author uncritically accepts the harshness of the lives of the blind, presenting their 'affliction' and their hard labour as God's will; the lack of any intellectual enrichment in a 'school' is neither remarked upon nor critiqued.

The depiction of blind schools in American children's fiction took on radically new forms after the founding of the first American institu-tions for the blind in 1832 in Philadelphia, Boston, and New York. These schools rejected the workhouse-based models used by most of the British school/asylums, preferring to adopt and modify the French model which

77   'A Visit to the Blind Asylum', 181.
78   'A Visit to the Blind Asylum', 169.
79   'A Visit to the Blind Asylum', 170.

focused on intellectual education: reading, arithmetic, geography, history, and music while also providing the children with instruction in life skills, trades (printing and weaving) and handicrafts (knitting and sewing). The schools also followed the French model of staging exhibitions as a way of publicizing their successes and raising funds,[80] a practice that had been in effect since before the founding of the first institution for the blind in France – in 1784 Valentin Haüy brought a young man named La Sueur, his first successful pupil with him to Paris, 'to exhibit him as an example of what might be achieved by his methods'.[81] The ploy was so successful that the Philosophical Society of Paris funded his first school: L'Institution Nationale des Jeunes Aveugles; and he continued to put on exhibitions right to the eve of the Revolution.[82] The American exhibitions began almost immediately after the founding of the schools, and were an immediate success. As Samuel Gridley Howe, founder of the Perkins School for the Blind reported:

> In January, 1833, the Treasury was empty, and the Institution in debt. An exhibition of the pupils was then given before the General Court, which afforded such complete and striking proof of the capacity of the blind for receiving an intellectual education, that the Legislature, as it were by acclamation, voted that $6000 per annum should be appropriated to the Institution, for the support of twenty poor blind persons belonging to the State.[83]

These exhibitions were widely reported in both the mainstream newspapers and in children's periodicals, and had a radical impact on both the public's awareness of the presence of the schools and on their perception of the intellectual and artistic capabilities of their students. It is likely that children in or near America's urban areas might be taken to see these exhibitions (and may, in turn, have written about them to further-flung friends and cousins).

---

80 Ernest Freeberg, 'The Meanings of Blindness in Nineteenth-Century America', *Proceedings of the American Antiquarian Society*, 110/1 (2000), 119–152, 122.

81 W. H. Illingworth, *History of the Education of the Blind* (London: Sampson et al., 1910), 5.

82 Illingworth, *History of the Education of the Blind*, 5.

83 Samuel Gridley Howe, 'Education of the Blind' *The North American Review* (1833), 98.

Whereas before the only images of blind people were those contained in sentimental, moralistic tales, now children had images of real blind boys and girls – in addition to the accounts of exhibitions prominently featured in contemporary newspapers, there were also periodicals written expressly for children, like Lydia Maria Child's *The Juvenile Miscellany* which featured accounts of visits to blind institutions and reported on actual conversations with blind children as early as 1833.

An early American title which describes one of these exhibitions also uses its title to play on the popular 'restoration of sight' narrative that such stories were replacing. Sarah Savage's *Blind Miriam Restored to Sight* is a tale which contrasts the situations and dispositions of two girls: Miriam, a spoiled rich girl being raised by her aunt, Mrs Cooper, and Sarah Thompson, a blind orphan being raised by her grandmother, a poor washer woman. Miriam's mother is impressed by the intelligence, industry and tranquillity of Sarah, and she discusses her with her friends, one of whom 'suggested that she was a fit subject for the New England Asylum for the Blind, which had lately gone into operation. 'Application was immediately made to the Trustees of the Asylum and Sarah Thompson was soon admitted to that admirable institution.'[84] Subsequently, Miriam and her aunt attend one of the institution for the blind's public exhibitions, where they see Sarah 'somewhat changed': '[there was a] soft and now joyous spirit to her features ... The pallid hue had disappeared, and the instruction of the brief period of six months had so quickened the spark within, that it sent its bright radiations through the whole countenance.'[85] They watch Sarah demonstrate her knowledge of geography, do mathematic calculations and read from a raised-print Bible. The effect this has on Miriam is immediate:

> No sooner was Miriam alone with her aunt, then throwing herself upon her neck, she sobbed out, 'Oh dearest aunt, it is not Sarah, it is I – it is I, who am blind' 'No, my dear, replied her aunt, 'you are this moment restored to sight. As soon as we

---

84   Sarah Savage, *Blind Miriam Restored to Sight* (Salem, MA: Registrar's Office, 1833),
      10–11.
85   Savage, *Blind Miriam Restored to Sight*, 12.

clearly discern our past negligence, the film is removed from our eyes. Take care that it never gathers over yours again.[86]

Miriam then repents of her spoiled, selfish ways and becomes a model of juvenile piety and devotion. In some ways this tale repeats the sins of previous stories: the working-class blind individual is largely a mechanism for growth and reform in her sighted (and upper-class) counterpart. However, the plot's affirmation that Sarah's blindness in no way prevents her from being a smart, competent and happy child is a long way from the earlier storylines which maintain that the only positive outcome for a blind character is the restoration of sight.

A British text written three years later, Eliza Paget's *The Blind Girl and Her Teacher*[87] does not include a precise account of the inmates or activities of the Blind Asylum, but it breaks away from the conventional 'sight restored' narrative and may indicate how the public's perception of the appropriate way to protect and support blind children was changing. The story presents Elizabeth Lee, nine years old, blind since infancy, the pinnacle of impoverished child piety, learning prayers by rote and eagerly attending a rural Sunday School. Although the story is told from the perspective of the unnamed, upper-class Sunday School teacher, unlike many of the other tales the focus of the story is on Elizabeth and her desire to achieve religious knowledge through education. Elizabeth Lee's rabid desire for education – demonstrated in her perilous solo journeys to Sunday School mark her as a transitional character, combining the piety of earlier blind characters with the thirst for knowledge of the later ones.

When her mother dies, Elizabeth is sent to the Riverston poorhouse where she was 'obliged to mingle amongst thoughtless and wicked children,'[88] and we learn that the other poor-house children 'took advantage of her blindness to create their own amusement; while all of them ridiculed her silent thoughtfulness, and purposely talked and laughed the loudest

86   Savage, *Blind Miriam Restored to Sight*, 15.
87   Eliza Paget, *The Blind Girl and Her Teacher* (London: Darton and Harvey, 1836).
88   Paget, *The Blind Girl and Her Teacher*, 100.

when, morning and night, she knelt to repeat her prayer'.[89] This description marks Elizabeth as a precursor of other famously bullied and mocked
heroines of children's literature – from the pious doomed girls of James
Janeway's morbid *A Token for Children* to the Golden Age resilience of Sara
Crewe and Anne Shirley. Distressed by Elizabeth's fate and impressed by
her pious resignation, the Sunday School teacher recalls that she has 'a very
rich godfather, who was a liberal supporter of the Asylum for the Blind, in
London; and she did not doubt that he had sufficient interest to procure
Elizabeth's admittance into this institution'.[90] The godfather, Mr Owenson,
visits Elizabeth and finds her worthy, and she is persuaded to leave her one
remaining friend by the school teacher's description of 'how many things
she would be taught, and how happy a home God had provided for her,
in which her blindness would subject her to no ridicule, and her desire of
instruction would be fully gratified'.[91] A bit of historical context makes
this assertion somewhat chilling. In 1833 Samuel Gridley Howe wrote that
contemporary British institutions for the blind: 'are not under the direction
of scientific men, nor is their object a scientific or intellectual education
of the blind: the one in London is merely for indigent blind, and they are
taught only handicraft work, and a little music; no books are used in the
establishment, and no intellectual education is given'.[92] Although it is to be
hoped that Elizabeth would have at least received some protection against
bullying in the blind school, it is to be feared that her desire for education
would have continued to be thwarted. It is possible that Paget was either
unaware of the true nature of the British schools, or she may also have
mistakenly assumed that the London school was run along the same lines
as the Edinburgh School for the Blind, which followed the French intellectually focused model and whose staged exhibitions were widely reported
in English and Scottish newspapers. The story ends with Elizabeth on her
knees thanking God for her good fortune, and we can only hope that her
next experience will be less painful than what has come before. However,

---

89   Paget, *The Blind Girl and Her Teacher*, 104.
90   Paget, *The Blind Girl and Her Teacher*, 101.
91   Paget, *The Blind Girl and Her Teacher*, 112.
92   Illingworth, *History of the Education of the Blind*, 64.

whether or not Paget's narrative reflects the reality of the relevant British institution, it does clearly signal that something has shifted both in the nature of the happy ending, and in the placing of a blind person in the centre of the narrative.

The pinnacle of this new theme can be found in the 1837 American book, *The Howard Family: or The Blind Made Happy*.[93] The book's author is anonymous, but it should be noted that the frontispiece and title page, which are executed in the raised type which was the forerunner of braille, were printed at the Perkins Institute for the Blind, indicating that individuals at the institution were directly connected to its creation. The book's preface begins by stating its intention, which is far more tightly focused than most of the 'conduct of life' literature. The book's goal is '[t]o awaken the attention and engage the sympathies of the young in their [the blind's] behalf', and specifically, to cause those who have the means to devote themselves to 'meliorating the evils of their condition' by supporting the schools for the blind; on the page adjacent to this preface is an etching of the Institution for the Blind at Philadelphia. The 108-page book follows the now-familiar format of so many of these conduct books in its use of a framing narrative in which an exemplary mother (the widowed Mrs Howard) educates her children about blindness. What sets this text apart is the wide range of blind characters who are introduced: a virtuous blind woman from the mother's youth who, in spite of living before the time when 'the blind are so well instructed that they may be useful in almost as many different ways as those who can see',[94] managed to make herself useful and beloved in her little rural village. The children are intrigued by the story and become keenly interested in the state of blindness; their mother educates them in a variety of ways – presenting statistics on the number of blind people in the United States, recounting biographies of 'uncommon' blind people from the past, including the British mathematician Nicholas Saunderson, the Viennese teacher Jacob Braun, an unnamed inventor from Normandy, an etymologist from Switzerland, and a French music teacher. The impression

---

93 Anonymous, *The Howard Family: or The Blind Made Happy* (New York: Scofield and Voorhies, 1839).
94 *The Blind Made Happy*, 21.

one gets is that blind people exist in all countries and in all times, and that many among them have been extraordinary. One of the children responds by saying that she now feels 'quite differently about them [the blind]. I have always pitied them, but I did not know before that they could be so instructed, and made almost as happy as we are.'[95]

The narrative continues with a short history of the founding of schools for the blind, followed by multiple visits to the local blind school where the family party sees an exhibition of accomplished pupils and also learns about the lives of the children who live there. In the course of the narrative, the sighted children also meet a blind street musician who is 'too old to enter the school'[96] and learn of a 'little blind boy' whose parents are soon convinced to enrol him in the school, where he is noted for his 'intelligence, animation, and rapid improvement'.[97] The text's inclusion of the 'raised let-ters' title page allows sighted children to gain first-hand knowledge of the texts used in the blind school, and its contents include etchings of blind people, poems about blindness, and a reference to a bible passage about a blind beggar. The overall effect is a normalization of blindness – the impression that blindness is a natural state experienced by people of all ages and from all times, countries, regions, and walks of life. Collectively, the blind are depicted as intelligent and resourceful, with a special emphasis placed on the benefits of the education that they can now receive through institutions for the blind – whereas the predominant emotions of virtuous blind people in earlier works were patience and resignation, the pupils of the blind school are described as 'joyous.'[98]

The Blind Made Happy builds on many of the previous children's publications in its use of the maternal narrator, 'real-life' experiences by its child-character, mixed with the recitation of historic/scientific facts, and anecdotes. Although the central figures, the Howard family, are sighted and the text is largely about their moral growth and education; the density of information about blindness and the proliferation of blind characters

95   *The Blind Made Happy*, 50.
96   *The Blind Made Happy*, 58.
97   *The Blind Made Happy*, 107.
98   *The Blind Made Happy*, 76.

reverses the usual practice of presenting a single blind individual isolated in a world of sighted characters. *The Blind Made Happy* provides an immersion in blind culture, creating an alternative world where blindness is an attribute rather than a character-defining disability. The texts which I have discussed leading to this final book – in both the sight-restoring and education categories – have shown a noticeable shift over the sixty years from *The Blind Child* to *The Blind Made Happy* towards presenting more of the internal lives of the blind characters, and also tracing the evolution of the exemplary blind character away from passive pious acceptance and towards an active quest to gain knowledge and skills. This can be attributed largely to the perception of the blind which was actively promoted by the blind schools with their exhibitions – and perhaps by the emergence of authors who had first-hand knowledge of blind individuals.

From 1780 to 1840 the stories of visual restoration initiated by *The Blind Child* languished into a hackneyed plot device, most frequently employed to reinforce rigid gender (marriage as woman's destiny) and class hierarchies – the curing of the blind characters in this narratives is sought so that they can return to their 'normal' position within the society – these texts celebrated the cultural dominance of the aristocratic class in Britain, and of the intellectual/medical elite in America. In contrast, the narratives about the institutions for the blind that emerged in 1815 initially celebrated blind people's being given an alternative space (the asylum) away from the larger society. This narrative of separation and difference grew stronger and richer with the advent of American texts which presented the model of the institution as not only asylum, but also as a source of intellectual education and practical/vocational training. These narratives promoted a reconfiguring of blindness from an affliction imposed by God into a practical problem to be solved through the establishment of specialized institutions and new systems of education. This led to the sighted public's increasing ability to see blind people as distinct individuals and paved the way for the emergence of the next phase in blind-narratives, such as the celebrity blind author, Helen De Kroyft, whose memoir *A Place in thy Memory* took America by storm in 1849.

It is hard to tell at this distance what the effect of children's texts depicting the blind had on their child readers in the late eighteenth and early nineteenth centuries. Today we recognize that children's views not only of their world, but also of themselves can be influenced by the books they read (or have read to them) in their early years. Children who are exposed to a more diverse cast of characters are more open-minded and empathetic to people who are different from themselves; children who differ from the majority in race, class, ability, or beliefs are bolstered by the appearance of fictional characters who are similar to themselves – they feel 'seen' by the larger community, and view books (and by extension, institutions like schools and libraries which house books) as a safe and welcoming space. We can thus extrapolate that the proliferation of images of blind people – especially blind children – during this time period would have had a positive impact on its readers in terms of making them aware of the state of blindness and encouraging them to consider the emotional and physical impact of this condition. The less positive messages conveyed in the earliest books: their focus on the helplessness of blind people and their isolation, and insistence upon blind people's inability to change or improve their situation certainly encouraged pity in young readers, but did little to promote empathy in sighted readers or pride in blind children who may have been exposed to these tales. In contrast, the later books which featured blind characters heroically struggling to gain education and independence undoubtedly inspired respect in the sighted, and promoted hope in the blind. It is impossible to say how much the evolution of these texts reflected the larger society's changing perception of the blind, or whether these texts played a significant role in shifting society's perceptions. In either case, they provide us with fascinating insights into the perception of blindness in the past.

CLARE WALKER GORE

'The awful individuality of suffering': Disabled Characterization in Dinah Mulock Craik's *Olive* and *A Noble Life*

ABSTRACT

This essay explores two rare examples of Victorian novels which have disabled protagonists, Dinah Mulock Craik's *Olive* (1850) and *A Noble Life* (1866). These novels are radical in being centred on the experience of disabled characters, and anticipate the social model of disability in their depiction of disability as a socially constructed category. However, I argue that Craik ultimately fails to construct fully functional disabled protagonists, and that it is this very failure which makes these novels so interesting. Craik's unwillingness to engage directly with certain aspects of disabled experience not only reveals something about contemporary constructions of disability, but speaks to the limitations of the social model of disability at the present time.

Introduction

Disabled characters are common in nineteenth-century fiction, but disabled protagonists are vanishingly rare. Disability plays an important part in many novels, but it is practically never the subject of the novel: Tiny Tim plays a crucial role in 'A Christmas Carol', but the story is not about him. The purpose of Tim's inclusion is to melt Scrooge's heart, his 'active little crutch' a device to aid Scrooge on his journey towards finding the spirit of Christmas, not to help Tim himself get anywhere in particular. Tim not only acquiesces in his narrative role but is made to voice his acquiescence, recognizing that he functions as a spectacle, 'hop[ing] the people saw him in the church, because he was a cripple, and it might be pleasant to them

to remember upon Christmas day, who made lame beggars walk'.[1] Tiny
Tim is only the most famous of many such characters, some of whom are
villains rather than victims, but all of whom exist on the margins of the
novels they inhabit.

So pronounced is this pattern that critics have theorized the marginalization of disabled characters as an inherent feature of the nineteenth-
century novel. Lennard J. Davis suggests that because 'novels are a social
practice that arose as part of the project of middle-class hegemony [...]
the plot and character development of novels tend to pull toward the normative [...] ideologically emphasizing the universal quality of the central
character whose normativity encourages us to identify with him or her.'[2]
Sharon Snyder and David Mitchell might seem to be taking up an opposing
position when they argue that disability is an essential part of the Western
narrative tradition 'as a stock feature of characterization and, second, as an
opportunistic metaphorical device', but they too contend that disability is
almost never the subject of narrative, noting that 'while stories rely on the
potency of disability as a symbolic figure, they rarely take up disability as
an experience of social or political dimensions.'[3]

This is what makes Dinah Mulock Craik's novels *Olive* (1850) and
A Noble Life (1866) so interesting and so important to the discussion of
disability in nineteenth-century literature. These once-popular, now lit-
tle-known novels both feature disabled characters as protagonists; Olive
Rothesay is described at her birth as 'deformed' because of her rounded
spine, which causes 'an elevation of the shoulders', while the Earl of
Cairnforth, more drastically, is said to be 'the smallest, saddest specimen
of infantile deformity', born with multiple physical impairments which
ultimately prevent him from walking and make it difficult for him to use

---

1   Charles Dickens, *A Christmas Carol and Other Christmas Books*, Robert Douglas-
     Fairhurst, ed. (Oxford: Oxford University Press, 2008), 50.
2   Lennard J. Davis, *Enforcing Normalcy: Disability, Deafness, and the Body* (London:
     Verso, 1995), 41.
3   David T. Mitchell and Sharon L. Snyder, *Narrative Prosthesis: Disability and the
     Dependencies of Discourse* (Ann Arbor, MI: University of Michigan Press, 2000), 48.

his arms and hands.[4] Not only are these characters at the centre of the novels they inhabit, but the novels are about their experiences of disability: both characters are shown to have a strong moral effect on those around them, but it is their own development which dominates the novels, and their experience into which the reader is drawn.

Moreover, Craik does represent what Mitchell and Snyder call the 'social [and] political dimensions' of disability. *Olive* stages the process by which the heroine comes to think of herself as 'deformed', and then depicts the reversal of this process, as Olive finally rejects this damaging self-image and begins to see herself as lovable. However, the process by which Craik enables Olive to come to this new self-understanding points to the major limitations of her achievement. Ultimately, she cannot enable Olive to function as a novelistic heroine and take up her rightful place as the wife of the novel's hero without re-forming her 'deformed' body: at a crucial point in the narrative, she writes out Olive's physicality. Having depicted disabling as a social process, Craik yet feels the need to erase the embodied aspects of disability completely, emphasizing Olive's physical normality at the point of her acceptance into the marriage plot.

In *A Noble Life*, Craik makes this manoeuvre impossible for herself by representing the Earl's body too vividly and too consistently as impaired – rather than simply unusual – for it to be 'normalized' at the novel's conclusion. Unfortunately, this has a disastrous effect upon her ability to enable him to function as a protagonist. Craik effectively stymies her own effort to represent the Earl of Cairnforth as a sentimental hero whose emotional development takes the place of the actions we might expect from the 'biography' of a great man by shutting the reader out of his inner life almost completely. The reason *A Noble Life* ultimately fails as a sentimental novel is not that the Earl is an insufficiently active protagonist, but that he is a remote one: Craik disables his characterization by relying almost entirely on paralepsis, inference, ellipsis and absence to communicate his experience to the reader. By a cruel irony, Craik's inability to engage directly with

4   Dinah Maria Mulock Craik, *Olive*, 3 vols (London: Chapman and Hall, 1850), 10–11; Dinah Maria Mulock Craik, *A Noble Life*, 2 vols (London: Hurst and Blackett, 1866), 23, 64, 155.

her own subject disables a novel that is ostensibly celebrating the abilities of its disabled hero.

In this essay, I want to examine what I see as the interesting failures of both novels, and ask why Craik found herself unable to create fully functional disabled protagonists. An indication of why this might be is, I think, provided by the internal contradictions of the very phrase, 'functional disabled protagonists'. As my usage of the term – as both verb and adjective – has already illustrated, 'disabled' is a word that can be used in two distinct but crucially overlapping ways. To 'disable' a device is to stop it from working; to 'be disabled' in this sense is to be 'rendered incapable of action or use; incapacitated; taken out of service'. The dictionary's second sense of the word, however, is now the predominant usage: here, 'to be disabled' means 'having a physical or mental condition which limits activity, movement, sensation, etc.'[5] As any disabled person can attest, to have such a 'condition' is not to be completely 'incapacitated', and there are few who would overtly claim such synonymy. Yet the older definition still haunts the modern usage: to be called 'disabled' is to be defined by negatively conceived difference, by incapacity measured against a functional 'norm'. As Irving Kenneth Zola puts it: '"a disabled car" is one which has totally broken down. Could "a disabled person" be perceived as anything less?'[6] Since a character in a novel is a representation of a person, might it be reasonable to suggest that a disabled character is disabled *as* a character by the ascription of disability, not merely debarred from certain plot roles, either by physical incapacity or by social prejudice, but actually unable to function as a novelistic character?[7]

5   'Disabled, Adj. and N.', *OED Online* (Oxford: Oxford University Press), accessed 6 January 2015, <http://libsta28.lib.cam.ac.uk:2123/view/Entry/53385>.

6   Irving Kenneth Zola, 'Self, Identity and the Naming Question: Reflections on the Language of Disability', *Social Science & Medicine*, 36/2 (1993), 170.

7   The question of how we should read novelistic characters in relation to persons is, of course, an extremely complicated one; so much critical ink has been spilt on the subject that is impossible for me to summarize the debate here. For my purpose, Martin Price's definition of characters as being 'within the frame of their fictional world, no less than fictional persons' is most helpful. (Martin Price, *Forms of Life:*

Zola's solution to the problematic nature of the phrase 'disabled person' is to advocate the use of the phrase 'person with a disability', suggesting that prepositions 'imply both "a relationship to" and "a separation from"' disability.[8] This is politically problematic in itself, however, for the slippage between the two senses of 'disabled' to which Zola (understandably) objects has the advantage of drawing our attention, almost inevitably, to the social aspect of disability. If some people 'are disabled' like broken-down cars, who or what, we must ask, is disabling them? The social model of disability theorizes that the dis/ability system disables them, by working to isolate and denigrate those who are defined by difference, pathologized as deviance. As Tobin Siebers cogently summarises this position:

> Disability is not a physical or mental defect but a cultural and minority identity. To call disability an identity is to recognize that it is not a biological or natural property but an elastic social category both subject to social control and capable of effecting social change.[9]

If we think about disability in this way, then it makes little sense to talk about 'characters with disabilities', as though disability could be an inherent property of persons, rather than 'disabled characters'. As disability theorist Rosemarie Garland-Thomson explains, 'disability is a reading of bodily particularities […] not so much a property of bodies as a product of cultural rules about what bodies should be or do.'[10] According to this logic, 'the object of disability studies', as Lennard J. Davis puts it, 'is not the person using the wheelchair or the Deaf person but the set of social,

---

Character and Moral Imagination in the Novel (New Haven, CT and London: Yale University Press, 1983), 64.).

8   Zola, 'Self, Identity and the Naming Question: Reflections on the Language of Disability', 170.

9   Tobin Siebers, *Disability Theory* (Ann Arbor, MI: University of Michigan Press, 2008), 4.

10   Rosemarie Garland-Thomson, *Extraordinary Bodies: Figuring Physical Disability in American Culture and Literature* (New York: Columbia University Press, 1997), 6–7.

historical, economic and cultural processes that regulate and control the way we think about and think through the body.'[11]

This statement, which encapsulates the shift of attention away from the body and towards the social processes by which it is read, perfectly captures both the power and the inadequacy, for readers like myself, of the social model of disability as a means to understand our own experience. Encountering such a statement, as I do, as an occupant of the identity category 'disabled' and from within a body which hurts, halts, fails, and insistently draws attention back to itself, it is impossible not to recognize that the 'social, historical, economic and cultural processes' that regulate how 'we think about and think through the body' are only one part of the story that this 'person using the wheelchair' needs to hear. As Susan Wendell, observes, speaking from her own experience of chronic pain:

> I do not think my body is a cultural representation, though I recognise that my experience of it is highly interpreted and very influenced by cultural (including medical) representations. Moreover, I think it would be cruel, as well as a distortion of people's lives, to erase or ignore the everyday, practical, experienced limitations of people's disabilities simply because we recognize that human bodies and their varied conditions are both changeable and highly interpreted.[12]

As Wendell explains here, to recognize that the body has a reality of its own, and that there are forms of bodily immobility, loss or pain which no amount of social reform could erase, is not to deny the socially mediated experience of the body, but rather to insist upon the interrelationship of the social and the embodied aspects of disability. Tobin Siebers conceptualizes this as 'complex embodiment', a model of disability which 'views the economy between social representations and the body not as unidirectional, as in the social model, or non-existent as in the medical model, but as reciprocal.'[13] It is at this intersection between representation

11   Davis, *Enforcing Normalcy*, 2–3.
12   Susan Wendell, *The Rejected Body: Feminist Philosophical Reflections on Disability* (New York: Routledge, 1996), 44.
13   Siebers, *Disability Theory*, 25.

and embodiment that I wish to situate this argument, in the interstice where we all of us live, whether disabled or not.

I may seem to have wandered some way from the mid-Victorian novels with which I began, but it is in fact this intersection between the social and embodied aspects of disability, and between the two senses of the word 'disabled' – between physical difference interpreted as lack, and actual incapacity – which the experience of reading these novels forces us to confront. Craik's inability to endow her disabled protagonist in *A Noble Life* with full subjectivity – and, in parallel, her decision to re-form Olive's 'deformed' body in order to enable her to take up a heroine's place at the novel's finale – has its source in the same fear of contemplating the bodily experience of disability which is at the root of the social prejudice that the social model of disability seeks to address, and which yet is replicated in the social model itself, in its flinching from the aspects of disabled experience which cannot be explained in purely social terms. Reading these neglected novels, nineteenth-century explorations of disabled subjectivity by a non-disabled writer, actually allows us to confront our own attitudes to the 'disabled' body and to disability itself, forcing us to consider the extent to which characterization is disabled by disability.[14] To be capable of being imagined as a novelistic character seems to me a crucial aspect of

14   I have called these novels 'neglected', but *Olive* at least has begun to attract critical attention in recent years, as a result of its subject matter. It was re-published in the Oxford Popular Classics series in 2000, and featured prominently both in the first book-length study devoted to disability in nineteenth-century British literature and culture, Martha Stoddard Holmes's *Fictions of Affliction*, and in the first special journal edition devoted to Craik's work (see Martha Stoddard Holmes, *Fictions of Affliction: Physical Disability in Victorian Culture* (Ann Arbor, MI: University of Michigan Press, 2004), 48–52; Tabitha Sparks, 'Dinah Mulock Craik's *Olive*: Deformity, Gender and Female Destiny', *Women's Writing*, 20/3 (2013), 358–369; Alisha R. Walters, 'Affective Hybridities: Dinah Mulock Craik's *Olive* and British Heterogeneity', *Women's Writing*, 20/3 (2013), 325–343. Increasing academic interest in disability has to some extent revived Craik's critical fortunes; as Karen Bourrier points out in her introductory essay to the special edition of *Women's Writing* on Craik, 'the majority of scholars at this critical moment are coming to Craik's work through a disability studies perspective.' (Karen Bourrier, 'Introduction: Rereading Dinah Mulock Craik', *Women's Writing*, 20/3 (2013), 2.)

personhood in a culture in which the novel is the major popular literary form. Meeting disabled protagonists is therefore a rare opportunity to peep through a window (or into a mirror) and see ourselves as we have been seen – or rather not seen. For if Craik cannot succeed at creating disabled protagonists, the terms on which she fails might have everything to tell us about how disabled people have been disabled as subjects – and why.

'Am I really deformed?': Negotiating Disability in *Olive*

The terms upon which we are to understand Olive's physical difference are clearly set out in the scene immediately after her birth. When the doctor notices the 'slight curve at the upper part of the spine, between the shoulder and neck', he revises his opinion that she is 'as nice a little girl as ever was seen' and instead pronounces her 'deformed', a 'terrible sentence' at which her nurse is 'overpowered with blank dismay'.[15] Nor is this an overreaction on Elspie's part, for Olive's 'deformity' is hugely significant in cutting her off from her parents' affection; when Olive's mother Sybilla is told of her 'hopeless deformity', the shock is 'to her almost more fearful than her child's death'.[16] She imagines that when her husband returns from his estates in the Caribbean and sees their daughter, he will 'turn away in disgust, and answer that it had better died'. Indeed, Olive almost does die as a result of Sybilla's total neglect in her 'temporary madness'.[17]

Although we are encouraged to see this reaction as 'exaggerated', arising from the 'exquisitely beautiful' Sybilla's vanity and excessive regard for physical beauty, which she has been taught to consider 'as the greatest good',[18] she is fundamentally right about how her husband Angus (supposedly so much more serious-minded) will react. When he first sees Olive,

15   Craik, *Olive*, 1.10–11.
16   Craik, *Olive*, 1.32.
17   Craik, *Olive*, 1.34
18   Craik, *Olive*, 1.15, 1.32.

she is five years old, and although she is described as 'almost pretty', her 'elevation of the shoulders, shortening the neck, and giving the appearance of a perpetual stoop' horrifies him, to such an extent that he experiences 'frenzied unbelief' before 'turn[ing] away, putting his hands before his eyes, as if to shut out the sight'.[19] Despite the fact that Olive's physical difference causes her no pain, nor any kind of impairment – the suggestion that she is slightly frail, and small for her age, is the sole indication that she is in anything other than good health – it is regarded by both her parents as supremely significant. While Sybilla does ultimately learn to appreciate her exceptionally sweet-natured and gifted daughter, repudiating her earlier attitude and coming to regard Olive as 'the most loving and duteous daughter that ever mother had',[20] this change of heart takes many years, and involves Sybilla herself going blind, perhaps as a narrative punishment for her earlier failure to 'see' Olive clearly. Angus is dealt a still harsher fate, sliding into alcoholism and bankruptcy and succumbing to an early death, not before he has further damaged Olive's self-esteem by calling her, in a drunken fit of temper, a 'white-faced mean-looking hunch-back!',[21] a 'cruel epithet' which comes back to her at crucial points in the novel.[22]

As this summary suggests, Olive's parents are shown to be fundamentally at fault in their estimation of the significance of her physical difference. Throughout the novel, characters' moral worth can be appraised by their reaction to Olive's appearance; where it seems highly significant to her first (and false) friend Sara, who turns out to be a faithless flirt, it is hardly regarded by the earnest clergyman, Harold Gwynne, Olive's eventual husband, who claims 'he had never noticed [her] being "slightly deformed"'.[23] 'Deformity' is shown to be significant only in the eyes of those who over-value physical perfection, and Olive's prejudiced father turns out to be quite wrong in thinking that she will 'never marry'.[24] Ultimately,

19   Craik, *Olive*, 1.58.
20   Craik, *Olive*, 2.313.
21   Craik, *Olive*, 1.211.
22   Craik, *Olive*, 2.15.
23   Craik, *Olive*, 3.59.
24   Craik, *Olive*, 1.139.

the only thing holding back Olive's matrimonial career is shown to be the sense of inadequacy he himself inculcated in her: she fails to recognize her beloved Harold's first declaration of love as such, because she believes it 'impossible' that anyone could love her,[25] something she re-iterates when her rejected suitor, Lyle Derwent has just proposed to her – declaring it 'utterly impossible that you can love me'[26] – an idea which only 'quit[s] her heart forever' after Harold, now her betrothed husband, unequivocally declares her to be 'beautiful'.[27] It is possible to read *Olive* as a radical text in which the heroine's journey is towards understanding that her physical dif-ference has no significance in and of itself, that she is not 'deformed' except when others see her as being so, and that she has the power to reject this reading of her body. Olive can be read as a disabled protagonist whose fully imagined personhood actually causes her author to explode the category of disability, revealing it to be a purely social construction.

This reading is strengthened by the fact that Olive is shown to have an instinctive sense of the truth and to be self-taught in all the most important things, and yet has to be taught to see herself as disabled. Craik depicts Olive as a Romantic child of Nature, who does not have to be taught to see the reality of the world surrounding her:

> She had never heard of Wordsworth; yet, as she listened to the first cuckoo note, she thought it no bird, but truly 'a wandering voice'. Of Shelley's glorious lyric ode she knew nothing; and yet she never heard the skylark's song without thinking it a spirit of the air, or one of the angels hymning at Heaven's gate. [...] She had never heard of Art, yet there was something in the gorgeous sunset that made her bosom thrill [...] No human being had ever told her of the mysterious links that reach from the finite to the Infinite, out of which, from the buried ashes of dead Superstition, great souls can evoke those two mighty spirits, Faith and Knowledge; yet she went to sleep every night believing that she felt, nay, could almost see, an angel standing at the foot of her little bed, watching her with holy eyes, guarding her with outstretched wings.[28]

---

25   Craik, *Olive*, 3.115.
26   Craik, *Olive*, 3.221.
27   Craik, *Olive*, 3.349.
28   Craik, *Olive*, 1.197.

The angelic Olive does not have to be taught how to read the natural world, nor the tenets or even the imagery of the Christian faith. She is similarly a self-made daughter, understanding how to be dutiful and loving to her parents even though they have not set her any kind of good example; she is 'prompted by her loving nature' to kiss her father, even after his rejection has 'gone deep to her child's soul',[29] and is even more adoring of her negligent mother, eagerly responding to her first overtures of affection, apparently entirely without resentment.[30] Olive seems able to intuit all the things that Craik depicts as having an essential and enduring reality: the beauty of Nature, the goodness of God, a daughter's duty to love her parents. The fact that *she* does not understand her physical difference as 'deformity', then, seems significant. Her father is mistaken in thinking that she understands why she will 'never marry'; in fact, the narrator tells us, the thought had merely 'come to her, as it does to most young girls who love their parents very dearly, too dearly to imagine a parting', and later on she wonders '"why papa said that, of course, I should never marry!"'[31] When she is going to her first ball at the age of seventeen, and her mother urges her to cover her shoulders with a mantle, she does not understand why, for 'the defect in her shape rarely crossed her mind'.[32] The scene at the ball in which Olive overhears Sara laughing with another girl at the idea '"of Olive's stealing any girl's lover!"', and then nerves herself to ask why, is painful for the reader precisely because Olive actually sees herself more clearly *before* the 'revelation' of her deformity. Sara's explanation is subtly shown to warp Olive's sense of self rather than to reveal an essential truth:

> 'Yes, I know,' she murmured, 'I am little, and plain, and in figure very awkward. Would that make people hate me, Sara?' 'Not hate you; but – ' 'Well, go on – nay, I *will* know all!' said Olive firmly; though, gradually, a thought – long subdued – began to dawn painfully in her mind. 'I assure you, dear,' began Sara, hesitatingly, 'it does not signify to me, or to any of those who care for you; you are such a gentle little creature, we forget it all in time. But perhaps with strangers, especially with men,

29   Craik, *Olive*, 1.73, 1.58.
30   Craik, *Olive*, 1.15.
31   Craik, *Olive*, 1.138–140.
32   Craik, *Olive*, 1.170.

who think so much about beauty, this defect' – She paused, laying her arm round
Olive's shoulders – even affectionately, as if she herself were much moved. [...] 'Do
not look so, my dear girl; I did not say that it was a positive *deformity*.' Olive faintly
shuddered: 'Ah, that is the word! I understand it all now.'[33]

We are surely prompted to ask ourselves what the difference between being
'little, and plain, and [...] awkward' and being 'deformed' really is; the true
significance appears to lie only in Olive's changed understanding of herself
as set apart from others. When she returns home, and asks her mother, '"am
I then so painful to look upon? Shall I, indeed, cause people to dislike me
wherever I go?"',[34] the reader's answer must surely be a resounding 'no', since
Olive is ultimately loved by all who know her. In her 1875 revision of the
novel, Craik reformulated the question as, '"am I really deformed?"'.[35] The
change is slight but hugely significant: does Olive question the reaction
of others to her difference, or the basis of that difference itself? The two
questions are ultimately shown to be indivisible, for Olive is 'deformed'
only when others see her as being so. The whole idea of 'deformity' is
thereby destabilized.

   This instability is greatly increased by the fact that Olive's identity
as 'deformed' is shown to be enabling in some respects, in freeing her to
pursue the career she loves. Clearly, Olive is not able to become an artist
because the shape of her shoulders enables her to paint better, but the
social identity that the reading of her physical difference as 'deformity'
confers upon her means that she feels herself to be free to pursue a career
as an artist, which is explicitly figured as an alternative to marriage. When
she first 'saw in herself a poor deformed being', she thought she would
be 'shut out from all natural ties', from 'the love which is the religion of a
woman's heart'.[36] Yet this exclusion from marriage and domesticity, which
appeared to her in the first volume of the novel as a tragedy, strikes her in
the second volume as a positive boon, as her 'sense of personal imperfection
which she deemed excluded her from a woman's natural destiny, gave her

---

33   Craik, *Olive*, 1.180–182.
34   Craik, *Olive*, 1.187.
35   Dinah Maria Mulock Craik, *Olive* (London: Macmillan and Co., 1875), 88.
36   Craik, *Olive*, 1.190–191.

freedom in her own';[37] in the revision, more explicitly still, it is her 'personal deformity' which so liberates her.[38] She finds herself able to 'do many things with an independence that would have been impossible to a beautiful and unguarded youth', able to study at the British Museum and walk to London alone, reassuring her mother that she is '"not like other girls. Who would notice me?"', and adding 'how happy she was in being so free, and how fortunate it seemed that there could be nothing to hinder her from following her heart's desire.'[39] As Antonia Losano and Dennis Dennisoff have pointed out, it is because Olive is not regarded as an aesthetic object that she is able to become an artist and earn her own living.[40] Moreover, her exclusion from 'a woman's natural destiny' means that she does not have to *reject* marriage in order to enjoy this freedom; Craik can maintain her commitment to the proposition that 'there scarcely ever lived the woman who would not rather sit meekly by her own hearth, with her husband at her side, and her children at her knee, than be crowned Corinne of the Capitol',[41] whilst also depicting her heroine as a flourishing female artist. As Tabitha Sparks suggests, 'Olive's deformity allows her to shape-shift into a number of conventionally exclusive destinies, including professional artist and wage earner, wife and mother.'[42] The disabling aspect of 'deformity' can be enabling when viewed from a different angle, conclusively showing that there is nothing immutable or even essential about what Olive's mother saw as the 'curse' of deformity.

Moreover, the one disabling aspect of deformity which remains – Olive's unmarriageability – is shown in the third volume also to be a matter of misperception. Once Olive has managed to put aside her sense

---

37 Craik, *Olive*, 2.58.
38 Craik, *Olive* (revised edn, 1875), 165.
39 Craik, *Olive*, 2.58–59.
40 Antonia Losano, *The Woman Painter in Victorian Literature* (Columbus, OH: Ohio State University Press, 2008), 182–183; Dennis Denisoff, 'Lady in Green with Novel: The Gendered Economics of the Visual Arts and Mid-Victorian Women's Writing', in Nicola Diane Thompson, ed., *Victorian Women Writers and the Woman Question* (Cambridge: Cambridge University Press, 1999), 165.
41 Craik, *Olive*, 2.55–56.
42 Sparks, 'Dinah Mulock Craik's *Olive*: Deformity, Gender and Female Destiny', 3.

of inadequacy sufficiently to recognize Harold's love for her and declare her love for him, the two are finally united. Moreover, Olive finally feels able to ask the question she put to her mother in the first volume, and to receive the reassurance that she, and the reader, have so long awaited:

> 'Sometimes I feel – as I once bitterly felt – how unworthy I am of you.' 'Darling! why?' Because I have no beauty; and, besides – I cannot speak it, but you know – you know.' She hid her face, burning with blushes. The words and acts revealed how deeply in her heart lay the sting which had at times tortured her her whole life through – shame for that imperfection with which Nature had marked her from her birth, and which, though now so slight as to be forgotten in an hour by those who learned to love her, still seemed to herself a perpetual humiliation. The pang came, but only for the last time, ere it quitted her heart for ever. For, dispelling all doubts, healing all wounds, fell the words of betrothed husband – tender, though grave: 'Olive, if you love me, and believe that I love you, never grieve me by such thoughts again. To me you are all beautiful – in heart and mind, in form and soul.' Then, as if silently to count up her beauties, he kissed her little hands, her soft smiling mouth, her long gold curls. And Olive hid her face in his breast, murmuring, 'I am content, since I am fair in your sight, my Harold – my only love!'[43]

In one sense, this wish-fulfilling scene marks the culmination of Olive's career as a novelistic heroine and the final proof that her 'deformity' has only ever existed in the minds of others. Once Olive sees herself through Harold's eyes, she can finally cease to see herself as 'deformed', and be free of the disabling self-hatred this has caused her.

At the same time, however, the scene marks the limitations of Craik's vision. Harold does not put his hand on Olive's shoulders and tell her that he sees nothing ugly in their shape. Nor does he reassure her that physical beauty is not the source of her worth. Instead, he 'silently count[s] up her beauties', which Craik lists, re-forming Olive in the image of a conventionally attractive heroine. There is nothing radical about admiring a woman with 'little hands', a 'soft smiling mouth', 'long gold curls': these are the attributes which are valued in the beauty system which the novel had seemed to discredit. If Olive is, in fact, beautiful, then perhaps the valuation of female beauty was not so misguided after all – and by implication,

43   Craik, *Olive*, 3.348–350.

it is not that Harold loves a woman who departs from the conventional standard of beauty, but that he does not see Olive as departing from it. No further mention is made of Olive's physical difference; when we see her standing beside Harold in the novel's final scene, 'the type of a true woman',[44] there is no reference to her 'elevation of the shoulders' – and, of course, no wheelchair to get in the way, because Olive's physical 'defect' has consistently been represented as aesthetic, never as functional.

It is in fact extremely easy for Craik to write Olive's physical difference out at the novel's conclusion, having sketched it so lightly to begin with. There is some truth in Elaine Showalter's complaint that the representation of Olive's body is inconsistent, her 'spinal curvature so serious that she is a source of anguish and self-recrimination to her parents; yet […] so slight that it can apparently be concealed by her flowing hair.'[45] If the moments at which Olive's body is described are examined closely, it becomes evident that Craik has repeatedly tried to have it both ways, representing Olive's difference as being, on one hand, unmissable, and on the other, as hardly noticeable. At the age of five, 'her lovely hair was arranged so as to hide, as much as possible, the defect, which, alas! was even then only too perceptible';[46] by the time she is seventeen, her 'defect was less apparent […] and the extreme sweetness of her countenance almost atoned for her figure', which can be 'effectually disguised' by a 'small mantle'[47] – and yet is apparently noticed by everyone at the ball. A few years later, she is wearing her beautiful hair in 'artistic confusion' over her shoulders 'in order to veil that defect which, though made far less apparent by her maturer growth, and a certain art in dress, could never be removed.'[48] Yet it does seem to be removed by Harold's kisses; tempting as it is to attempt to argue that Craik un-disables her heroine as part of a radical re-imagining of disability as pure social construction, I think it would be truer to say

44   Craik, *Olive*, 3.375.
45   Elaine Showalter, 'Dinah Mulock Craik and the Tactics of Sentiment: A Case Study in Victorian Female Authorship', *Feminist Studies*, 2/2–3 (1975), 15–16.
46   Craik, *Olive*, 1.56–57.
47   Craik, *Olive*, 1.169.
48   Craik, *Olive*, 2.80.

that Craik draws back from representing a disabled woman as an object of sexual desire. She cannot bring herself fully to commit to the position that physical perfection does not matter; repeatedly, she stresses Olive's physical attractiveness, and finally seems to capitulate completely to some unspoken pressure, and remove the one obstacle to her 'beauty'.

The revisions I have already mentioned which Craik made to the novel in 1875 support the idea that Craik struggled with the definition of Olive's difference and the question of whether she was 'really deformed'. Craik returned to almost every point at which Olive's 'deformity' is mentioned and made changes, but taken together, the revisions do not represent clarifications so much as thickenings of the complexity which characterizes these moments. Craik seems to have been unable to commit herself to the representation of a 'deformed' heroine, hesitating at crucial moments over the depiction and definition of her physical difference. In her next attempt to create a disabled protagonist in her 1866 novel, *A Noble Life*, Craik moves past this prevarication in one sense, describing her protagonist's body and its functional limitations without hesitation. However, the disastrous effect this has upon her ability to characterize the Earl of Cairnforth with anything like the boldness that she showed in her creation of Olive, points to the fearfulness that underpins both novels.

'He never put forth his suffering': Paralepsis, Paralysis and Unspeakable Disability in *A Noble Life*

Craik introduces *A Noble Life* as a radical attempt to write a 'biography' of a man whose nobility rests upon his affective and spiritual development and influence, rather than upon more conventionally masculine feats of derring-do, or even upon practical achievements. Seemingly pre-empting criticism of her choice of subject, the narrator acknowledges that the reader 'will not find his name in "Lodge's Peerage"', for the title that 'had been borne for centuries by many noble and gallant men' became 'with him [...] extinct', foregrounding his failure to fulfil his most fundamental obligation as a man of property and ensure the succession – a failure that is explicitly linked to his disability later on in the novel.[49] Yet she insists that 'amongst what we call "heroic" lives – lives, the story of which touches us with something higher than pity and deeper than love – there never was any of his race who left behind a history more truly heroic than he.'[50] Re-defining heroism enables her disabled protagonist to play the role of hero, and it is upon stimulating certain kinds of affect – 'something higher than pity and deeper than love' – that this new kind of heroism is made to depend.

Given the 'connection between emotion and impairment' which Martha Stoddard Holmes has identified as 'a kind of cultural shorthand' in the Victorian age (and in our own), it might be thought that a disabled character would be ideally fitted to play such a role, what Holmes calls 'habitual association [...] between physical disability and emotional excess' enabling the Earl easily to prompt our tearful identification with the sufferings he surmounts.[51] Mary Klages has pointed out that sentimental novels opened up new possibilities for disabled characters, as subjectivity was 'defined as a fundamentally embodied and also universal form of self, one that considers bodies similar on the basis of their capacity to feel and express emotions', a construction which 'produced new possibilities of selfhood for the disabled', who could 'encourage and strengthen the empathetic capacities of the able-bodied' and 'feel for [...] the suffering of others.'[52] Craik's attempt to situate a disabled character at the centre of a sentimental novel seems logical rather than revolutionary, when selfhood is defined by the capacity to feel, and disability so insistently associated with affect.

However, something disrupts the formula that ought to ensure Craik's success. The Earl of Cairnforth ultimately fails as a sentimental protagonist because the reader is consistently prevented from identifying with him. Throughout the novel, we are not allowed to witness his struggles, except at a remove which chills our emotional reaction, and so, although

49   Craik, *A Noble Life*, 1.3, 1.238
50   Craik, *A Noble Life*, 1.3–4.
51   Stoddard Holmes, *Fictions of Affliction*, 3–4.
52   Mary Klages, *Woeful Afflictions: Disability and Sentimentality in Victorian America* (Philadelphia, PA: University of Pennsylvania Press, 1999), 6–7.

we witness every major event in his life – as Craik fulfils her promise that
the novel will be 'like a biography'[53] and we follow the Earl from birth to
death – we remain at a distance from the character supposedly at the centre
of the novel. One contemporary reviewer complained that despite being
morally praiseworthy, the novel was 'monotonous' and 'tedious', noting
particularly that '[t]oo much is left to the imagination of the reader' in the
depiction of Helen Cardross, supposedly the heroine.[54] This distance from
the characters whose emotional experiences ought to form the crux of our
sentimental engagement – as we engage with Scrooge's fear that Tiny Tim
will die, if not with Tiny Tim himself – seems to me to go to the heart of
the novel's failure as a sentimental text, and the Earl of Cairnforth's ineffectiveness as a protagonist.

While it might be tempting to attribute the Earl's ineffectiveness as
a character to his incredible virtue, in fact, Olive Rothesay is every bit as
(improbably) saintly as he is. The real difference between Olive and the
Earl[55] is that we witness the process by which she comes to see herself as
'deformed', and have access to her thoughts and feelings as she negotiates
this identity in her interactions with others. On the night of the ball, for
example, we hear her 'bitter murmur' against the injustice of her situation,
before she immediately 'tremble[s] at its impiety' and sets about resigning

53   Craik, *A Noble Life*, 1.3.
54   'A Noble Life', *John Bull*, 2355 (27 January 1866), 59.
55   Another major difference between the two novels is, of course, the gender of the
      protagonists. I have written elsewhere about the gender politics of *A Noble Life* (see
      'Noble Lives: Writing Disability and Masculinity in the Late Nineteenth Century',
      Nineteenth-Century Contexts, 36/4 (2014), 363–375; '"The Right and Natural Law
      of Things": Disability and the Form of the Family in the Fiction of Dinah Mulock
      Craik and Charlotte M. Yonge', in Duc Dau and Shale Preston, eds, *Queer Victorian
      Families: Curious Relations in Literature* (New York: Routledge, 2015), 116–133). For
      articles on the gender politics of *Olive*, see Showalter, 'Dinah Mulock Craik and the
      Tactics of Sentiment'; Sparks, 'Dinah Mulock Craik's *Olive*: Deformity, Gender
      and Female Destiny'; and Robyn Chandler, 'Dinah Mulock Craik: Sacrifice and
      the Fairy-Order', in Brenda Ayres, ed., *Silent Voices: Forgotten Novels by Victorian
      Women Writers* (Westport, CT: Praeger, 2003), 173–201.

herself.[56] There is no comparable moment in *A Noble Life*; when the Earl is of a similar age, he undergoes a series of medical experiments to improve his mobility, and after their failure has to resign himself to the permanence of his disability, but this happens off-stage, when he is absent from the scene of the novel. We do witness his conversation about it with Helen, but this only serves to underscore what we are not being told. He tells Helen that she knows "'as much as [she] can know'" about his experience, a statement which causes her to recognize 'as she had never recognized before, the awful individuality of suffering which it had pleased God to lay upon this one human being'.[57] Craik could leave it there, but she elaborates, as if to highlight her own omissions: 'What was the minute history of the experiments he had tried, how much bodily pain they had cost him, and through how much mental pain he had struggled before he attained that "content", he did not explain even to Helen.'[58] When the narrative pauses in this way, our attention is drawn to what is being left out of this 'life'. The equivocation in phrases such as, '[p]erhaps it was one of those merciful compensations that what he could not have he was made strong enough to do without',[59] further leads us to question the completeness of the picture we are being offered.

By drawing our attention to the gaps in her account, Craik forces the reader to consider what the Earl might have to suppress in order to play his inspirational part, suggesting that there are aspects of his experience which he does not share with anyone. Reminding us that 'he was exceedingly self-contained from his childhood', apparently 'feel[ing] by instinct that to him had been allotted a special solitude of existence, into which [...] none could ever fully penetrate and with which none could wholly sympathise',[60] Craik introduces doubt into our minds as to whether Helen

---

56   Craik, *Olive*, 1.190.
57   Craik, *A Noble Life*, 1.181.
58   Craik, *A Noble Life*, 1.182
59   Craik, *A Noble Life*, 1.157, emphasis added.
60   Craik, *A Noble Life*, 1.156–157.

is right in being 'forced to believe' that the Earl's faith is a compensation for his disability, rather than something imperfectly attained through struggle.[61]

It is by no means obvious why we are not allowed to see more of the Earl's 'mental pain'. Sentimental texts frequently thrive on the portrayal of anguished cries to heaven and tearful crises; if we could enter into the Earl's frustration, and then witness his spiritual triumph over it, surely we would be moved even more effectively, and sentimental communion would flourish? Clearly, there is something in the Earl's particular condition which renders it unrepresentable, something in his pain which is unspeakable. It is this 'something' which disrupts the sentimental paradigm that Craik has set up.

We are given an indication of what it might be when the narrator depicts the Earl's successful entry into Edinburgh society. At this point, we are told that 'he never put forward his affliction so as to make it painful to those around him'.[62] The Earl can become the centre of 'a knot of real friends', he can even 'go out a little into society [...] with some personal difficulty and pain', his 'chief difficulty' being 'the practical one of locomotion', which can be overcome 'by a good deal of ingenious contrivance'[63] – but all this must be done in a way that does not 'put forward' his affliction. The Earl's disability is shown to be no bar to respect, to friendship, even to parenthood, provided he does not speak of it: the Earl's own acceptance that 'by instinct that to him had been allotted a special solitude of existence'[64] appears to be the condition of his acceptance by others. We do not have to insist upon the Earl's difference, because he insists upon it himself; we can open our hearts to him because he does not 'put forward' his claim to be there. At one and the same time, the Earl is allowed to take up a central place in the narrative, his physical difference represented as something to which his friends can become accustomed, a chiefly practical inconvenience which can be overcome through 'ingenious contrivance' – and yet this physical difference is represented throughout as an experience

61   Craik, *A Noble Life*, 1.126–128.
62   Craik, *A Noble Life*, 2.10.
63   Craik, *A Noble Life*, 2.7–8.
64   Craik, *A Noble Life*, 1.156–157.

so absolutely 'other' that it is one with which no-one can sympathize. The Earl can take up a place at the centre of the novel and at the centre of his community, but the price is his own recognition of his difference, and total abstention from any attempt to cross the distance this puts between himself and those around him.

Where Olive's sense of herself as deformed could be erased by 'the words of [a] betrothed husband', 'dispelling all doubts, healing all wounds',[65] and subsequently her very difference erased from the text, no such reformation is possible for the Earl. Although he loves Helen Cardross, he does not ask her to marry him; when she marries someone else, the narrator insists that the Earl's feelings cannot be discussed: 'Whatever emotions the earl felt – and it would be almost sacrilegious to intrude upon them, or to venture on any idle speculation concerning them – one thing was clear; in losing Helen, the light of his eyes, the delight of his life, was gone.'[66] Craik's insistence that it would be 'sacrilegious' to 'intrude' or 'speculate' upon the Earl's feelings represents a form of paralepsis, for these feelings are invoked by the very statement that they will not be shown, made present by their announced absence from the text. After Helen's unhappy marriage is speedily ended by her wicked husband's premature death, she returns to Cairnforth to live near the Earl and he adopts her son, Boy, as his heir, but the couple never marry.

The compromise that Craik reaches through the thwarted marriage plot opens up a space for the disabled protagonist to be in a relationship and at the centre of a family in which he and his beloved are 'not unhappy',[67] but the negative terms of this formulation reveals how unsatisfactory this relationship is at the level of plot. The couple cannot move forward: the plot of the novel stalls when Helen returns to Cairnforth and yet refuses the Earl's invitation to live with him at the castle, limping towards a conclusion which is reached only in the Earl's death. We are assured that '[i]n spite of its outward incompleteness, it had been a noble life – an almost

65   Craik, *Olive*, 3.349.
66   Craik, *A Noble Life*, 2.27–28.
67   Craik, *A Noble Life*, 2.207.

perfect life,'[68] but it is the incompleteness which leaves the strongest impression. Moreover, by refusing to 'intrude' upon the Earl's feelings for Helen, or hers for him, Craik renders the central relationship of the novel utterly unsatisfactory, little more than a space where the emotional heart of the novel should be. The sentimental possibilities of a thwarted love relationship should have been as great – if not greater – than those of a successful marriage plot such as Olive's, but Craik squanders them in her refusal to break the Earl's silence.

Yet she does draw our attention both to the Earl's silence and to her own, reminding the reader repeatedly of all that we are not shown of his experience. For example, when Helen thanks the Earl for leaving her side and travelling to St Andrews to keep an eye on her son, we are bleakly told, 'she knew not half of what she thanked him for.'[69] Neither can the reader know – but at least we know that we don't know. Craik creates a certain pathos out of her own narrative omissions: whether it is sufficient to save the novel from failure as a sentimental text is debatable.

Perhaps the novel's true value lies in prompting us to assess the *source* of its failure as a sentimental text. I would suggest that Craik's first biographer, Sally Mitchell, gives us a vital clue here when she claims that:

> *A Noble Life* is embarrassing to read. [...] We feel uncomfortable in the presence of deformity and pain; we feel sensitive about staring so openly at a cripple. It becomes even more embarrassing when we realize that Craik's friend Frank Smedley died not long before the book was written.[70]

Mitchell is able to deal with her own embarrassment only by translating disability into gender, treating Craik's 'biography' of the Earl as an extended metaphor for women's experience under patriarchy.[71] Mitchell's remarks

---

68   Craik, *A Noble Life*, 2.299.
69   Craik, *A Noble Life*, 2.55.
70   Sally Mitchell, *Dinah Mulock Craik* (Boston: Twayne Publishers, 1983), 64.
71   This manoeuvre had already been used by Showalter in order to discuss four of Craik's novels (*Olive, John Halifax, Gentleman, The Little Lame Prince and His Travelling Cloak* and *A Noble Life*) without acknowledging any of them to be *about* disability. (Showalter, 'Dinah Mulock Craik and the Tactics of Sentiment').

strongly call to mind Lennard J. Davis's appeal – made some thirty years later – that 'before we can leap to the metaphor, we need to know the object.'[72] Clearly, Mitchell 'leaps to the metaphor' because she is embarrassed by the object, because she feels 'uncomfortable in the presence of deformity and pain'. The fact that Craik's portrayal of a disabled character may have been inspired by a real disabled person – her wheelchair-using friend and publisher, Frank Smedley – only heightens Mitchell's embarrassment, which she assumes will be shared by her fellow able-bodied readers, the 'we' who shrink from the sight of 'deformity and pain'. Perhaps I extrapolate too far in suggesting that this 'we' must necessarily be able-bodied; perhaps for Mitchell, such embarrassment is universal, even for those who have experienced such pain.

I do not quote Mitchell's verdict upon the novel in order to score cheap critical points off a scholar writing long before the advent of disability studies, and at a time when the political implications of such a judgement were obscured by sheer ubiquity. Rather, I quote it because the novel itself seems to anticipate exactly this reaction; Craik seems to lack confidence in the reader's willingness to contemplate the spectacle she sets before them, unless she veils it in indirection. Perhaps she cannot quite bear to contemplate it herself, drawing back from the Earl's 'mental pain'. Yet why should disappointed hopes, physical pain, or mental anguish, be so incommunicable that the Earl must 'stand aloof' in 'the awful individuality of suffering' them?[73] These are fundamental human experiences: readers who have no difficulty in walking will still have experienced disappointment, humiliation, frustration or incapacity in some form; those who have never yet been forced to confront their own physical frailties will have to do so eventually. Frustration and limitation are as much a part of the human experience as triumph and capability; disabled people do not have a monopoly on the former any more than 'able-bodied' people do

---

72 Lennard J. Davis, 'Seeing the Object as in Itself It Really Is: Beyond the Metaphor of Disability', Foreword to Julia Miele Rodas, David Bolt, and Elizabeth J. Donaldson, eds, *The Madwoman and the Blindman: Disability in Jane Eyre* (Columbus, OH: Ohio State University Press, 2012), xi.

73 Craik, *A Noble Life*, 1.181.

upon the latter. Why, then, refuse to allow readers to attempt to identify with a disabled man's embodied experience, which, however remote from the reader's own, cannot be distant in all respects, when all human bodies are subject to deterioration, illness, and injury? Perhaps to put the Earl of Cairnforth on a spectrum which contains all bodies is simply too painful or frightening for Craik. Mitchell's critical verdict shows that her very partial attempt to do so – present mostly in the gaps to which she draws attention – clearly pained and frightened one reader honest enough to admit to 'embarrassment'.

The desire to cordon off pain, suffering, frailty and weakness, and attribute them to a deviant minority – rather than to acknowledge them as aspects of human experience – seems to me a crucial motivation for creating and enforcing the category of disability in the first place. Disability studies scholars themselves have sometimes struggled, I think, to accommodate physical pain and bodily suffering in their own account of disability, which is why the social model of disability, in Tobin Siebers's words, 'collaborates with the misrepresentation of the disabled body in the political sphere.'[74] As Mark Jeffreys indignantly points out: 'The constructivist invalidation of physicality is no more helpful to the person with a disability than the empiricist objectification of it.'[75] To acknowledge this is not to argue against the tremendous utility of the social model of disability as a political tool, but to recognize that it is far more useful to a person like Olive than a person like the Earl of Cairnforth. The difference between Craik's representation of the two characters indicates that the fear she could not quite overcome was not the fear of 'deformity' in the sense of stigmatized physical difference, but the fear of physical pain arising from physical impairment, and its attendant emotional suffering. To suggest that we embrace the experience of impairment – explore it, talk about it, write about it – is not to advocate a miserablist model of disability, but rather to acknowledge the

74   Siebers, *Disability Theory*, 61.
75   Mark Jeffreys, 'The Visible Cripple (Scars and Other Disfiguring Displays Included)', in Sharon L. Snyder, Brenda Jo Brueggemann, and Rosemarie Garland-Thomson, eds, *Disability Studies: Enabling the Humanities* (New York: Modern Language Association of America, 2002), 33.

co-existence, in *all* our experience, of frustration and achievement, pleasure and pain, limitation and overcoming. A truly human model of disability has to accommodate these things because they are aspects of human experience. Acknowledging Craik's failed attempts to do so is just one way to tell a story we have not yet finished writing.

WILL VISCONTI

Constructing La Goulue: The Queer, the Criminal and the Cancan

ABSTRACT

Using textual analysis and oft-overlooked materials documenting the rise, reinventions and eventual decline of the performer La Goulue (Louise Weber), I aim to shed new light on a celebrity simultaneously marketed as the embodiment of Paris and criticized for her sexual, spatial and social alterity; and how the moralizing of the fin-de-siècle has left an enduring legacy of scandal-mongering and interwoven presumptions around sexuality, crime and performance not only in relation to La Goulue but more broadly.

Introduction

In 1963, Armand Lanoux suggested, provocatively, 'Le quadrille, comme la Goulue, était né du pave' [The quadrille, like La Goulue, was born on the street],[1] putting into words a legend famously embodied by Henri de Toulouse-Lautrec's paintings of the Moulin Rouge. Over the course of five decades, Louise Weber (better known as La Goulue, 'The Glutton') was a fixture of popular entertainment in Paris, as a dancer, animal-tamer, and celebrity who was active between the 1880s and the 1920s. The stage name that she took when she made her debut as a paid dancer at the age of sixteen was one she kept all her life. With it came a reputation as a cheeky, fiery, and distinctively working-class performer who was identified on one hand as embodying modern Paris through her *gouaille* (street patter) and

---

1   Armand Lanoux, "Moulin-Rouge", *Les oeuvres libres*, 205 (1963), 97.

her status as a star dancer of the cancan. On the other she was the embodi-ment of the city's unsavoury side – its roughness and its bawdiness, seen in her associations, be they real or imagined, with prostitution, crime, or criminality and vulgarity. Intertwined with Louise Weber's public persona was a tendency to mythicize her origins and her biography, so as to suit prevailing moral codes of the late nineteenth and early twentieth centuries. This paper attempts to examine the gaps in Weber's story and the gossip or misinformation that has warped her representation over time, creating an image of her that has implicitly linked her perceived queerness to perceived wickedness, making a morality play of her life, by turns with and without taking into account her experiences before and after the Moulin Rouge. The underlying thread within the narrative or narratives of Louise Weber's story, aside from the fact that her onstage persona and offstage nature have bled into one another and become indistinguishable, is the forced redac-tion of Louise's life story to fit prevailing ideas regarding morality and existing narratives around prostitution, female sexuality, class and space. In Weber's case the details of her life have been edited and moulded to fit more closely with the plot of Emile Zola's *Nana*, a novel that depicts the lives of courtesans, prostitutes and stage performers at the height of the Second Empire, and the time preceding the Franco-Prussian War.[2] As a result, gossip and hearsay emphasizing her apparent otherness has become accepted as fact, and has become exaggerated along with other aspects of her life, which was sufficiently over-the-top without alterations. Much of what has been said about La Goulue has a kernel of truth in one way or another, however the popular press (and one assumes the popular imagi-nation and popular opinion of the late nineteenth century) manipulated elements of these stories and Weber's background.

In performing as a public figure, and having a public image, La Goulue became quite literally a public woman, but during the nineteenth cen-tury she was perceived as 'une fille publique' in all possible senses. This meant that her character was called into question and her career or rela-tionships were tainted by association with people labelled as 'unsavoury'.

---

2   Emile Zola, *Nana* (Paris: Charpentier, 1880).

Unfortunately, the period when she managed to move beyond such stereo-typed and negative images was the same period that has been overlooked by contemporary audiences. One of the reasons for this is the lack of media attention. While dancing at the Moulin Rouge, and certainly after being painted by someone with as high a profile as Lautrec (as well as others like Charles Conder, Emile Bernard and Jean-François Raffaëlli), Weber, as one of the star dancers, had a publicity juggernaut behind her that extended into press reports and photography.

The sections of this article, after providing some biographical details about Louise Weber, deal first with the contrast between representations of Weber and the facts of her situation, and a discussion of La Goulue in relation to ideas or trends of embodiment in nineteenth-century Paris, and then the spaces inhabited by La Goulue, her career, and her sexuality. There are frequent intersections of all of these areas, which may have con-tributed to the image promulgated of Weber as being identified as queer or criminal, along with links to spaces seen more broadly as 'bohemian' or 'rough'. Her familiarity with these spaces, however, is not indicative of the extent of her involvement – consider her relationship with Lautrec, whom she saw as a 'drinking buddy' rather than a fellow bohemian.[3]

Intertwined with this identification (however erroneous) is the vari-ability of Weber's body over time. Despite assumptions to the contrary, Weber sought, and to a degree succeeded, in reinventing herself in her later years, just as she had reinvented herself professionally since her teens. She managed to be abreast of emerging trends in popular entertainment throughout her career, always moving to remain at the forefront of what would bring in audiences and incorporate trends into her performances including the dance hall scene of the late 1800s, the fin-de-siècle vogue for Orientalism, the popularity of funfairs, or post-war nostalgia for the Belle Époque.

The key assumption underpinning narratives about Louise Weber is that she was a coarse, sexually incontinent diva. In fact, Weber was acting in a manner similar to numerous performers today. She grew up in poverty,

3   Jean Castarède, *Moulin Rouge: Reflets d'une époque* (Paris: France-Empire, 2001), 103, 131.

and wrote in her diary that she saw celebrity status as a means of elevating herself, and being able to provide for her family (and, being thrust into the limelight as a teenager, may well have struggled to cope with her situation, as can be seen with some contemporary celebrities).[4] The moves made from one style of performing to another are, I would argue, more indicative of securing income and planning for the next performance rather than a sense of exhibitionism or vanity, and were timed to capitalize on the shifting popularity of various entertainments.

Who was La Goulue?

Louise Weber was born in Clichy-la-Garenne in 1866 to parents who had migrated to Paris from Alsace-Lorraine. As a child she worked with her mother as a laundress, and as a teenager began frequenting local dance halls. There she distinguished herself as a gifted amateur, and was engaged as a paid dancer in venues around Montmartre, possibly as early as 1882.[5] In 1889 she began dancing at the Moulin Rouge (along with concurrent engagements at other venues on the *bal public* circuit in Montmartre and across Paris), and in 1895 she left the Moulin to open a sideshow and reinvent herself as a *dompteuse* (animal tamer). Between 1895 and approximately 1920 Weber performed with her menagerie at *fêtes foraines* (funfairs) around France and other countries, forming an act with her husband José Droxler, a former stage magician, whom she married in 1900.[6] During the 1920s Weber, now usually known as Madame La Goulue, sold her remaining animals and took on jobs including selling vegetables, lollies and matches in the street – sometimes outside the Moulin Rouge – and possibly working as a maid

---

4   Louise Weber, 'No title', in *Mémoires de Louise Weber dite la Goulue* (Paris: Archives du Moulin Rouge, n.d.), n.p.

5   Georges Montorgueuil, *La vie à Montmartre* (Paris: G. Baudet, 1898), 236.

6   Bernard Delmont, 'La Goulue, qui fut dompteuse', *Le Cirque dans l'univers*, 6 (1966), 21.

in a brothel.[7] She died in 1929 and was buried in Pantin, but her remains were moved in 1992 to the Cimetière de Montmartre, near the Moulin.

Truth and Representation

An integral factor to consider regarding La Goulue's representation is the shorter collective cultural memory in the absence of significant markers or evidence, such as artworks. Her representation effectively charts the appearance, reappearance and disappearance of her body or persona in terms of popular memory and embodiment throughout her life and following her death. During her life, this extended from photographs and racy *cartes de visite* to portraits, artworks and popular songs, and since her death has included plays, burlesque performances and film appearances. What is most remembered is, however, generally limited to her representation in Lautrec's iconic (or iconoclastic) lithographs and paintings, and contemporary representations of Weber are most commonly inspired by and anchored around her time at the Moulin Rouge. As a result, the myth of Weber's anonymity beyond the Moulin is perpetuated by the lack of images or documents that can match the cachet of Lautrec's posters and paintings. While working as an independent artist, she was not only without a fixed venue in which to perform, but she also lacked the access to publicity in the same manner as she had at the Moulin.

The mainstay of her publicity was her stage name and the weight that it carried, be it in a nostalgic sense or on the merits of her current act. Despite being given the sobriquet La Goulue as a teenager, she kept it all her life, and despite the problems caused by being so fully enveloped within a public persona that was created in her teens, Weber turned this to her advantage, even if she adapted it slightly as an older woman and was often

---

7   Jacqueline Baldran, *Paris, Carrefour des artistes et des lettres 1880–1918* (Paris: l'Harmattan, 2002), 81.

referred to as Madame la Goulue, with her husband becoming 'Monsieur la Goulue' or even 'Monsieur Weber'.[8]

The main sources of material cited in the representation of La Goulue are not by her own hand (such as surviving diary entries and interviews), but include pure fiction, such as Emile Zola's *Nana*. There are parallels between Louise Weber and Nana Coupeau in quite a broad sense – comparable looks and backgrounds, associating with both the upper echelons of society and the underbelly of nineteenth century Paris: fantastic wealth and decadence alongside poverty, and her son predeceasing her (although where Nana's son died as a child, Louise Weber's son died in his twenties, after surviving World War One).[9] Within *Nana*, however, all of this is compressed into a shorter timeframe, culminating in Nana's premature death from smallpox, unlike Louise, who died of cervical cancer at the beginning of 1929 in the Hôpital Lariboisière. Nana was created by Zola to embody destructive female sexuality, as well as the decadence (in the sense of decay) of Second-Empire France, and La Goulue was, and became, a similar figure incarnating the image of 'Gay Paree' as much as the sins of the age.

The image of Weber as a real-life Nana was reinforced by texts such as the 1885 chapbook *Grille d'Égout et La Goulue: histoire réaliste*. The work purports to tell the stories of the two dancers, devoting most of the narrative to Weber's time as a kept woman, establishing both figures as 'fallen women'. The opening pages include a dedicatory passage listing '*hétaïres*' of history,[10] thereby reinforcing the dancer's similarity with Phryne, Messalina, Cleopatra and other infamous women commonly represented as sexual or

---

8   Anonymous, '*Le Journal* (13 July 1902), 2.
9   While Simon Colle's cause of death is not clear, all that is known is that it was sudden, and that Colle died in 1923. See, Francesca Canadé Sautmann, 'Invisible Women: Working Class Culture in France, 1880–1930', in Jeffrey Merrick and Bryant Ragan, eds, *Homosexuality in Modern France* (Oxford: Oxford University Press, 1996), 184–185.
10   A *hetaera* or *hetaira* (Plural *hetaerae* or *hetairai*) was the equivalent of the fin-de-siècle *grande horizontale*, an elite courtesan in ancient Greece who served as a companion to men of the wealthy class.

lustful.[11] The narrative of La Goulue as a sex worker is reinforced by artworks including Auguste Roedel's *Legende de la Goulue*, and subsequently carried through journalistic representations of Weber, more frequently than other dancers like Grille d'Égout ('Gutter Grate', a dancer whose nickname referred to the gap between her front teeth).

The link to prostitution has been challenged by some, with varying levels of success. Michel Souvais, the great-grandson of La Goulue, established himself as the official biographer of Louise Weber as well as the actress Arletty for whom he acted as secretary, while working as an actor and later a painter, often appropriating works depicting La Goulue.[12] When Souvais first wrote a biography of La Goulue, it was a slim volume composed in the style of a narrative with La Goulue herself telling the story of her life, as if to an interviewer or journalist paying her a visit in her *roulotte* (caravan). There were two expanded re-editions of Weber's biography, with further embellishments. The book has its basis in several interviews Weber gave towards the end of her life, visited by journalists often seeking to write articles about the 'good old days' of the fin-de-siècle.[13]

What is most curious about Souvais' work is that despite mythicizing La Goulue even further, and embellishing stories about her, Souvais is quite prudish when it comes to her sexuality, and constructs her as quite coy regarding her sex life. This extends, I would argue, to projecting narratives of transgressive or same-sex desire away from Weber and onto other

---

11   Anonymous, *Grille d'Égout et la Goulue: Histoire Réaliste* (Paris: H. Marot, 1885), 6–7.

12   Souvais claimed that he only found out about his great-grandmother when he was an adult, since his mother, Weber's granddaughter, had been ashamed of the connection. Alain de Keramoal, 'La Goulue ressuscitée par son arrière petit-fils', Dossier *La Goulue/ML Weber/La Glu* (Paris: Musée de Montmartre, c.1997), 68.

13   On occasion, however, she actively courted publicity, as when she wrote an open letter to a newspaper about a dancer copying her stage name, and when she spoke out after newspaper reports falsely claimed that she had died in 1918. Georges Montorgueuil, 'Au jour le jour: La Goulue', Dossier *DOS GOU: Goulue, La (Weber, Louise)* (Paris: Bibliothèque Marguerite Durand, c.1929), n.p.; Anonymous, 'Mort de la "Goulue"', *Le Rappel* (24 February 1918), n.p.

figures who appear within the book, such as other cancan dancers and the music-hall star Thérésa (born Emma Valadon). Souvais claims that Thérésa was gay and that she and Weber lived together for a time, but emphatically denies that Weber herself was anything other than heterosexual, perhaps as part of an effort to rehabilitate Weber's image and emphasize her generosity and her own attempts to portray herself as a 'mother hen' figure later in her life.[14] He does, however, claim that she was a great ally of the queer community, such as it would have existed in Montmartre during her lifetime, and that she was never a prostitute herself, but again had many friends who were homosexual or sex workers and whom she helped (something reinforced elsewhere).[15]

More recently there have been parallels made with the story of Edith Piaf, who, like Weber, has been identified as quintessentially Parisian and working-class – a French equivalent of someone like Marie Lloyd or Barbara Windsor. Neither Weber nor Piaf acquired the polish or appearances of the moneyed classes, despite their wealth, and their public personae were inextricably linked to their class and the fact that they inhabited the same spaces: that is, Pigalle, Montmartre, Clichy and Belleville, and the night-spots in these districts. Michel Souvais attempts to create a similar link, while emphasizing the pathos of Weber's story. Regardless of the author's intention, the editing of La Goulue's story over time has denied her a degree of agency and perpetuated myths about her, even if those myths, such as those around her sexuality, have been reclaimed or come to be viewed in a more positive light.

---

14   Michel Souvais, *La Goulue: Mémoires d'une insolente* (Paris: Bartillat 1998), 29; Michel Souvais, *Moi, La Goulue de Toulouse-Lautrec: Les mémoires de mon aïeule* (Paris: Publibook, 2008), 87.

15   Louise Weber, 'Fêtes concours Galerie des Machines', in *Mémoires de Louise Weber dite la Goulue* (Paris: Archives du Moulin Rouge, n.d.), n.p.; Louise Weber, 'Mon voyage avec le marquis de Biron', in *Mémoires de Louise Weber dite la Goulue* (Paris: Archives du Moulin Rouge, n.d.), n.p.; Souvais, *Moi, La Goulue de Toulouse-Lautrec*, 33, 35, 78.

Embodiment and Space

Where Paris had previously been incarnated by Mary, St Genevieve or La Marianne; or the dangerous if mythic *pétroleuses* of the Commune in 1871 within Montmartre, by the 1880s it was the *cancaneuse* who was the most emblematic figure, more so than even the Eiffel Tower (as evidenced by the cover of the *Courrier Français* on 12 May 1889).[16] In the 1880s Weber was engaged by the Cirque Médrano in a pageant to embody La Parisienne, however some detractors argued that she embodied the vices of the city more strongly than its modernity, and was not fit to appear in a show intended for family audiences.[17]

Elizabeth Grosz has written of the link of the female body to urban space, and one can definitely draw this same parallel with La Goulue.[18] In fact, the reactions against La Goulue feed directly into on-going debates regarding space, gender and sexuality of the fin-de-siècle, alongside her broad popularity, as well as her evolution as a performer, her aging and decline. La Goulue embodied the modernity of the age as a cancan dancer and a Montmartroise – the *arrondissement* being centre of some of the fiercest fighting during the Paris Commune, and a hub of the creative avant-garde. The cancan came to be associated with spaces of modernity during the Universal Exhibition in 1889, when it was performed in custom-built venues, and with La Goulue as one of the most recognized dancers, she was seen as the Queen of Paris.[19] This image was promoted in photographs

16   Richard Thomson, 'Representing Montmartre', in Claire Frèches-Thory, Anne Roquebert and Richard Thomson, eds, *Toulouse-Lautrec* (London: South Bank Centre, 1990), 239.

17   Jules Roques, *Courrier Français* (1889), 4; cited in Richard Thomson, 'The Circus', in Phillip Dennis Cate, Richard Thomson and Mary Weaver Chapin, eds, *Toulouse-Lautrec and Montmartre* (Washington, DC: National Gallery of Washington, 2005), 238.

18   Elizabeth Grosz, 'Bodies/Cities', in Beatriz Colomina, ed., *Sexuality and Space* (New York: Princeton University Press, 1992), 250–252.

19   Anonymous, *Guide des Plaisirs à Paris* (Paris: Édition Photographique, 1899), 71; Pierre Lazareff, 'La triste fin de La Goulue qui fut la reine de Paris', *Paris Midi* (31

as well, showing La Goulue wearing a crown and seated at a table laden with food, smoking and quaffing champagne. Conversely, as Louise Weber aged and moved from the dance halls and belly dancing to funfairs to becoming a 'living relic' and making a brief appearance on film, her career and its decline mirror the changing landscape of Paris and the entertainment industry, in terms of both the tides of fashion and the rise of film and revue at the expense of vaudeville and the dance halls.

In their heyday, the venues where La Goulue performed were ambiguous spaces of public spectacle, mixing onstage performance with people-watching and sex tourism. Artworks like those by Xavier Sager depict the 'types' of women in different bars or nightspots including the Moulin, Tabarin and Rat Mort, and in publications like the *Guide des Plaisirs à Paris*, an entire chapter is devoted to Montmartre. In an entry about the Moulin Rouge the author mentions specifically that there are varied entertainments and sights, from the 'battalion' of *chahuteuses* (dancers of the *chahut*/cancan) to the *amies* (girlfriends) present, and the ladies who line the *promenoir* 'comme en une foire d'amour' [as in a fair of/for love] alongside the tables of ever-thirsty 'petites dames' ('little ladies', a reference to sex workers).[20] Others refer to the Moulin as a 'temple d'Aphrodite de la Butte'.[21]

Some dancers no doubt supplemented their income with, or came from a background of prostitution, either casually or otherwise, and their names reflected this – or made a joke of the possibility of their disreputable backgrounds. Some of these are explicit, as in the case of Jeanne Beaunichons (Jeanne Pretty-Tits), others less so, such as La Môme Fromage ('The Cheese Kid', *môme* being either slang for a kid or urchin, or for a prostitute), and Camélia Trompe-la-Mort (Camellia Death-Dodger).[22] The name Camellia was also unremarkable on one hand, since many dancers

January 1929), n.p.; Georges Montorgueuil, *Paris dansant* (Paris: Théophile Belin, 1898), iv; Louise Weber, 'Fêtes concours Galerie des Machines', in *Mémoires de Louise Weber dite la Goulue* (Paris: Archives du Moulin Rouge, n.d.), n.p.

20   Anonymous, *Guide des Plaisirs à Paris*, 72–73.

21   Auguste Pawlowski, *Plaisirs de la vie de Paris (guide du flâneur)* (Paris: Librairie L. Borel, 1900), 101.

22   Charles Virmaître, *Trottoirs et lupanars* (Paris: H. Perrot, 1893), 145.

had names of flowers, like Serpolette, Muguet and Myosotis (Wild Thyme, Lily-of-the-Valley and Forget-Me-Not), but on the other, *Camélia* was a slang name for a prostitute. The association of the flower with prostitution is possibly traceable to *La Dame aux Camélias*, a novel inspired by the courtesan Marie Duplessis. Another name with a *double entendre*, possibly at the expense of the visitors to the Moulin, was Georgette la Vadrouille. *Vadrouiller* is the verb to wander, which could refer equally to the popularity of flânerie among bourgeois and wealthy men at the Moulin and within Montmartre, as well as to streetwalking, which also touches on the notion of the *flâneuse* as a female counterpart to the *flâneur*, and whether such a thing indeed exists, or positioning the prostitute as a comparable – and equally modern – figure.[23]

Space, sex and sexuality were frequently elided in fin-de-siècle Paris. Venues like the Moulin Rouge were known to be frequented by prostitutes, and it was said at the Moulin that lesbianism was 'good for business' to create an added voyeuristic frisson for bourgeois male visitors.[24] The Moulin was a space of performed sexuality, and the performance of La Goulue's character as what could today be termed queer (and more broadly as non-normative sexuality in its expression), is a key part of that.[25] Beyond voyeurism for bourgeois consumption, there was a taste for queer erotica, as shown in the works by Adolphe Willette, some of which were set in, or decorated, the Moulin Rouge. As a result of the decisions made by the venue's management and the works shown within (and advertising) the

23   Kelly Conway, *Chanteuse in the City: the Realist Singer in French Film* (Berkeley: University of California Press, 2004), 19.

24   David Sweetman, *Toulouse-Lautrec and the fin-de-siècle* (London: Simon & Schuster, 1999), 362. Elsewhere in Montmartre there was a thriving lesbian scene, with bars like the Rat Mort and Hanneton painted by Lautrec.

25   For further discussion of the performance of sexuality and its representation at the Moulin, see Pip Muratore, 'Sexuality and Voyeurism from le Moulin-Rouge to *Moulin Rouge!*', in Matthew Ball and B. Scherer, eds, *Queering Paradigms II* (New York: Peter Lang, 2010), 49–60.

Moulin, La Goulue, and the dancers generally, would have been assumed
to be sexually available, an implication which rankled some of the troupe.[26]

Outside of the Moulin, the sexuality or status of Weber and other
dancers was suggested through the spaces they occupied, and exacerbated
the stigma of the questionable virtue of the dancer (much less of the *cancaneuse*). A reference to Weber living in the Bréda district, for instance,
was a coded allusion to her being a kept woman (since many mistresses and
lorettes lived in the area). Nini Pattes-en-l'Air's dance school is identified by
a contemporary account as being in the same *quartier*, which on one hand
makes sense given the proximity to the 18th district and the dance halls,
but also reinforces the link between negotiable virtue and the cancan.[27] La
Goulue's sexuality was ambiguously coded, despite descriptions of where
she lived. After leaving the Moulin and performing the *danse à l'almée*,
Weber wore Orientalist-inspired slave bracelets and similar accessories with
her costume (again linking to bourgeois fantasies of sexual availability),
but carrying potential additional meanings, since her choice of accessories
paralleled those used to encode or 'out' lesbianism during the period.[28]

An explicit link between La Goulue and sex or sex work was made in
1886, when Weber was called to testify in a procurement case. One gets the
impression, however, that her appearance as a witness for the prosecution
against the procuresses is treated as something of a joke.[29] Because of the

---

26   Montorgueil, *Paris dansant*, 192. La Goulue apparently made joking references to
      her questionable reputation, keeping a pet goat on a leash and possibly living for a
      time in the Hôtel de la Païva on the Champs-Elysées, a baroque building once owned
      by La Païva, a famous courtesan. I have not found documentation proving Weber's
      residence there, which may suggest further rumour-mongering and the construction
      of a mythology around Weber as a sex worker and venal character. See also Yvette
      Guilbert, *La chanson de ma vie* (Paris: Bernard Grasset, 1927), 75.

27   Jean Morel, 'Nini Patte-en-l'Air, Une école de dressage', in Claudine Brécourt-Villars
      and Jean Morel, eds, *Jane Avril: Mes mémoires, suivi de Erastène Ramiro: Cours de
      danse fin-de-siècle* (Paris: Phébus, 2005), 137–138.

28   Emily Apter, *Continental Drift: From National Characters to Virtual Subjects*
      (Chicago: University of Chicago Press, 1999), 135.

29   Albert Bataille, 'Police correctionnelle: Deux matrones. La *Goulue* devant la 10e
      Chambre. Nouvelles Judiciaires', *Le Journal* (1 April 1886), 2.

nature of her profession, and her existing reputation within Montmartre, when La Goulue again took to the stand for the prosecution in the Bal des Quat'z'Arts case in 1893, her appearance was largely laughed at, despite her efforts to apparently distance herself from the commonly held image of her as wanton or sluttish. Four female models were accused of indecency during their appearances on floats from artists' *ateliers*, and La Goulue, who had participated in the same procession, appeared as a witness for the prosecution. The coverage is contradictory, even within one article, which both highlights the irony of her appearance alongside conservatives like Senator Bérenger despite her own seemingly disreputable career, and her naïveté or ignorance at the same time as she is depicted again as a fallen woman, repentant and past her prime, escaping from the iniquity of the dance hall to avenge her damaged reputation.[30] The media attention at the time of the case was similarly varied, with some decrying Weber's behaviour as a publicity stunt and others pitying 'poor La Goulue'.[31]

There is another curious contrast: Weber reputedly wrote against the striptease, and made a show of her sensibilities being offended by the Bal.[32] Her presence is ascribed to bruised pride for being overlooked as a star performer losing out to rivals, but her criticism could as easily be recognition of the threat posed by stripping to her own act and its primacy in popular entertainment.[33] Weber was no stranger to public indecency trials; she and Grille d'Égout had been defendants in a case of 'moral corruption' in 1885 following their engagement at the Alcazar d'Été. Both women were acquitted, with their defence counsel declaring that the quadrille and cancan were essential parts of the French national spirit and character.[34]

30 Lucien Perrin, 'Le Bal de Quatr'z'Arts', *Le Courrier Français* (c.23 June 1893), 3–6.

31 Caribert, 'Les Quatr'z'Arts', *Le Courrier Français* (19 February 1893), 3.

32 Rachel Shteir, *Striptease: The Untold History of the Girlie Show* (New York: Oxford University Press, 2004), 36; Maître Z., 'Chronique des tribunaux', *Le Gaulois* (24 June 1893), 3.

33 Caribert, 'Les Quatr'z'Arts', 3; Perrin, 'Le Bal de Quatr'z'Arts', 3–6.

34 Artus, 'Elysée-Montmartre', *Le Vieux Montmartre*, vol. IV (1906–1910), 304. Again, a link was insinuated between the dancers and prostitution, which their defense counsel dismissed, saying 'Sont-elles des marchandes d'amour? J'opine negativement' [are they selling love? I opine in the negative] (Artus, 'Elysée-Montmartre', 303).

In the same year as the Bal des Quat'z'Arts trial, a poem was composed in the *Gil Blas* by way of apparently condensing an interview with La Goulue at the Moulin Rouge. In it, Weber is described as the most beautiful of the *houris* known in Paris. This reinforces the image of La Goulue, and to an extent the other dancers, as sexually available, and the Moulin Rouge as a paradisiacal space for male visitors, potentially undermining Weber's indignation at the models' appearance at the Bal.[35]

Sexuality

There were rumours about Weber's sexuality beyond the question of her 'appetite' and extending to her preference. One of the reasons for the assumption that she was sexually omnivorous is the conflation with moralizing writings by figures like Alexandre Parent-Duchâtelet in the early 1800s and Pauline Tarnowsky or Cesare Lombroso towards the end of the century. They theorized that deviant sexuality and criminal behaviour were linked, writing that predispositions to lesbianism, criminality and overt sexuality or engaging in prostitution were symptomatic of defects in one's character or nature.[36] Lombroso was among the authors who took this further, asserting that prostitutes could be identified by physical traits like body shape and facial structure; similarly, Tarnowsky's research continued from works dating to the 1860s that suggested a link between physical traits and 'degeneracy' or predisposition towards criminality and specifically prostitution.[37] By these standards, Louise Weber's tattoo (the initials of an old lover), feistiness, sexual assertiveness and even her body shape would

---

35   Albert Callarias, 'Actualités', *Gil Blas* (30 November 1893), 2.

36   Nickie Roberts, *Whores in History: Prostitution in Western Society* (London: Grafton, 1993), 224, 226.

37   Pauline Tarnowsky, *Étude anthropométrique sue les prostituées et les voleuses* (Paris: E. Lecrosnier et Babé, 1889), 1–2, 33–42, 205; Cesare Lombroso and Giuliano Ferrero, *La donna delinquente, la prostituta e la donna normale* (Turin: Roux, 1893), 284–334.

likely have been seen as proof of her degeneracy (she was described as fat by some commentators; Lombroso identified prostitutes as frequently overweight).[38]

The rumours exaggerating Weber's queerness and conflating the queer elements around her were therefore more akin to slights against her than contemporary readers' assumptions about her sexuality. Another story illustrating this is the assertion at the Musée de l'Érotisme in Pigalle that La Goulue was at one point the lover of Casque d'Or, an equally mythicized character within the Parisian underworld over whom battles between gangsters had been fought, and at least one man killed. This simultaneously fuses rumours of Weber's 'deviant' sexuality with her links to prostitution and the underworld of Paris.[39]

Weber herself told stories that emphasized her precocious, head-strong nature and sexual experiences even at an early age, which would have shocked bourgeois readers and lent weight to later representations of Weber as sexually 'other'. A story told to an interviewer in the 1920s was that she attended her first communion wearing a borrowed tutu and slippers left at her mother's laundry by a client; another detailed her first sexual experience at the age of about thirteen with an artilleryman.[40] As an adult, she quipped 'the soldiers, they bring you luck!'[41]

When discussing Louise Weber's relationships and inclinations, some authors have simply labelled her as a lesbian, others as bisexual, but often pairing her with La Môme Fromage, another dancer with whom she often

38 Le Greffier, 'Grande Mise en accusation par devant la cour de *La Vie Moderne* des demoiselles la Goulue et Grille d'Égout accusées de malversation morale', *La Vie Moderne* (7 November 1885), n.p., Dossier *La Goulue/ML Weber/La Glu* (Paris: Musée de Montmartre, n.d.); Jacques Crépineau and Jacques Pessis, *Le Moulin Rouge* (Paris: Éditions de la Martinière, 1990, 2002), 16.

39 James Morton, *Gangland: The Early Years* (London: Time Warner, 2003), 525–528.

40 Michel Georges-Michel, 'Madame la Goulue', in Dossier *DOS GOU Goulue, La (Weber, Louise)* (Paris: Bibliothèque Marguerite Durand, n.d.); Michel Georges-Michel, *En jardinant avec Bergson* (Paris: Albin Michel, 1926), 146–147.

41 Lanoux, 'Moulin Rouge', 95.

performed.[42] This reinforces the point that her life and career outside of the Moulin was effectively erased from public consciousness, despite public heterosexual relationships, her marriage and eventual separation.[43] Artworks by Lautrec inadvertently exacerbated the confusion about Weber's sexuality – *La Goulue et sa soeur* (1892) shows a woman often identified as La Môme Fromage alongside La Goulue. This has prompted an understanding of the work's title as euphemistic and positions the women as lovers, however it is actually Jeanne Weber, Louise's sister. Jeanne appears again in *La Goulue entrant au Moulin Rouge* (also from 1892), arm in arm with her sister and another woman, possibly Nini Patte-en-l'Air. Both women have occasionally been identified as La Goulue's lover.

The origins of Weber's rumoured queerness are often traced to one story told by the *diseuse* Yvette Guilbert, in which she mentions that Weber, when asked about her preferences, demurred. La Môme Fromage, hearing her, cried 'comment tu peux nier que tu m'aimes? Tu t'embêtes pourtant pas quand tu m'friandes!' [how can you deny that you love me? You don't complain when you're nibbling on me!].[44] This may easily be a fabrication, but it fits conveniently with the image of Weber as sexually omnivorous, and strengthens the parallel with Zola's Nana, who has a relationship with Satin the street prostitute, and with whom she visits *brasseries à femmes*. Conversely, one journalist spoke to her much later (during her time as a *dompteuse*), when some of her animals had been poisoned. She accused jealous ex-lovers of being responsible, and when asked 'homme ou femme?', she replied 'les deux!' [both!][45]

42   Edward Shorter, *Written in the Flesh: A History of Desire* (Toronto: University of Toronto Press, 2005), 163; Crépineau and Pessis, *Le Moulin Rouge*, 36. It should also be noted that several other performers known to frequent the Moulin (and featured in Lautrec's works) have been identified at various times as lesbians, including May Milton, Georgette Macarona, Cha-U-Ka-O (and with her the dancer Gabrielle), and even Yvette Guilbert.

43   Richard Thomson, 'Representing Montmartre', 252, 254; Philippe Huisman and M. G. Dortu, *Lautrec par Lautrec* (Paris: La Bibliothèque des Arts, 1964), 84.

44   Yvette Guilbert, *La chanson de ma vie*, 77–78.

45   Lanoux, 'Moulin Rouge', 128.

Same-sex behaviour in the nineteenth century was seen as linked to both the 'criminal classes' and to counterculture, both of which were incarnated in constructions of La Goulue.[46] This carried the added fear of each leading to the others; certainly expressions of 'deviant' sexuality and behaviour were seen by authors like Lombroso as inseparable, and often tied in with prejudices or anxieties about class.[47] Queerness was also linked to the combined implications of creativity, eccentricity and otherness in the public imagination of the fin-de-siècle, and Weber's joking approach meant that audiences might interpret her behaviour as an external signifier in relation to her preferences or personality.[48]

In truth, there is little known of Weber's sexuality, since she herself seemed to have been often remarkably quiet about her personal life, which is somewhat odd given her larger-than-life personality, and the sole explicit reference to her sexuality comes from another performer. Looking at surviving pages of Weber's diary, little is said. Even when writing about events including the suicide of her sister or the death of her mother, Weber refrains from divulging details, or indeed her own state of mind, though her description of her paying for the funeral and the arrangements made is telling when borne in mind alongside her references to stardom as an escape from poverty. When writing about the Marquis de Biron, whom it can be inferred had taken her as a mistress while she was a teenager, she either self-censors or neglects to give too much information, focusing instead on what she wore or the fact that a trip with him was the first time she saw the sea.

Throughout her life, Weber was seen as threatening for two primary reasons. Firstly, her manner and aggressively working-class nature posed a

---

46   Jane Kinsman et al., 'Houses of Tolerance', in Jane Kinsman and Stéphane Guegan, eds, *Toulouse-Lautrec: Paris and the Moulin Rouge* (Canberra: National Gallery of Australia, 2012), 135; Alain Corbin, *Filles de noce* (Paris: Aubier Montaigne, 1978), 19, 22, 43, 47.

47   Nancy Harrowitz, *Antisemitism, Misogyny, and the Logic of Cultural Difference: Cesare Lombroso and Matilde Serao* (London: University of Nebraska Press, 1994), 30–31.

48   Francesca Canadé Sautmann, 'Invisible Women', 184; John Berger et al., *Ways of Seeing* (London: British Broadcasting Corporation and Penguin Books, 1972), 47.

challenge to social hierarchies of the age. Secondly, the manner in which she exercised her sexuality and the agency afforded her as a star did not fit neatly within the boundaries of bourgeois morality. Furthermore, the rumours about her (by others and of her own making) contributed to her reputation as not only different, but dangerously so.[49] This is exacerbated by the shifts between the different 'bodies' inhabited and performed or incarnated by La Goulue, and her manipulation of her representation for the sake of profit, playing to and confounding expectations in equal measure but always trading on the nebulous cachet of her celebrity.

Conclusion

The liberties taken with Weber's story throughout her life have had long-lasting repercussions that are still felt today, and are evidenced by suppositions upheld as fact ('sans doute prostituée occasionnelle'), and not interrogated fully by audiences and readers when she appears, invariably in relation to Lautrec – that is, as a bit-player in a man's narrative.[50] What this paper has sought to do is redress the imbalance in the representation of La Goulue and demonstrate how the details surrounding Weber's life have been altered over time, to create a specific image of La Goulue as embodying her name and onstage persona in a way that was both derogatory and couched in the prejudices of her age. However, despite the negative connotations of her class and career, and speculation about her sexuality, Weber herself managed to wrest some degree of control from her situation. She turned her reputation to her advantage as a publicity tool, reinventing herself where possible and prolonging her career in a manner that has so far been generally overlooked.

49   Roberts, *Whores in History*, 203–204.
50   Farid Abdelouahab, *Muses: elles ont conquis les cœurs* (Paris: Flammarion, 2011), 69.

Epilogue

BEE SCHERER

Variable Bodies, Buddhism and (No-)Selfhood: Towards Dehegemonized Embodiment

ABSTRACT

Following on from current discourses within critical disability studies I investigate the parameters, opportunities and challenges of some Buddhist responses to variable bodies. Negotiating the different Buddhist modes between 'karmatic' sociology and 'nirvāṇic' soteriology, I develop outlines of Socially Engaged Buddhist 'theology' of bodily inclusiveness, arguing for a person-centred, non-judgemental approach to bodily variability and neuro-diversity. I conclude with critical ruminations about oppressive normalcy and by pointing out some pathways to navigating variability-affirming 'anthroposcapes' – landscapes of embodied human experiences.

Introduction

Recently, Chris Mounsey has proposed a shift in critical disability studies, away from the Foucauldian emphasis on the notion of compulsory ableism – as, for example, in McRuer's *Crip Theory*[1] – toward a fuller emphasis on and an appreciation of the individual embodied experience.[2] Mounsey theorizes this approach under the concept of *variability*, 'same

1   Robert McRuer, *Crip Theory: Cultural Signs of Queerness and Disability* (New York: New York University Press, 2006).
2   Chris Mounsey, 'Introduction: Variability – Beyond Sameness and Difference', in Chris Mounsey, ed., *The Idea of Disability in the Eighteenth Century* (Lewisburg, PA: Bucknell University Press: 2014), 1–27.

only different'[3] as a discursive replacement to 'disability'. Consciously or not, Mounsey's radical reconceptualization and celebration of sameness in difference contrast-imitates Homi Bhabha's observations on the oppressive fixation as 'a 'partial' presence' of the colonial subject through 'the ambivalence of mimicry (almost the same, *but not quite*)'.[4] The postcolonial critique of oppressive identity construction through mimicry is transformed for critical disability theory into the variability approach: Mounsey's 'same only different' affords, without centre and margin, any variable body the complete autonomy of an embodied presence while leaving empathic, unoppressive recognisability in sameness intact.

The chapters in this volume testify to the fact that the focus on the body can facilitate history speaking to the presence – without the necessity of anachronistic categorizations and retro-diagnoses. This does not preclude – or devalue the usefulness of – diachronic phenomenological and philosophical meanderings, in particular when the focus, limitations and parameters of such enquiries are clearly defined. With these caveats, I would like to open up a dialogue between contemporary critical disability theory with Buddhist thought, moving in this chapter from investigating selected variable bodies within the circumscribed yet still somewhat fluid, fuzzy and messy discursive context of Buddhist practices, narratives and philosophies[5] to infusing 'variability' as a critical angle with Buddhist 'theology' (i.e. Buddhist constructive-critical thought). I aim to demonstrate how embodied and body-oppressive normativities – and the margins they produce – can successfully be challenged through the lens of the conjunct Buddhist principles of interdependency, cause and effect; and no-self. In

3   Mounsey, 'Introduction: Variability', 18.

4   Homi Bhabha, *The Location of Culture* (New York and London: Routledge, 2012), 123; emphasis in the original.

5   In this chapter I do not attempt to provide a survey of the vast streams of Buddhist traditions in their relationship to 'disability'. A useful – yet by its lack of direct access to primary texts quite limited – compilation of literature on Buddhism and disability in Asia is M. Mills, 'Buddhism and Responses to Disability, Mental Disorders and Deafness in Asia. A bibliography of historical and modern texts with introduction and partial annotation, and some echoes in Western countries' (West Midlands, 2013), <http://cirrie.buffalo.edu/bibliography/buddhism/>, accessed 12 April 2016.

conclusion I dare to finish this non-Foucauldian volume with a (post-) Foucauldian critique of oppressive normalcy and I will attempt to point out some pathways to navigating variability-affirming 'anthroposcapes'[6] – landscapes of embodied human experiences.

Buddhist Variable Bodies

Buddhist approaches to the body flow from two pivotal angles: soteriology and sociology, i.e. aspiration and (conditioned) socio-cultural reality. On the level of aspiration and soteriology the Buddhist traditions approach bodies as fields of transformative virtue while, on the level of socio-cultural realities, bodies are seen as limiting or expedient expressions of past actions and ripened conditions. Both approaches are based on the key Buddhist tenets of *karma* as the law of cause and effect; and of the *pratītyasamutpāda* – 'dependent arising'. Buddhist bodies are constructed within the parameter of Buddhist (virtue) Ethics or virtuosity.[7] However, variant embodied abilities, while linked to past actions, are not attributable to individualized (non-)virtue, since the Buddhist key tenet of 'no-self' (*anātman*) precludes the judgemental attribution of causal agency to an individual core, self or soul: instead, phenomena and empiric persons manifest as karmic continuities without essential identities attached. The ensuing conundrum of cause & effect and rebirth without a Self is itself

6   Bee Scherer, 'Crossings and Dwellings: Being behind Transphobia', paper given at the conference 'Fear and Loathing: Phobia in Literature and Culture', University of Kent, UK, 9–10 May 2014. Available at the Queering Paradigms blog, <http://queering-paradigms.com/2014/08/11/crossings-and-dwellings-being-behind-transphobia/>, accessed 12 April 2016.

7   Susanne Mrozik, *Virtuous Bodies: The Physical Dimensions of Morality in Buddhist Ethics* (Oxford: Oxford University Press, 2007).

the subject of intensive philosophical and doctrinal debate;[8] however, Buddhist Modernisms[9] have mostly solved the riddle by firmly pointing to the non-ontological nature of the Buddhist teachings: Without ontological assumptions of, e.g. 'self', 'soul' or even 'mind' and without any essentialized notion of ultimate reality, a particular meaningful way to understand the framework of the Buddhist intention-led, yet subject-essence-free karmatic theory arises as an exercise in deconstruction of essentialism by practice (or *performance* in Butlerian terms).

In this pedagogical or 'andragogical'[10] reading of Buddhism and Buddhist *praxis* – i.e. thought and performance – questions of ontologically essentialized selfhood and truths are rendered obsolete in favour of the soteriological pragmatics, experience-oriented andragogy aiming only at showing methods to enduring happiness. In the famous *Snake Simile Sutta* of the Pāli canon's *Middle Length Discourses*, the Buddha as interlocutor proclaims 'I only teach suffering and its ending.'[11] This can be read as the Buddha saying that he does not concern himself with essentialized identities; ontology, cosmology and other conceptualizations of reality. Instead, the focus of his teachings is freedom from *dukkha*: 'pain', 'unsatisfactoriness' or 'suffering'. *Dukkha* in Buddhist terms is juxtopposed to *sukha*: 'happiness', and points to the lack (*duḥ-*) of permanent happiness (*kha*). The Buddhist concept of sufffering includes the inextricably interpellated complexes of individual psycho-physical integrity as the *dukkha-dukkhatā*, the pain of experiencing pain, within ever-changing and fluid conditioned reality as the *sankhāra-dukkhatā*, the pain of karmatic flux, and the ensuing experience of lack, due to the constant change, the *vipariṇāma-dukkhatā*.

---

8   B. Scherer, 'Karma: The Transformations of a Buddhist Conundrum', in Chetyrova, L. B. et al., eds, *Vajrayana Buddhism in Russia: History and Modernity* (St Petersburg: St Petersburg State University, 2009), 259–285.

9   David L. McMahan, *The Making of Buddhist Modernism* (Oxford: Oxford University Press, 2008).

10   Scherer, 'Karma', 265 and 277–278.

11   *dukkhañceva paññāpemi dukkhassa ca nirodhaṃ* M 22 I 140. Pāli texts referred to are the editions of the Pali Text Society, London. Abbreviations follow the *Critical Pāli Dictionary* (see the *Epilegomena* to Vol. 1 and online at <http://pali.hum.ku.dk/cpd/intro/vol1_epileg_abbrev_texts.html>, accessed 12 April 2016).

The Buddhist notion of karma without individually essentialized agent and of rebirth without anyone who is reborn, hence, points to the experience of our ever-changing spatial, temporal and 'cosmic' (psycho-spiritual) context as a continuity without ontological, fixed identity – a flow without essence. In this reading of Buddhist philosophy, widening Butler's concept of performativity to the extreme, reality itself is performance. The view of simple, variable causalities without selves – without judging, blaming, shaming, and guilt-tripping variable embodiments – mitigates the Buddhist karmatic views on 'disability' or embodied variabilities: it can be argued that that from a Buddhist point of view body variances express genealogies or actualizations of generic human potentials rather than essentialized, individual histories of (non-)virtue.

This non-judgemental and in its potential arguably dehegemonic Buddhist approach does not preclude the moralizing of (un)virtuous Buddhist bodies in cautionary narratives; nor has it on the level of socio-cultural organization and expression prevented Buddhists and Buddhisms from variability-based discriminatory practices – most importantly on the level of the monastic discipline. All extant and still valid and mostly enforced Buddhist monastic codes preclude applicants with physical and mental variabilities from ordination. For example, in the Theravāda tradition the Pāli canon's section on monastic discipline or *vinaya* congenital and acquired impairment are physiomorally grouped together with those having received corporeal punishments – such as branding, scourging, marking as robber, cutting off of hands, feet, ears, nose, fingers, thumb, tendons – with congenital and/or acquired variabilities – such as webbed fingers, humpback, dwarfism, deformity, blindness, dumbness, deafness, lameness and other walking impairments, and paralysis – and general medical problems such as infirmity, bad health, contagious disease, goitre and elephantiasis.[12] The list is quite consistent across the five extant early *vinaya* traditions.[13]

---

12 Mahāvagga Vin I 71 i 91; cp. IX, 4, 10–11 i 322; Vin I 76 i 93–95 adds leprosy, boils, eczema and epilepsy.

13 For the parallels on 'cripples' in the other four early Buddhist *vinaya* traditions see the references in Erich Frauwallner, *The Earliest Vinaya and the Beginnings of Buddhist Literature* (Rome: Is.M.E.O., 1956), 77.

Equally, those seen as having non-normative sex/gender – i.e. the 'neither-male-nor-female' *paṇḍakas* and the 'both-and' intersex[14] – were and are prohibited from ordination; interestingly, were they inadvertently ordained their ordination was deemed annulled[15] while the inadvertent ordination of those disqualified due to impairments such as various degrees of blindness, deafness, skeletal deformation, etc. was and is still deemed as valid.[16]

Ordination to the Buddhist monastic community was and is not governed by soteriology but according to social context and societal pragmatics. The *vinaya* rules establish a physiomoral elite in-group, which feels the need guard itself from societal damage both by behaviour and by association. However, Buddhist modernisms are challenging the elite status of the monastics by privileging soteriology above sociology. Modernist lay movements in particular in the Global North vocally advocate equality of *virtuosi* status for householders and non-monastic 'yogis' in Buddhist praxis; transnationally, many 'new' lay Buddhist modernists move their traditions along onto a path of democratization, dehierarchization and counter-heteropatriarchal reform. In this context, it is relevant to keep in mind that the traditional monastic rules are, indeed, limited to the governance of a monastic elite: they cannot be argued to establish a universal ethical governance or code, which could be utilized to encouraging discrimination.

In doctrinal terms, the imperative of universal compassion is absolute paramount in Buddhisms and explicitly includes 'out-groups' and the marginalized. All variabilities – within and without the normative boundaries – are seen as manifestation of karma. Those physically and/or socially afflicted by these manifestations are prominently deserving of love-in-action. In canonical stories we can find that caring for 'the blind and old parents'[17] is narratively constructed as a valid reason for refusing to become a monk, as happened in the case of the potter Ghāṭikāra. And

---

14   Vin I 61 i 85–86; see Bee Scherer, 'Variant Dharma: Buddhist Queers, Queering Buddhisms', in *Queering Paradigms VI* (Oxford: Peter Lang, 2016).
15   Vin IX, 4, 10 i 322.
16   Vin IX, 4, 11 i 322.
17   *andhe jiṇṇe mātāpitaro* M. 81 ii 48 and 51–52.

Buddhist rulers regularly are praised in chronicles as sustaining institutions for the blind and sick and otherwise variable.[18]

From a Buddhist modernist point of view it can be argued that, what has opened up Buddhist traditions to discriminatory interpretations of – and practices with regard to – variabilities, is the popular and unsophisticated utilization of karma theory in the form of attributing guilt and shame for past(-lives) actions. This form of moralizing ignores the intricacies of Buddhist psychologies of (no-)selfhood and is based on cautionary explanations of karma abounding in Buddhist scriptures. In the Buddhist canonical texts karmatic 'foolishness', equalling to non-virtuous behaviour, is directly linked to non-favourable physical variability, e.g. prominently in the Theravāda Pāli canon in the *Discourse on the Fool and the Wise*;[19] although the judging and moralizing is aimed at the non-virtue which causes the variability it is difficult to ignore the real socially stigmatizing consequences for the subjects of embodied variability whose physicality is traced back to human non-virtue – however non-essentializing and 'no-self-ed' such causality philosophically is meant to be. The non-virtuous fool (*bāla*) experiences embodied aspects of his moral deficit in a variety of impairments, combined in the following stock phrase list in the Pāli canon: 'ugly (or: of inferior class), unsightly, deformed, diseased, or blind or crooked or lame or paralysed'.[20] This mnemonic list is usually preceded by a paragraph detailing (re-)birth into a socially abject group or caste (*nīcakula*) such as the untouchables.[21] The list-heading term *dubbaṇṇo*, 'of bad colour', implies both aesthetical and social abjection:[22] the overlaying of physical and social

18   For example, the *Lesser Chronicle* of the Buddhist rulers of Sri Lanka, the *Cūḷavaṃsa*, mentions such charity for the 4th century CE king Buddhadāsa (Mhv 37. 148 and 182); the 7th century CE ruler Aggibodhi (Mhv 45.43) and the eighth-century king Udaya I (Mhv 49. 20).

19   *Bālapaṇḍita-sutta*, M. 129, iii 167–178.

20   *dubbaṇṇo duddasiko okoṭimako bavhābādho, kāṇo vā kuṇi vā khañjo vā pakkhahato vā*, Vin II 90 S I 194 A I 107, II 85, III 385 Pug 51; the *Bālapaṇḍita-sutta* M 129 III 169 substitutes *khañjo* 'lame' for *khujjo* 'humpbacked'.

21   E.g. M III 169; S I 194 A I 107, II 85, III 385 Pug 51. Additionally, parts of the stock phrase occur separately throughout the Pāli canon.

22   Sanskrit *varṇa* (Pāli *vaṇṇo*) denotes both colour and caste.

appearances is paramount in the South Asian social context of the Buddhist sources, in which social inferiority was and largely still is equivalent with corporeal unattractiveness. The description of a boy in the Buddhist Sanskrit *Avadāna-Śatakam*, a collection of religious-didactic poetic narratives probably redacted around the first century, drastically exemplifies this marriage of social abjection to the non-normative physicality: the youngster is depicted as 'ugly (or: of inferior class), unsightly, deformed, his body smeared all over with faeces, and foul-smelling'.[23]

The Buddhist 'physiomoral discourse of the body'[24] includes abject class and non-normative sex/gender[25] and the inferior female birth.[26] Any progress on the Buddhist path towards enlightenment is impeded by physiomoral problematic rebirth as the Pāli commentarial list of eighteen 'impossible states' (*abhabbaṭṭhāna*) shows:[27] among humans, the list features the physical abject as blind, deaf, dumb, deformed and leper together with the sex/gender abject and the social abject as 'barbarian', slave, notorious criminal and heretic.[28] Within the early Sanskritic Buddhist traditions, such 'inopportune' (*akṣaṇaprāpta*) birth as result of karma is described in the *Pravrajyāntarāya-sūtra* as quoted in Śāntideva's eighth-century *Compendium of Discipline*:

23   *durvarṇo durdarśano avakoṭimako 'medhyamrakṣitagātro durgandhaś ca* Av 50 i 280; p. 125 Vaidya (abbreviations and editions of Sanskrit texts refer to Franklin Edgerton, *Buddhist Hybrid Sanskrit Grammar and Dictionary* (1953) with occasionally relevant alternative or newer editions added by editor's name only).
24   Mrozik, *Virtous Bodies*, Chapter 4.
25   *paṇḍaka* and intersex; see above Scherer, *Variant Dharma*.
26   *itthibhāva* (cp. Mrozik, *Virtuous Bodies*, 70–71). See, for example, the list in the para-canonical verses in the *Jātaka commentary* (J-a I 44) and the statement in the *Milindapañha* Mil 93 PTS on the inferiority (*ittaratā*) of woman (*itthi*, note the wordplay!).
27   *Suttanipāta commentary* Sn-a i 50 and *Apadāna commentary* Ap-a 141.
28   See Toshiichi Endo, *Buddha in Theravada Buddhism: A Study of the Concept of Buddha in the Pali Commentaries* (Dehiwala, Sri Lanka: Buddhist Cultural Centre, 2002), 160–164, and Mrozik, *Virtuous Bodies*, 71.

He is born blind, stupid, dumb, an outcaste – certainly not privileged, a notorious slanderer; a sex/gender deficient and deviant (*ṣaṇḍaka* and *paṇḍaka*), a perpetual slave, a woman, a dog, a pig, a donkey, a camel and a poisonous serpent.[29]

Another Mahāyāna discourse quoted in the same compendium, the *Inquiry of the Girl Candrottarā*, enumerates being 'blind, lame, without tongue, and deformed' among the karmic results of sense-attachment or desire (*rāga*):[30] 'Those who lead the low-life of lust become party to the various multitude of defects.'[31] And again, as in the case of the earlier quoted *Pravrajyāntarāya-sūtra*, mental disabilities or learning difficulties[32] and various animal rebirths are included in the shortly following summary of such physiomoral expressions of causality: 'Truly, those lustful will continuously be born as blind, deaf, and idiotic [...]'.[33] With the self-referential 'cult of the book' emerging within Mahāyāna praxis, disregard for the respective scripture becomes another karmic cause for disadvantageous births with variable bodies. The *Lotus Sūtra* illustrates this when it claims that 'those who do not have faith in this discourse I dispense, when they are born human again are then born idiots, lame, crooked, blind and dull'. The blasphemer, 'foolish and deaf, does not hear the *dharma* (liberating teaching)'; 'and when he obtains human birth he becomes blind, deaf and idiotic; he is a slave, always poor'.[34]

---

29   *jātyandhaś ca jaḍaś câjihvakaś ca caṇḍālaś [ca] {na} jātu | sukhito bhavaty abhyākhyānabahulaś ca ṣaṇḍakaś ca paṇḍakaś ca nityadāsaś ca | strī ca bhavati śvā ca śūkaraś ca gardabhaś côṣṭraś ca āśīviṣaś ca bhavati tatra tatra jātau ||* Śikṣāsamuccaya Śikṣ p. 69; all translations are my own unless indicated otherwise.

30   *kāṇāś ca khañjāś ca vijihvakāś ca | virūpakāś câiva bhavanti rāgāt* Candrottarādārikāparipṛcchā, Śikṣ, 80.

31   *bhavanti nānāvidhadoṣabhājāś caranti ye kāmacarīṃ jaghanyām* Candrottarādārikāparipṛcchā, Śikṣ, 80.

32   Here denoted by the term *visaṃjña* cp. above *jaḍa*.

33   *jātyandhabhava vadhirā visaṃjñā | [...] bhavanti nityaṃ khalu kāmalolāḥ ||* Śikṣ 80.

34   *Saddharmapuṇḍarīka-sūtra* SP 3 verses 122; 129ab; 132 a-c: *puruṣātmabhāvaṃ ca yada labhante te kuṇṭhakā laṅgaka bhonti tatra | kubjātha kāṇā ca jaḍā jaghanyā aśraddadhantā ima sūtra mahyam ||* 122; *na cāpi so dharma śṛṇoti bālo badhiraśca so bhoti acetanaśca |* 129ab; *manuṣyabhāvatvamupetya cāpi andhatva badhiratva jaḍatvameti | parapreṣya so bhoti daridra nityaṃ* 3.132a-c.

However, the karmic ripening of impairing conditions within one's lifetime does not necessarily preclude spiritual progress and realization. The canonical texts testify to the achievement of variable-bodied and/or impaired monastics; famously, the Ven. Bhaddiya 'the dwarf' is depicted in the very terms of physiomoral rejection discussed above as 'ugly (or of inferior class), unsightly, deformed' and as 'shunned by most monks'[35] – yet he is praised by the Buddha for his high spiritual achievements. Another example is the story of the blind Elder Cakkhupāla as told in the commentary to the famous collection of doctrinal verses, the *Dhammapada*. The narrative illustrates the *Dhammapada's* very first verse on intention-led and mind-governed karma; it relates how Cakkhupāla, by accepting the loss of its sight during rigorous asceticism dissolves a great karmic obstacle on the spiritual path.

As has become clear, the Buddhist physiomoral encoding of variable corporealities through the doctrine of karma can be – and is only – resolved by the nirvāṇic soteriology. Such nirvāṇic or *bodhi* orientation projects a utopia of invariable bliss and translates this salvific impetus into the healing activities of enlightenment. In fact, the Buddha had compared the non-essentializing pragmatics of his liberating teachings to a physician removing a poisonous arrow without the delay of forensic over-scrutinizing.[36] Following on from Early Buddhist praises of the Buddha as the unrivalled physician of humanity, the 'supreme surgeon'[37] who removes the poisons of attachment, aversion and ignorance which fuel the ego-delusion, Mahāyāna scriptures metaphorize the spiritual transformation of suffering as healing rays born out of the deep contemplative trance and fuelled by the higher compassion of enlightened beings.[38] For example, the influential Mahāyāna

---

35   *dubbaṇṇaṁ duddasikaṁ okoṭimakaṁ yebhuyyena bhikkhūnaṁ paribhūtarūpaṁ* Ud VII 5, 76.
36   M 63 i 429.
37   *sallakato anuttaro* Sn 560; Mil 215.
38   For Buddhism and Healing see [Paul Demiéville], *Buddhism and Healing: Demiéville's Article 'Byo' from Hōbōgirin*, Mark Tatz, trans. (Lanham, NJ: University Press of America, 1985); Raoul Birnbaum, *The Healing Buddha* (Boston: Shambhala, 1989); Tadeusz Skorupski, 'Health and Suffering in Buddhism: Doctrinal and Existential Considerations', in J. R. Hinnells and R. Porter, eds, *Religion, Health and Suffering*

scripture *Discourse of the Golden Light* describes in its second chapter the healing contemplation rays emitted by the Bodhisattva (enlightenment-being) Ruciraketu, whose name can be translated as 'Radiant Brightness':[39]

> And all the beings in this triple-thousand great-thousand world-sphere by the Buddha's power became possessed of divine happiness.[...] And beings blind from birth see forms with the eye. And deaf beings hear sounds with the ear. And unconscious beings regain their mindfulness. And beings whose minds were distraught were no longer distraught in mind. (9) And naked beings became clothed in robes. And hungry beings became full-bellied. And thirsty beings became thirstless. And disease-afflicted beings became diseaseless. And beings whose bodily organs were defective became possessed of complete organs. (trans. Emmerick)[40]

The salvific power of the Bodhisattvas is described in similar ways in the *Ratnolkadhāraṇī* as quoted in Śāntideva's *Compendium*, Chapter 18.[41]

The Enlightenment-being's salvific aspiration is founded upon the wish for universal happiness. Hence, the confessional aspiration liturgies include the prayer that all varieties of suffering in sentient beings cease. The *Discourse of the Golden Light* includes in Chapter Three, the 'confession

---

(London: Kegan Paul International, 1999), 139–165; and Analayo, 'Healing in Early Buddhism', *Buddhist Studies Review*, 32/1 (2015), 19–33.

39   *Suvarṇaprabhāsottama-sūtra* Sv 8–9 *sarve cāsmiṃstrisāhasramahāsāhasralokadhātau sattvā buddhānubhāvena divyasukhena samanvāgatā babhūvuḥ | jātyandhāśca sattvā rūpāṇi paśyanti sma | vadhirāśca sattvāḥ sattvebhyaḥ śabdāni śṛnvanti | unmattāśca sattvāḥ smṛtiṃ pratilabhante 'vikṣiptacittāśca smṛtimanto babhū-| vuḥ | nagnāśca sattvāściivaraprāvṛtā (Bagchi 5) babhūvuḥ | jighatsitāśca sattvāḥ paripūrṇagātrā babhūvuḥ | tṛṣitāśca sattvā vigatatṛṣṇā babhūvaḥ | rogaspṛṣṭāśca sattvā vigatarogā babhūvuḥ | hīnakāyāśca sattvāḥ paripūrṇendriyā babhūvuḥ | (I have omitted [...] 'Beings whose senses were incomplete became possessed of all their senses', which is most likely an interpolation duplicating the concluding sentence quoted and only found in the Tibetan and Chinese versions, but not in the Sanskrit manuscripts. Nobel conjected and added this passage as *aparipūrṇendriyāḥ sattvāḥ sarvendriyasamanvāgatā babhūvuḥ*).

40   Ronald E. Emmerick, *The Sutra of Golden Light: Being a Translation of the Suvarnabhasottamasutra* (Oxford: Pali Text Society, 2001), 4.

41   See in particular Śikṣ 341–2.

chapter' (*deśanā-parivarta*), such an elaborate aspirational prayer of hope and healing for all kind of variably disadvantaged:[42]

> And may the blind see the various forms, the deaf hear delightful sounds, the naked obtain various garments, poor beings obtain treasures [...] May the experience of woe harm no one. May all beings be good-looking. May they have beautiful, gracious, auspicious forms and continually have a heap of numerous blessings. (trans. Emmerick)[43]

The popularity of the aspirational hope for those in disadvantaging variabilities is evidenced by the intertextual variation of key formulations found throughout Buddhist literatures. For example, most influentially, the seventh- to eighth-century Buddhist poet-philosopher Śāntideva, in the concluding chapter of his seminal *Entering the Path to Enlightenment* (*Bodhicaryāvatāra*), concisely includes an only slight alteration to a central verse in the Sūtra's wishing prayer: 'May the blind see and may the deaf hear always.'[44]

What emerges from the discussion above are contradicting and idiosyncratic Buddhist approaches to embodied variance and impairment which exemplify attempts to negotiate different hegemonic social regimes of bio-power with soteriological universalism and inclusiveness. Buddhist modernisms with their main modes of detraditionalization, demythologization and psychologization[45] have found creative ways to propagate the demarginalization of the Buddhist 'un-ordainable', including, in modern terms, convicts; LGBT people; sex workers; and the 'disabled' variable.[46]

---

42 Sv verses 3.81–83 (p. 39 Nobel) *andhāśca paśyantu vicitrarūpān vadhirāśca śṛṇvantu manojñaghoṣān* || 81 *nagnāśca vastrāṇi labhantu citrā daridrasattvāśca dhanāṃllabhantu* | 82ab *mā kasyaciddhāvatu duḥkhavedanā sudarśanāḥ sattva bhavantu sarve* | *abhirūpaprāsādikasaumyarūpā anekasukhasaṃcita nitya bhontu* || 83
43 Emmerick, *The Sutra of Golden Light*, 16.
44 *Bodhicaryāvatāra* BCA 10.19ab *andhāḥ paśyantu rūpāṇi śṛṇvantu badhirāḥ sadā* (ed. Minaev 1889; the tenth chapter is missing in Prajñākaramati's commentary ed. by de la Vallée Poussin 1904–1914).
45 McMahan, *The Making of Buddhist Modernism*, 45–57.
46 Cf. Christopher Queen, 'Introduction: From Altruism to Activism', in Christopher Queen, Charles Prebish and Damien Keown, eds, *Action Dharma: New Studies in Engaged Buddhism* (London: Routledge Curzon, 2003), 1–35, 18.

Within the heterogeneous plethora of contemporary Buddhist modernist groups and flows called 'Socially Engaged Buddhism' karma is inventively rethought in terms of social justice and human rights advocacy.[47] Socially Engaged Buddhists most visibly aim their activism at ecological and socio-economic cause and they campaign for peace and gender equality. But just as in the case of Buddhist LGBT liberation, Buddhist 'disability' activism appears to be comparably underdeveloped,[48] with the exception of Buddhist and Buddhist-derived approaches to depression and anxiety such as *Mindfulness-Based Cognitive Therapy* or *Mindfulness Based Stress Reduction.*[49] Still, variable-bodied people are able to self-narrate meaning and hope through Buddhism.[50] Buddhist Modernist 'disabled' writers such as postpolio paraplegic Lorenzo Milam in his *CripZen: A Manual for Survival*, and right-hand-lacking Joan Tollifson in her *Bare-Bones Meditation* are utilizing the experience of variability for spiritual transformation and offer pathways to variable Buddhist empowerment.[51]

The time seems ripe for Socially Engaged Buddhist *Crip Liberation* and a fuller Buddhist 'theology' of embodied variability. The idiosyncratic and contradictory orientations of social marginalizing and soteriological inclusiveness found within Buddhist thought on human embodied variance by karma theory can firmly be reintegrated and dissolved by refocusing embodied experience from an essentialized individual subject and its misconstrued individualized past, to the opportunity in the here and now for the future. As leading socially engaged Buddhist theorist David Loy so points out:

---

47   See Sally B. King, *Socially Engaged Buddhism* (Honolulu: University of Hawai'I Press, 2009).

48   See King, *Socially Engaged Buddhism*, 163–164.

49   See, e.g., Jon Kabat-Zinn, 'Some Reflections on the Origins of MBSR, Skillful Means, and the Trouble with Maps', *Contemporary Buddhism*, 12/1 (2001), 281–306.

50   For example, see Darla Y. Schumm and Michael Stoltzfus, 'Chronic Illness and Disability: Narratives of Suffering and Healing in Buddhism and Christianity', *Journal of Religion, Disability & Health*, 11/3 (2004), 5–21 and Kampol Thongbunnum, *Bright and Shining Mind in a Disabled Body* (Bangkok: Friends of Morak Society, 2007).

51   See Susan Squier, 'Meditation, Disability, and Identity', *Literature and Medicine*, 23/1 (2004), 23–45.

Karma is better understood as the key to spiritual development .. When we add the
Buddhist teaching about not-self [...] We can see that karma is not something the
self *has*, it is what the sense of self *is* [...].[52]

By utilizing a twofold Buddhist hermeneutics of preliminary (socio-cultural) and ultimate (soteriological) contexts, I argue accordingly for a
Buddhist liberation 'theology' and praxis as non-judgemental, demarginal-
ized and dehegemonized, celebratory approaches to bodily variability and
neuro-diversity, in the full acknowledgment of the universal principle of
saṃsāric conditionality and the individual expression of *saṃsāric* challenges.

Despite the multiple examples of missed opportunities to challenge
embodied and body-oppressive normativities – and the margins they produce – in Buddhist cultural contexts, I maintain that Buddhist notions
such as (re)birth as a 'continuity without identity', 'no-self' and 'interdependency' or 'inter-being'[53] and as karma taking charge of the future rather
than paying a debt to the past offers a wide array of emancipatory impulses,
which can provide new tools to critical 'disability' theory and advocacy.
Oppressive body-normalcy as regimes of bio-power can be successfully
critiqued through Buddhist (modernist) social theory which provides
pathways for navigating variability-affirming anthroposcapes.

Conclusion

Buddhist realities and Buddhist utopias clash and their battleground are
real, historical defined and culturally refined embodied experiences of variance, marginalization, stigmatization, but also experiences of emancipation,
transformation and liberation. The shift advocated in this edited volume

52   David R. Loy, *Money, Sex, War, Karma: Notes for a Buddhist Revolution* (Boston:
     Wisdom, 2008), 61.
53   'Inter-being' is a term coined and popularized by Thich Nhat Hanh, a Vietnamese
     Zen teacher who also is credited with coining the term 'Socially Engaged Buddhism'.

toward telling historical bodies, far from heralding an end of theory, ought to decisively (in)form contemporary practical philosophy, social theory and cultural critique from the grassroots and is bound to co-create new accents and insights in critical theory, including Foucauldian derived approaches; Feminist; and Queer Theories. The human journey through the temporal and spatial landscape of our embodied experiences manifests within primary parameters of identity and difference; inside and outside; sameness and otherness; inclusion and rejection. Rather than being binary absolutes, the fundamental parameters of identitarian belonging form in protean, shifting ways with situation, context, time and space always in orientation to an underlying 'prototype'[54] centre attracting the most enduring, extreme and recognizable example. The Lakoffian prototype distribution and its centre(s) for psycho-social identitarian recognition is hence paradoxically oriented at an almost impossible (hence extreme) ideal; while each individual's embodied human experience is unique and varied, it is co-shaped by parameters gauging its distance to the centre of the human prototype, which in many cultures through history manifests as the essentialized ideal of the (binary, cisgender) male (patriarchal bias; sexism; cisgenderism; transphobia); racially elite-constructed (as for example in white supremacy; racism; colourism); heterosexual (homo-, lesbo-, bi-, queerophobia); abled-bodied (ableism), young (ageism), healthy (nosemaphobia) and beautiful (lookism; beauty-fetishism; fat-ism; cacophobia) person. The closer to the centre individuals performs their embodiment, the stronger is their participation in psycho-social power (the *phallus* in Lacan's terms). In particular in relationship to transphobia, homophobia and sexism I have suggested to think of the underlying power dynamic as *aphallophobia*:[55] the very fear of losing that individually channelled societal power of the essentialized, ideal centre. Extending the aphallophobia-principle to intersections beyond heteropatriarchal oppressions with regard to gender and sexuality, I maintain that the key struggle for inclusion and social justice lies exactly in the rethinking of the illusion of identitarian stabilities, essentialism or

54 George Lakoff, *Women, Fire, and Dangerous Things: What Categories Reveal about the Mind* (Chicago and London: University of Chicago Press, 1987).

55 Scherer, 'Crossings and Dwellings'.

in other words the ideal yet illusionary and random centres of belonging. The radical acceptance of human variability transforms the struggle to *include* variabled embodiments within a projected centre of 'ontological security'[56] into the celebratory recognition of belonging as being the 'same only different': varyingly performed embodiment, flowing from time and space and context and situation. Inhabiting such variable anthroposcapes without centre and margin restores the possibility of (biographically fluid or relatively static) individual body-performances without creating oppressive body-normativities.

In terms of post-phallic forms of governmentality, after heteropatriarchy and theocracy, the ethical imperative of social action can re-establish itself as aiming at the full protection of the integrity of the variably embodied individual. Where freedom from harm and suffering is established as highest legal good, competing societal discourses of meaning-making are disempowered to affect oppressively the variable embodied individual. These discourses include the two dominant exponents of oppressive cultural modes, the medical-pathologizing and the religious-stigmatizing discourses.[57] Culturally harmful practices, disconnected from hegemonizing and essentializing discourses, can on this basis be discontinued for the benefit of the suffering individual. If the individuals' rights to being asserted within their own variable centre and their freedom from harm become the key parameters of trans-national solidarity, embodied experiences can become the pivotal angles to challenge oppression without the need to navigate a jungle of competing hierarchies of rights and cultural relativisms: this individual, 'body-without-centre-and-margin' angle changes the evaluation of both contested and mainstream harmful practices, including the binarist sex inscription through mutilation of healthy infant intersex bodies; the pseudo-medical and/or religious scarring and penile desensitizing of healthy male infant bodies in the form of circumcision; the dramatic heteropatriarchal mutilation of healthy female bodies in the form

---

56   Anthony Giddens, *Modernity and Self-Identity: self and Society in the Late Modern Age* (Cambridge: Polity Press, 1991), Ch. 2.
57   Bee Scherer, '*Queer* Thinking Religion: Queering Religious Paradigms', *Scholar & Feminist Online* (forthcoming 2016).

of Female Genital Cutting (FGC); and the ageist, sexist and misogynic re-'normatizing' mutilation of healthy bodies through cosmetic surgeries, only to name a few examples. Within these debate, the proposed dehegemonic and aphallic affirmation of variable-bodily integrity differs from some arguments around individual 'agency', which dominate contemporary postcolonial, feminist and queer intersectional discourse and which in their well-meant privileging of decolonization and postcolonial and subaltern agency sometimes disempower inter-human solidarity and hence ignore the real, embodied suffering of the subject constructed as agentive. The here proposed approach is capable of devaluing the oppressive contexts (rather than affirming it), which co-shape 'agentive' decisions manifested as pseudo-agency or disempowered agency such as is the case in women's complicity to oppressive heteropatriarchy in the context of, among others, dowry; behavioural prohibitions and prescriptions, e.g. regarding clothes; FGC and other culturally harmful practices; or in the case of developing 'Stockholm syndrome' among queer subjects in fundamentalist queerophobic religious contexts.[58]

Infusing the concept of variability and, more broadly, critical social theory with the opportunities afforded by Buddhist (modernist) philosophies I maintain that pathways appear for navigating variability-affirming 'anthroposcapes'. By relaxing the artificial boundaries of our anxious Selfhood into the ravishing of ontological uncertainty and fluidity we are able to perform compassion without essentialized Self; solidarity without colonizing and hegemonizing overpowering; and dehegemonized embodiment, same only different.

58   Scherer, '*Queer* Thinking Religion.'

Bibliography

Abdelouahab, Farid, *Muses: Elles ont conquis les* coeurs (Paris: Flammarion, 2011).

Adelson, Betty, *The Lives of Dwarfs: Their Journey from Public Curiosity Toward Social Liberation* (New Brunswick: Rutgers University Press, 2005).

Agrimi J., and C. Crisciani, 'Wohltätigkeit und Beistand in der mittelalterlichen christlichen Kultur', in M. D. Grmek ed., *Die Geschichte des medizinischen Denkens. Antike und Mittelalte*r (Munich: C. H. Beck, 1996), 182–215.

Ahl, Frederic, 'The Art of Safe Criticism in Greece and Rome', *American Journal of Philology*, 105/2 (1984), 174–175.

Anālayo, 'Healing in Early Buddhism', *Buddhist Studies Review*, 32/1 (2015), 19–33.

Andrews, Jonathan, 'Identifying and providing for the mentally disabled in early modern London', in Anne Digby and David Wright, eds, *From idiocy to mental deficiency* (London: Routledge, 1996), 59–76.

Angenendt, Arnold, *Religiosität im Mittelalter* (Darmstadt: Primus, 1997).

Anonymous, *An Address in the Favour of the School for the Blind* (Liverpool: G. F. Harris, 1817).

Anonymous, 'The Blind Boy', in *The Keepsake: or Poems and Pictures for Childhood and Youth* (London: Darton and Harvey, 1818).

Anonymous, *Charles Liston, or Self-Denial* (Higham, MA: C & E. B., 1834).

Anonymous, *Grille d'Égout et la Goulue: Histoire Réaliste* (Paris: H. Marot, 1885).

Anonymous, *Guide des Plaisirs à Paris* (Paris: Édition Photographique, 1899).

Anonymous, *Hell upon earth: or the town in an uproar* (London, 1729).

Anonymous, *The Howard Family: or The Blind Made Happy* (New York: Scofield and Voorhies, 1839).

Anonymous, 'Le revolver de la Goulue', *Le Journal* (13 July 1902).

Anonymous, *The merry medley, or, a Christmass-box, for gay gallants and good companions* (London: J. Robinson 1750).

Anonymous, 'Mort de la "Goulue"', *Le Rappel* (24 February 1918).

Anonymous, 'Sophie Lefevre, or The Poor Blind Girl', in *The Fatal Mistake* (Hartford, CT: John Babcock, 1801).

Apophthegmes, that is to saie, prompte, quicke, wittie and sentencious saiynges (London: typis Ricardi Grafton, 1542).

Apter, Emily, *Continental Drift: From National Characters to Virtual Subjects* (Chicago: University of Chicago Press, 1999).

Archenholz, Johann Wilhelm von, *A Picture of England: containing a description of the laws, customs, and manners of England* (London: Edward Jefferey, 1789).

Aristotle, *Physiognomonica*, 805a; *The Complete Works of Aristotle*, Jonathan Barnes, ed., T. Loveday and E. S. Forster, trans, vol. 1 (Princeton, NJ: Princeton University Press [Bollingen Series, 71, 2], 1984).

Artus, Maurice, 'Elysée-Montmartre', *Le Vieux Montmartre*, vol. IV, 1906–1910 (1910), 269–332.

Axton, Marie, *Three Tudor Classical Interludes* (Cambridge: D. S. Brewer, Rowman & Littlefield, 1982).

Bacon, Francis, *The Essayes or Counsels, Ciuill and Morall, of Francis Lo. Verulam, Viscount St. Alban* (London: Printed by Iohn Haviland for Hanna Barret, 1625).

Baldran, Jacqueline, *Paris, Carrefour des artistes et des lettres 1880–1918* (Paris: l'Harmattan, 2002).

Baldwin, T. W., *William Shakspeare's Small Latine and Lesse Greeke*, 2 vols (Urbana, IL: University of Illinois Press, 1944).

Ballaster, Ros, 'Aphra Behn and the Female Plot', in Heidi Hutner, ed., *Re-Reading Aphra Behn: History Theory and Criticism* (Charlottesville, VA: University of Virginia Press, 1993), 191–203.

Barasch, Moshe, *Blindness: The History of a Mental Image in Western Thought* (New York and London: Routledge, 2001).

Barbauld, Anna Laetitia, 'The Blind Fiddler', in *Lessons for Children* (London: J. Johnson, 1781), 136–138.

Barnes, C., G. Mercer and T. Shakespeare, *Exploring Disability: A Sociological Introduction* (Cambridge: Polity Press, 1999).

Barnes, Colin, 'Theories of disability and the origins of the oppression of disabled people in western society', in L. Barton, ed., *Disability and Society: Emerging Issues and Insights* (London and New York: Longman, 1996), 43–61.

Bataille, Albert, 'Police correctionnelle: Deux matrones. La *Goulue* devant la 10e Chambre. Nouvelles Judiciaires', *Le Journal* (1 April 1886).

Behn, Aphra, *The Forc'd Marriage* (London: Printed by H. L. and R. B. for James Magnus, 1671).

——, *The Unfortunate Bride: or, the Blind Lady a Beauty* (London: Printed for Samuel Priscoe, 1698).

Beier, Lee, 'Anti-language or jargon? Canting in the English underworld in the sixteenth and seventeenth centuries', in P. Burke and R. Porter eds, *Languages and jargons: Contributions to a social history of language* (Cambridge: Polity Press, 1995), 64–101.

Berger, John, Sven Blomberg, Michael Dibb, Chris Fox, and Richard Hollis, *Ways of Seeing* (London: British Broadcasting Corporation and Penguin Books, 1972).

Berland, Kevin Joel, 'Inborn Character and Free Will in the History of Physiognomy', in Melissa Percival and Graeme Tytler, *Physiognomy in Profile: Lavater's Impact on European Culture* (Newark, NJ: University of Delaware Press, 2005), 25–39.

Bernhardt, W. W., 'Shakespeare's Troilus and Cressida and Dryden's Truth Found too Late', *Shakespeare Quarterly*, 20/2 (1969), 129–141.

Bersani, Leo, 'Is the Rectum a Grave?' *October* Special Issue: AIDS: Cultural Analysis/ Cultural Activism, 43 (1987), 197–222.

Bhabha, Homi, *The Location of Culture* (New York and London: Routledge, 2012).

Birnbaum, Raoul, *The Healing Buddha* (Boston, MA: Shambhala, 1989).

Blount, Thomas Pope *Essays on Several Subjects* (London: Printed for Richard Bently, 1697).

Bolt, David, *Changing Social Attitudes to Disability* (Abingdon: Routledge, 2014).

——, Julia Miele Rodas, and Elizabeth J. Donaldson, *The Madwoman and the Blindman: Jane Eyre, Discourse, Disability* (Columbus, OH: Ohio State University Press, 2012).

Bosl, K. 'Armut, Arbeit, Emanzipation', in *Beiträge zur Wirtschafts- und Sozialgeschichte des Mittelalters. Festschrift für Herbert Helbig* (Cologne and Vienna: Böhlau, 1976), 128 ff.

——, 'Potens und Pauper. Begriffsgeschichtliche Studien zur gesellschaftlichen Differenzierung im frühen Mittelalter und zum "Pauperismus" des Hochmittelalters', in *Frühformen der Gesellschaft im mittelalterlichen Europa. Ausgewählte Beiträge zu einer Strukturanalyse der mittelalterlichen Welt* (Munich and Vienna: R. Oldenbourg Verlag, 1964), 106–34.

Bourrier, Karen. 'Introduction: Rereading Dinah Mulock Craik', *Women's Writing*, 20/3 (2013), 1–6.

Brathwait, Richard, *The English Gentleman* (London: Printed by Iohn Haviland, for Robert Bostock, 1630).

——, *The Schollers Medley, or, An Intermixt Discovrse Vpon Historicall and Poeticall Relations* (London: Printed by N. O. for George Norton, 1614).

Breval, John, *The Confederates* (London: n.p. , 1719).

Brewer, Derek, 'Prose jest books, mainly in the sixteenth to eighteenth centuries in England', in J. Bremmer and H. Roodenburg, eds, *A Cultural History of Humour* (Cambridge: Polity Press, 1997) 97–99.

Brewer, John, *The pleasures of the imagination: English culture in the eighteenth century* (London Harper Collins, 1997).

Brothwell, D., and A. T. Sandison, eds, *Diseases in Antiquity* (Springfield, IL: C. C. Thomas, 1967).

Buckley, Stephen, 'Slow Change of Heart', *St Petersburg Times* (2 September 2001), <http://www.sptimes.com/News/090201/State/Slow_change_of_heart.shtml>, accessed 26 September 2015.

Burdett, Emmeline, 'Disability History: Voices and Sources', London Metropolitan Archives', in *Journal of Literary & Cultural Disability Studies*, 8/1 (2014), 97–103.

Burney, Frances, *Camilla, or a picture of youth* (Oxford: Oxford University Press, 1972).

Burr, David , *Olivi and Franciscan Poverty: The Origins of the Usus Pauper Controversy* (Philadelphia, PA: Pennsylvania University Press, 1989).

Callarias, Albert, 'Actualités', *Gil Blas* (30 November 1893), 2.

Canadé Sautmann, Francesca, 'Invisible Women: Working Class Culture in France, 1880–1930', in Jeffrey Merrick and Bryant Ragan, eds, *Homosexuality in Modern France* (Oxford: Oxford University Press, 1996), 177–201.

Caribert, 'Les Quatr'z'Arts', *Le Courrier Français* (19 February 1893). Dossier *Bal des Quat'z'Arts* (Paris: Musée de Montmartre).

Carnell, Rachel, 'Slipping from Secret History to Novel', *Eighteenth-Century Fiction*, 28/1 (2015), 1–24.

Castarède, Jean, *Moulin Rouge: reflets d'une époque* (Paris: France-Empire, 2001).

Caulfield, James, *Blackguardiana, or a dictionary of rogues, pimps, whores etc.* (London, 1795).

Chandler, Robyn, 'Dinah Mulock Craik: Sacrifice and the Fairy-Order', in Brenda Ayres, ed., *Silent Voices: Forgotten Novels by Victorian Women Writers* (Westport, CT: Praeger, 2003), 173–201.

Cheselden, William, *Appendix to the Fourth Edition of the Anatomy of the Human Body* (London: William Bowyer, 1730), 19.

Cicero, Marcus Tullius, *De Fato*, J. E. King, trans. (Cambridge, MA: Harvard University Press, 1927), 203–205.

——, *De Fato* V.10, H. Rackham, ed. (Cambridge, MA: Harvard University Press, 1927).

Clark, Anna, *The struggle for the breeches: gender and the making of the British working class* (Berkeley: University of California Press, 1997).

Colman, Julie, *A history of cant and slang dictionaries, Vol. 1 1567–1784* (Oxford: Oxford University Press, 2004).

Conner, Mr, *Adultery. The trial of Mr. William Atkinson, linen-draper, of Cheapside, for criminal conversation with Mrs. Conner, wife of Mr. Conner, … which was tried in Hilary term, 1789, in the Court of King's Bench, before Lord Kenyon* (London, [1789]).

Conway, Kelly, *Chanteuse in the City: the Realist Singer in French Film* (Berkeley, CA: University of California Press, 2004).

Cooke, J., *The Macaroni jester and pantheon of wit* (London: T. Shepherd 1773).

Cooke, Thomas, *A Compleat Collection of all the Verses, Essays, Letters and Advertisements, Which Have been occasioned by the Publication of Three Volumes of Miscellanies by Pope and Company* (London: Printed for A. Moore, 1728).

——, 'Thersites, from the second Book of the Iliad', in *Tales, Epistles, Odes, Fables, &c. With translations from Homer and other antient Authors* (London: Printed for T. Green, 1729), 173–185.

Cooper, Richard, 'The Theme of War in French Renaissance Entries', in J. R. Mulryne, Maria Ines Aliverti, Anna-Maria Testaverde, eds, *Ceremonial Entries in Early Modern Europe: The Iconography of Power* (London: Routledge, 2015).

Copley, Anthony, *Wits fits and fancies* (London: Edw. Allde, 1614).

Corbin, Alain, *Filles de noce* (Paris: Aubier Montaigne, 1978).

Cradock, Joseph, *The Life of John Wilkes, Esq; in the manner of Plutarch*, 2nd edn (London: Printed for J. Wilkie, 1773).

Craik, Dinah Maria Mulock, *A Noble Life* 2 vols (London: Hurst and Blackett, 1866).

——, *Olive* (London: Macmillan and Co., 1875).

——, *Olive*, 3 vols (London: Chapman and Hall, 1850).

Crépineau, Jacques, and Jacques Pessis, *Le Moulin Rouge* (Paris: Éditions de la Martinière, 1990, 2002).

Cubero, Jose, *Histoire du vagabondage du Moyen Age à nos jours* (Paris: Imago, 1998).

Davis, Lennard J., 'Dr. Johnson, Amelia, and the Discourse of Disability in the Eighteenth Century', in Helen Deutsch and Felicity Nussbaum, eds, *'Defects': Engendering the Modern Body* (Ann Arbor, MI: University of Michigan Press, 2000), 54–75.

——, *Enforcing Normalcy: Disability, Deafness, and the Body* (London; New York: Verso, 1995).

——, 'Foreword: Seeing the Object as in Itself It Really Is: Beyond the Metaphor of Disability', in Julia Miele Rodas, David Bolt and Elizabeth J. Donaldson, eds, *The Madwoman and the Blindman: Disability in Jane Eyre* (Columbus, OH: Ohio State University Press, 2012), ix-xii.

Day, Thomas, 'The Good-natured Boy/The Ill-Natured Boy', in *The History of Sandford and Merton* (London: Stockdale, 1783), 43–52.

Dayton, Cornelia H. '"The Oddest Man that I Ever Saw": Assessing Cognitive Disability on Eighteenth-Century Cape Cod', *Journal of Social History*, 49/1 (2015), 77–99, 79–80.

Delmont, Bernard, 'La Goulue, qui fut dompteuse', *Le Cirque dans l'univers*, 6 (1966), 19–23.

Demers, Patricia, *From Instruction to Delight* (Oxford: Oxford University Press, 2004), 190.

DeMolen, Richard, *Richard Mulcaster (c.1531–1611) and Educational Reform in the Renaissance* (Nieuwkoop: De Graaf, 1991).

Denisoff, Dennis. 'Lady in Green with Novel: The Gendered Economics of the Visual Arts and Mid-Victorian Women's Writing', in Nicola Diane Thompson, ed.,

Victorian Women Writers and the Woman Question (Cambridge: Cambridge University Press, 1999), 151–169.

Deutsch, Helen, 'The Body's Moments: Visible Disability, the Essay and the Limits of Sympathy', in Brueggemann and Lupo, eds, *Disability and/in Prose* (Abingdon: Routledge, 2008), 1–16.

——, 'Deformity', in Rachel Adams, Benjamin Reiss, David Serlin, eds, *Keywords for Disability Studies* (New York: New York University Press, 2015).

——, 'The "Truest Copies" and the "Mean Original": Pope, Deformity, and the Poetics of Self-Exposure', *Eighteenth-Century Studies*, 27/1 (1993), 1–26.

Dickens, Charles, *A Christmas Carol and Other Christmas Books*, Robert Douglas-Fairhurst, ed. (Oxford: Oxford University Press, 2008).

Dickie, Simon, *Cruelty and Laughter: Forgotten comic literature and the unsentimental eighteenth century* (Chicago: University of Chicago press, 2011).

——, 'Hilarity and Pitilessness in the Mid-Eighteenth Century: English Jestbook Humor', *Eighteenth-Century Studies*, 37/1 (2003), 1–22.

Doggett, Thomas, *Hob, or the country wake: A farce* (London: D. Brown, 1715).

Donoghue, Emma, *Life Mask* (London: Hachette Digital, 2004), Kindle edition.

Douglas, Mary, *Purity and Danger: An Analysis of Concepts of Pollution and Taboo* (London and New York: Routledge, 1966).

Dryden, John, *Fables Ancient and Modern; Translated into Verse, from Homer, Ovid, Boccace, & Chaucer* (London: Printed for Jacob Tonson, 1700).

——, *The Satires of Decimus Junius Juvenalis: Translated into English Verse. &c.* (London: Jacob Tonson, 1693)

——, *Troilus and Cressida, or, Truth Found too Late. A Tragedy* (London: Printed for Abel Swall and Jacob Tonson, 1679), 20.

Durant, Will, *The Life of Greece* (New York: Simon and Shuster, 1939).

Durfey, Thomas, *Sir Barnaby Whigg, or, No Wit like a Womans: A Comedy* (London: Printed by A. G. and J. P. for Joseph Hindmarsh, 1681).

E. B., *A new dictionary of the terms ancient and modern of the canting crew* (London: T. Hawes, 1699).

Eco, Umberto, 'Dreaming of the Middle Ages', in *Travels in Hyperreality*, W. Weaver, trans. (London: Harvest, 1987), 61–72.

Edgeworth, Maria, 'Blind Kate', in *Rosamond, A Sequel to Early Lessons* (Philadelphia, PA: J. Maxwell, 1821; London: J. Johnson, 1801).

Edgeworth, Richard Lovell, *Poetry Explained for the Use of Young People* (London: J. Johnson, 1802).

Egan, Piers, *Grose's classical dictionary of the vulgar tongue, revised and corrected* (London, 1823).

Elias, Norbert, *On the Process of Civilisation*, Stephen Mennell, with Eric Dunning, Johan Goudsblom and Richard Kilminster, eds (Dublin: University College Dublin Press, 2012).

Emmerick, Ronald E., *The Sutra of Golden Light: Being a Translation of the Suvarnabhasottamasutra* (Oxford: Pali Text Society, 2001).

Emmett, James, 'The Blind Authoress of New York: Helen De Kroyft and the Uses of Disability in Antebellum America', *American Quarterly*, 51/2 (1999), 385–418.

Endo, Toshiichi, *Buddha in Theravada Buddhism: A Study of the Concept of Buddha in the Pali Commentaries* (Dehiwala, Sri Lanka: Buddhist Cultural Centre, 2002), 160–164.

Enlightenment and Disability, <https://enlightanddis.wordpress.com/sensory-impairments/blindness/behns-unfortunate-bride-1688/>, accessed 14 June 2015.

Ermarth, Elizabeth Deed, *Sequel to History: Postmodernism and the Crisis of Historical Time* (Princeton, NJ: Princeton University Press, 1992).

Ernest Freeberg, 'The Meanings of Blindness in Nineteenth-Century America', *Proceedings of the American Antiquarian Society*, 110/1 (2000), 119–152.

Evans, R. J., *In Defence of History* (London: Granta, 1997).

Evelyn, John, *The Diary of John Evelyn*, 2 vols (New York and London: Walter Dunne, 1901).

Fagles, Robert, *The Iliad* (New York: Penguin, 1990).

Farmer, Sharon 'Introduction', in Sharon Farmer and Barbara H. Rosenwein, eds, *Monks and Nuns, Saints and Outcasts: Religion in Medieval Society: Essays in Honor of Lester K. Little* (Ithaca, NY and London: Cornell University Press, 2000).

——, 'Manual Labor, Begging, and Conflicting Gender Expectations in Thirteenth-Century Paris', in S. Farmer and C. B. Pasternack, eds, *Gender and Difference in the Middle Ages* (Medieval Cultures), vol. 32 (Minneapolis: University of Minnesota Press, 2003), 261–87.

Fay, Elizabeth 'Mary Robinson: On Trial in Public Court', *Studies in Romanticism*, 45/3 (2006), 397–423.

Feldman, Abraham, 'The Apotheosis of Thersites', *The Classical Journal*, 42/4 (1947), 219–221.

Foot, Ferdinando, *The nut-Cracker* (London: J. Newbery, 1751).

Fowler, J., 'On a window representing the life and miracles of S. William of York, at the north end of the eastern transept, York Minster', *Yorkshire Archaeological and Topographical Journal*, 3 (1873–4), 260.

Frauwallner, Erich, *The Earliest Vinaya and the Beginnings of Buddhist Literature* (Rome: Is.M.E.O., 1956).

Freedberg, David, *The Power of Image: Studies in the History and Theory of Response* (Chicago, IL: University of Chicago Press, 1989).

Freud, Sigmund, *The joke and its relation to the unconscious* (Harmondsworth: Penguin, 2002).

Frugoni, Chiara, *Books, Banks, Buttons and Other Inventions of the Middle Ages*, William McCuaig, trans. (New York: Columbia University Press, 2003).

Galloway, Joseph, *Considerations upon the American Enquiry* (London: printed for J. Wilkie, 1779).

Garland-Thomson, Rosemarie, *Extraordinary Bodies: Figuring Physical Disability in American Culture and Literature* (New York: Columbia University Press, 1997).

——, *Staring: How We Look* (New York: Oxford University Press, 2009).

Genlis, Stephanie de, *Tales of the Castle*, Thomas Holcroft, trans. (London: Scatcherd and Letterman, 1819).

George, M. D., *Catalogue of Prints and Drawings in the British Museum*, vol. 7. 1793–1801. (London: Trustees of the British Museum by British Museum Publications, 1954. Reprint, 1978).

Giddens, Anthony, *Modernity and Self-Identity: self and Society in the Late Modern Age* (Cambridge: Polity Press, 1991).

Goadby, Robert, *An apology for the life of Mr Bampfylde-Moore Carew* (London: W. Owen, 1750).

Goodey, C. F., *A history of intelligence and 'intellectual disability': The shaping of psychology in early modern Europe* (Farnham: Ashgate, 2011).

Goodman, Nelson, *Languages of Art* (Inaianapolis: Hackett Publishing Company, 1976).

Greig, Hannah, *The Beau Monde: Fashionable Society in Georgian London* (Oxford: Oxford University Press, 2013), 203–11.

Grose, Francis, *A classical dictionary of the vulgar tongue*, 2nd edn (London: S. Hooper, 1788).

Grosz, Elizabeth, 'Bodies/Cities', in Beaztriz Colomina, ed., *Sexuality and Space* (New York: Princeton University Press, 1992), 241–253.

Guilbert, Yvette, *La chanson de ma vie* (Paris: Bernard Grasset, 1927).

Hammond, Brean, *Pope* (Brighton: Humanities Press International, 1986).

Harrowitz, Nancy, *Antisemitism, Misogyny, and the Logic of Cultural Difference: Cesare Lombroso and Matilde Serao* (London: University of Nebraska Press, 1994).

Harvey, A. D., *Sex in Georgian England: Attitudes and Prejudices from the 1720s to the 1820s* (London: Gerald Duckworth, 1994).

Hay, William, *Deformity: An Essay*, Kathleen James-Cavan, ed. (Victoria: University of Victoria Press [English Literary Studies Monographs 92], 2004).

——, *Deformity: An Essay* (London: Printed for R. and J. Dodsley, and Sold by M. Cooper, 1754).

——, *Religio Philosophi: Or, the Principles of Morality and Christianity, Illustrated from A View of the Universe, and of Man's Situation in it* (London: Printed for R. Dodsley, 1753).

Heninger, Jnr, S. K., *A Handbook of Renaissance Meteorology: with Particular Reference to Elizabethan and Jacobean Literature* (Durham, NC: Duke University Press, 1960).

Herzlich, C., and J. Pierret, *Illness and Self in Society*, E. Forster, trans. (Baltimore, MD: Johns Hopkins University Press, 1987).

Heywood, Thomas *The Iron Age, Contayning the Rape of Hellen: The siege of Troy: The Combate between Hector and Aiax: Hector and Troilus slayne by Achilles: Achilles slaine by Paris: Aiax and Vlisses contend for the armour of Achilles: The death of Aiax, &c.* (London: Printed by Nicholas Okes, 1632), sig. F.II.r.

Hickes, William, *Coffee house jests, being a merry companion* (London: S. Crowder, 1760).

Hill, Elizabeth, *A Sequel to the Poetical Monitor*, 2nd edn (London: Longman et. al, 1815).

Hobgood Allison P., and David Houston Wood, *Recovering Disability in Early Modern England* (Columbus, OH: Ohio State University Press, 2013).

Hofland, Barbara, *The Blind Farmer and His Children* (London: Harris and Son, 1819).

Homer, *Chapman's Homer: The Iliad*, Allardyce Nicoll, ed., vol. 2 (Princeton, NJ: Princeton University Press [Bollingen Series XLI], 1998).

——, *Homer's Iliads in English*, Thomas Hobbes, trans. (London: Printed by J. C. for William Crook, 1676).

——, *Ten books of Homers Iliades, translated out of French, by Arthur Hall* (London: Imprinted by [Henry Bynneman for] Ralph Nevvberie, 1581).

Hornback, Robert, 'Lost Conventions of Godly Comedy in Udall's Thersites', *SEL* 47/2 (2007), 281–303.

Horsley, Henry Sharpe, 'A Visit to the Blind Asylum', in *The Affectionate Parent's Gift and the Good Child's Reward* (London: T. Kelly, 1828), 168–174.

Howard, Robert, *Poems* (London: Henry Herringman, 1660).

Howe, Samuel Gridley, 'Education of the Blind' *The North American Review* (1833), 98, <http://www.historyofparliamentonline.org/volume/1690-1715/member/norton-richard-ii-1666-1732>, accessed 15 September 2015.

Huffer, Lynne, *Are the Lips a Grave?* (New York: Columbia University Press, 2013).

Huisman, Philippe, and M. G. Dortu, *Lautrec par Lautrec* (Paris: La Bibliothèque des Arts, 1964).

Hurault, Iaques, *Politicke, Moral, and Martial Discourses*, Arthur Golding, trans. (London: Printed by Adam Islip, 1595).

Illingworth, W. H., *History of the Education of the Blind* (London: Sampson et al,, 1910).

James-Cavan, Kathleen, '"[A]ll in me is nature": The values of deformity in William Hay's *Deformity: An Essay*', in Brenda Jo Brueggemann and Marion E. Lupo, eds, *Disability and/in Prose* (Abingdon: Routledge, 2008), 17–28.

Jeffreys, Mark, 'The Visible Cripple (Scars and Other Disfiguring Displays Included)', in Sharon L Snyder, Brenda Jo Brueggemann and Rosemarie Garland-Thomson, eds, *Disability Studies: Enabling the Humanities* (New York: Modern Language Association of America, 2002), 31–39.

Jessop A., and M. R. James, eds and trans, *The Life and Miracles of St William of Norwich by Thomas of Monmouth* (Cambridge: Cambridge University Press, 1896).

Jusserand, J. J., *English Wayfaring Life in the Middle Ages*, Lucy Toulmin Smith, trans. (London: T. Fisher Unwin, 1888).

Jütte, Robert, *Poverty and Deviance in Early Modern Europe* (Cambridge: Cambridge University Press, 1994), 14.

Juvenal, *The Satires of Decimus Junius Juvenalis. Translated into English Verse by Mr. Dryden and Several other Eminent Hands* (London: Printed for Jacob Tonson, 1693).

Kabat-Zinn, Jon, 'Some Reflections on the Origins of MBSR, Skillful Means, and the Trouble with Maps', *Contemporary Buddhism*, 12/1 (2001), 281–306.

Kamenetz, Herman L., 'A Brief History of the Wheelchair', *Journal of the History of Medicine and Allied Sciences*, 24 (1969) 205–10.

Keener, Frederick M., 'On the Poets' Secret: Allusion and Parallelism in Pope's "Homer"', *Yearbook of English Studies*, 18 (1988), 159–170.

Kelly, Gary, 'Revolution, Reaction, and the Expropriation of Popular Culture: Hannah More's Cheap Repository', *Man and Nature/L'homme et la nature*, 6 (1987), 147–159, 152.

Keramoal, Alain de, 'La Goulue ressuscitée par son arrière petit-fils', in Dossier *La Goulue/ML Weber/La Glu* (Paris: Musée de Montmartre, c.1997).

Kimbrough, Robert, 'The Problem of Thersites', *The Modern Language Review*, 59/2 (1964), 173–176.

King, Sally B., *Socially Engaged Buddhism* (Honolulu: University of Hawai'I Press, 2009).

Kinsman, Jane, Jaklyn Babington, and Simeran Maxwell, 'Houses of Tolerance', in Jane Kinsman and Stéphane Guégan, eds, *Toulouse-Lautrec: Paris and the Moulin Rouge* (Canberra: National Gallery of Australia, 2012), 109–153.

Klages, Mary, *Woeful Afflictions: Disability and Sentimentality in Victorian America* (Philadelphia, PA: University of Pennsylvania Press, 1999).

Knauer, Nancy, 'Legal Fictions and Juristic truth', *St Thomas Law Review*, 23 (2010), 1–51.

Knoppers Laura L., and Joan B. Landes, *Monstrous Bodies/Political Monstrosities in Early Modern* Europe (Ithaca, NY: Cornell University Press, 2004).

Korhonen, Anu, 'Disability humour in English jestbooks of the sixteenth and seventeenth centuries', *Cultural History*, 3/1 (2014), 27–53.

Korobkin, Laura Hanft, *Criminal Conversations: Sentimentality and Nineteenth-Century Legal Stories of Adultery* (New York: Columbia University Press, 1998).

La Fountain-Stokes, Lawrence, 'Gay Shame, Latina- and Latino Style: A Critique of White Queer Performativity', in Michael Hames-Garcìa and Ernesto J. Martìnez, eds, *Gay Latino Studies: A Critical Reader* (Durham, NC: Duke University Press, 2011), 55–80.

Lakoff, George, *Women, Fire, and Dangerous Things: What Categories Reveal about the Mind* (Chicago and London: University of Chicago Press, 1987).

Langbein, John H., *The Origins of Adversary Criminal Trial* (Oxford: Oxford University Press, 2003).

Lanoux, Armand, 'Moulin-Rouge', *Les Oeuvres libres*, 205 (1963), 81–136.

Latham, R. E., *Revised Medieval Latin Word-List from British and Irish Sources* (London: British Academy, 1965).

Lattimore, Richard, The Iliad of Homer (Chicago: University of Chicago Press, 1951).

Lazareff, Pierre, 'La triste fin de La Goulue qui fut la reine de Paris', *Paris Midi* (31 January 1929).

Le Goff, Jacques, 'Laughter in the Middle Ages', in Bremmer and Roodenburg, *A Cultural History of Humour* (Cambridge: Polity Press, 1997).

Le Greffier, 'Grande Mise en accusation par devant la cour de *La Vie Moderne* des demoiselles la Goulue et Grille d'Égout accusées de malversation morale', in *La Vie Moderne* (7 November 1885). Dossier *La Goulue/ML Weber/La Glu* (Paris: Musée de Montmartre).

Linehan, Peter, *The Ladies of Zamora* (Manchester: Manchester University Press, 1997), 1.

Loftis, J. E., 'Congreve "Way Of The World" And Popular Criminal Literature', *Studies in English Literature, 1500–1900*, 36/3 (1996), 561–578.

Lombroso, Cesare, and Giuliano Ferrero, *La donna delinquente, la prostituta e la donna normale* (Turin: Roux, 1893).

Losano, Antonia Jacqueline, *The Woman Painter in Victorian Literature* (Columbus, OH: Ohio State University Press, 2008).

Loy, David R., *Money, Sex, War, Karma: Notes for a Buddhist Revolution* (Boston, MA: Wisdom, 2008).

Lund, Roger, 'Laughing at Cripples: Ridicule, Deformity, and the Argument from Design', *Eighteenth-Century Studies*, 39/1 (2005), 95–114.

M. of Lowell, *Blind Susan, or the Affectionate Family* (New York: Mahlon Day, 1832)

McCreery, Cindy, *The Satirical Gaze: Prints of Women in Late Eighteenth-Century England* (Oxford: Clarendon Press, 2004).

McDonagh, Patrick, *Idiocy: a cultural history* (Liverpool: Liverpool University Press, 2008).

Mack, Maynard, '"The Least Thing like a Man in England": Some Effects of Pope's Disability on his Life and Literary Career', in Maynard Mack, *Collected in Himself* (Newark, NJ: University of Delaware Press, 1982), 372–392.

McMahan, David L., *The Making of Buddhist Modernism* (Oxford: Oxford University Press, 2008).

McRuer, Robert, *Crip Theory: Cultural Signs of Queerness and Disability* (New York: New York University Press, 2006).

Maître Z, 'Chronique des tribunaux', *Le Gaulois* (24 June 1893).

Manningham, Richard, *An abstract of midwifry, for the use of the lying-in infirmary: which with due explanations by anatomical preparations, &c. the repeated Performances of all Kinds of Deliveries, on our great Machine, with the Ocular Demonstration of the Reason and Justness of the Rules to be observed in all genuine and true Labours, in the Lying-in Infirmary, on our Glass Machine, makes a complete method of teaching midwifry; by giving the Pupils the most exact Knowledge of the Art, and perfectly forming their Hands, at the same time, for the safe and ready practice of midwifry* (London: T. Gardner, 1744).

Marjorie Nicolson and G. S. Rousseau, *'This Long Disease, My Life': Alexander Pope and the Sciences* (Princeton, NJ: Princeton University Press, 1968).

Meier, Frank *Gaukler, Dirnen, Rattenfänger. Außenseiter im Mittelalter* (Ostfildern: Jan Thorbecke, 2005).

Metzler, Irina, 'Hermaphroditism in the western Middle Ages: Physicians, Lawyers and the Intersexed Person', in S. Crawford and C. Lee, eds, *Bodies of Knowledge: Cultural Interpretations of Illness and Medicine in Medieval Europe* (Studies in Early Medicine 1) (Oxford: Archaeopress, 2010), 27–39.

Miller, Joe, *Joe Miller's Jests*, 4th edn (London: T. Read 1740), 28.

Mills, M., 'Buddhism and Responses to Disability, Mental Disorders and Deafness in Asia. A bibliography of historical and modern texts with introduction and partial annotation, and some echoes in Western countries' (West Midlands, 2013), <http://cirrie.buffalo.edu/bibliography/buddhism/>, accessed 12 April 2016.

Mitchell, David, and Sharon Snyder. *Narrative Prosthesis: Disability and the Dependencies of Discourse* (Ann Arbor, MI: University of Michigan Press, 2000).

Mitchell, Sally, *Dinah Mulock Craik* (Boston, MA: Twayne Publishers, 1983).

Montolieu, Isabelle *La Jeune Aveugle* (Paris: Bertrand, 1819).

Montorgueil, Georges, 'Au jour le jour: La Goulue', in Dossier *DOS GOU: Goulue, La (Weber, Louise)* (Paris: Bibliothèque Marguerite Durand, c1929).

——, *La vie à Montmartre* (Paris: G. Baudet, 1898).

——, *Paris dansant* (Paris: Théophile Belin, 1898).

Mora, María José, 'The political is personal: The attack on Shadwell in Sir Barnaby Whigg', *Sederi*, 15 (2005), 115–128.

Morel, Jean-Paul, 'Nini Patte-en-l'Aire, Une école de dressage', in Claudine Brécourt-Villars and Jean Morel, eds, *Jane Avril: Mes mémoires, suivi de Erastène Ramiro: Cours de danse fin-de-siècle* (Paris: Phébus, 2005), 137–140.

Morris, Corbyn, *An essay towards fixing the true standards of Wit, Humour, Raillery, Satire and Ridicule* (London: J. Roberts, 1744).

Morton, James, *Gangland: The Early Years* (London: Time Warner, 2003).

Mounsey, Chris, 'A Manifesto for a Woman Writer: Letters Writen as Varronian Satire', in Aleksondra Hultquist and Elizabeth Matthews, eds, *New Perspectives on Delarivier Manley and Eighteenth Century Literature: Power, Sex, and Text* (London: Routledge, 2016), 171–187.

——, *The Birth of a Clinic* (Lewisburg, PA: Bucknell University Press, 2016).

——, 'Edward Rushton and the First British Blind School', in *LA QUESTIONE ROMANTICA* (forthcoming 2016).

——, 'Variability: Beyond Sameness and Differences', in Chris Mounsey, ed., *The Idea of Disability in the Eighteenth Century* (Lewisburg, PA: Bucknell University Press, 2014), 1–21.

Mrozik, Susanne, *Virtuous Bodies: The Physical Dimensions of Morality in Buddhist Ethics* (Oxford: Oxford University Press, 2007).

Mulcaster, Richard, *Elementarie*, E. T. Campagnac, ed. (Oxford: Clarendon Press, 1925).

——, *Positions Concerning the Training Up of Children*, William Barker, ed. (Toronto: Toronto University Press, 1994).

Muratore, Pip, 'Sexuality and Voyeurism from le Moulin-Rouge to *Moulin Rouge!*', in Matthew Ball and B. Scherer, eds, *Queering Paradigms II* (New York: Peter Lang, 2010), 49–60.

Nash, Richard, *The Jests of Beau Nash* (London: W. Bristowe, 1763).

Natalis, Hervaeus, *The Poverty of Christ and the Apostles*, John D. Jones, trans. (MSDT 37) (Toronto: PIMS, 1999).

Nyquist, Mary, 'Contemporary Ancestors of de Bry, Hobbes, and Milton', *University of Toronto Quarterly*, 77/3 (2008), 837–875.

Oakley, Warren L., *A Culture of Mimicry: Laurence Sterne, His Readers and the Art of Bodysnatching* (Modern Humanities Research Association), vol. 73 (London: Maney Publishing, 2010).

Ober, William B., *Boswell's Clap and and Other Essays: Medical Analyses of Literary Men's Afflictions* (Carbondale, IL: Southern Illinois University Press, 1979).

Oexle, O. G., 'Armut und Armenfürsorge um 1200. Ein Beitrag zum Verständnis der freiwilligen Armut bei Elisabeth von Thüringen', in *Sankt Elisabeth: Fürstin, Dienerin, Heilige: Aufsätze – Dokumentation – Katalog* (Sigmaringen: Thorbecke, 1981).

Oldys, William, *Observations on the Cure of William Taylor … Also, Some Address to the Publick, for a Contribution towards the Foundation of an Hospital for the Blind* (London: E. Owen, 1753).

O'Malley, Andrew, *The Making of the Modern Child* (New York: Routledge, 2003).

O'Quinn, Daniel, 'Diversionary Tactics and Coercive Acts: John Burgoyne's Fête Champetre', *Studies in Eighteenth-Century Culture*, 40 (2011), 133–155.

Paget, Eliza, *The Blind Girl and Her Teacher* (London: Darton and Harvey, 1836).

Pawlowski, Auguste, *Plaisirs de la vie de Paris (guide du flâneur)* (Paris: Librairie L. Borel, 1900).

Perrin, Lucien, 'Le Bal de Quatr'z'Arts', *Le Courrier Français* (c.23 June 1893). Dossier *Bal des Quat'z'Arts* (Paris: Musée de Montmartre).

Pinchard, Elizabeth, *The Blind Child, or Anecdotes of the Wyndham Family* (London: E. Newbury, 1791).

Pinkethman, William, *Pinkethman's jests, or wit refined*, 2nd edn (London: T. Warner, 1721).

Plutarch, 'Of Envie and Hatred', *The Philosophie, commonlie called, the Morals written by the learned Philosopher Plutarch of Chaeronea*, Philemon Holland, trans. (London: Printed by Arnold Hatfield, 1603).

Pope, Alexander, *An Epistle from Mr. Pope, to Dr. Arbuthnot* (London: Printed by J. Wright for Lawton Gilliver, 1734).

—— *The Iliad of Homer, translated by Mr. Pope*, vol. 1 (London: Printed by W. Bowyer, for Bernard Lintott, 1715).

——, *The Works of Mr. Alexander Pope, in Prose*, vol. 2 (London: Printed for J. and P. Knapton, C. Bathurst, and R. Dodsley, 1741).

Postlethwaite, N., 'Thersites in the "*Iliad*"', *Greece & Rome*, 2nd ser., 3/2 (1988), 123–136.

Potter, Humphrey Tristram, *A new dictionary of all the cant and flash languages* (London: J. Downes, 1787).

Preson S. D., and F. B. M. de Waal, 'Empathy: Its Ultimate and Proximate Bases', *Behavioral Brain Science*, 25/1 (2002), 1–20.

Price, Martin, *Forms of Life: Character and Moral Imagination in the Novel* (New Haven, CT: London: Yale University Press, 1983).

Pufendorf, Samuel, *Of the Law of Nature and Nations*, Basil Kennet, trans., 3rd edn (London: Printed for R. Sare, et al., 1717).

Queen, Christopher 'Introduction: From Altruism to Activism', in Christopher Queen, Charles Prebish and Damien Keown, eds, *Action Dharma: New Studies in Engaged Buddhism* (London: Routledge Curzon, 2003), 1–35.

Renaudaut, Theophraste, *A General Collection of the Discourses of the Virtuosi of France, Upon Questions of All Sorts of Philosophy, and other Natural Knowledg*, G. Havers, trans. (London: Printed for Thomas Dring and John Starkey, 1664).

Rieu, E. V., *The Iliad* (Harmondsworth: Penguin, 1966).

Rivera-Cordero, Victoria, 'Spatializing Illness: Deafness in Teresa of Cartagena's *Arboleda de los enfermos', La corónica: A Journal of Medieval Hispanic Languages, Literatures, and Cultures*, 37/2 (2009), 61–77.

Rizzo, Betty, 'Equivocations of Gender and Rank: Eighteenth-Century Sporting Women', *Eighteenth-Century Life*, 26/1 (2002), 70–118.

Roberts, Nickie, *Whores in History: Prostitution in Western Society* (London: Grafton, 1993).

Robertson, Kellie, *Keeping Paradise: Labor and Language in Late Medieval Britain* (Basingstoke: Palgrave Macmillan, 2004).

Rouse, W. H., *The Iliad* (1938; New York: Signet, n.d.).

Rubin, Miri, *Charity and Community in Medieval Cambridge* (Cambridge: Cambridge University Press, 1987).

Rushton, Peter, 'Idiocy, the family and the community in early modern north-east England', in Anne Digby and David Wright, eds, *From idiocy to mental deficiency* (London: Routledge, 1996), 44–58.

S. J., *England's Merry Jester* (London: N. Boddington, 1694).

St Jerome, 'Against Vigilantius', 14, in *The Principal Works of St. Jerome*, W. H. Freemantle, trans. (The Nicene and Post-Nicene Fathers 6) (Grand Rapids, MI: Christian Classics Etherial Publisher, 1954).

Salisbury, G. T., *Street Life in Medieval England* (London: n. p., 1939).

Sanders, Edward, *The three royall cedars or Great Brittains glorious diamonds, being a royal court narrative of the proceedings ... of ... Charles by the grace of God, King of Great Brittain, France and Ireland, His Highness Prince James Duke of York, and the most illustrious Prince. Henry Duke of Glocester. With a brief history of their memorable transactions ... since their too-much-lamented Exile [sic] in Flanders, and the Lord Chancellour Hide, the Marquess of Ormond, the Earl of Norwich, the Lord Wentworth, the Lord Digby, and many other nobles and gentlemen, created lords of his Majesties privie-council. Also, the resplendent vertues appearing in these princely pearles, to the great joy of all loyal subjects ... By E. Sanders Esq; a lover of his countries liberty, and a loyal subject and servant to his Sacred Majesty* (London: printed for G. Horton, living near the three Crowns in Barbican, 1660).

Savage, Sarah, *Blind Miriam Restored to Sight* (Salem, MA: Registrar's Office, 1833), 10–11.

Scherer, B., 'Crossings and Dwellings: Being behind Transphobia', paper given at the conference 'Fear and Loathing: Phobia in Literature and Culture', University of Kent, UK, 9–10 May 2014. Available at the Queering Paradigms blog, <http://queeringparadigms.com/2014/08/11/crossings-and-dwellings-being-behind-transphobia/>, accessed 12 April 2016.

——, 'Karma: The Transformations of a Buddhist Conundrum', in L. B. Chetyrova et al., eds, *Vajrayana Buddhism in Russia: History and Modernity* (St Petersburg: St Petersburg State University, 2009), 259–285.

——, '*Queer* Thinking Religion: Queering Religious Paradigms', *Scholar & Feminist Online* (forthcoming 2016).

——, 'Variant Dharma: Buddhist Queers, Queering Buddhisms', in *Queering Paradigms VI* (Oxford: Peter Lang, 2016).

Schmeising, Ann, *Disability, Deformity, and Disease in the Grimm's Fairy Tales* (Detroit, MI: Wayne State University Press, 2014).

Schumm, Darla Y., and Michael Stoltzfus, 'Chronic Illness and Disability: Narratives of Suffering and Healing in Buddhism and Christianity', *Journal of Religion, Disability & Health*, 11/3 (2004), 5–21.

Scott, Anne M., *Piers Plowman and the Poor* (Dublin: Four Courts Press, 2004).

Seidenspinner-Núñez, Dayle, *The Writings of Teresa de Cartagena: Translated with Introduction, Notes, and Interpretive Essay* (Cambridge: D. S. Brewer, 1998).

Shadwell, Thomas, *The Sullen Lovers* (London: Henry Herringman, 1668).

Shakespeare, Tom, 'Joking a part', *Body and Society*, 5/47 (1999).

Shakespeare, William, *The History of Troilus and Cressida*, I.iii.192–196.

——, *The Tempest* (New York: Signet., 2005).

Shepherd, Geoffrey, 'Poverty in Piers Plowman', in T. H. Aston, P. R. Coss, C. Dyer and J. Thirsk, eds, *Social Relations and Ideas: Essays in Honour of R. H. Hilton* (Cambridge: Cambridge University Press, 1983), 169–89.

Shirley, John, *The scoundrel's dictionary* (London: J. Brownell, 1754).

Shorter, Edward, *Written in the Flesh: A History of Desire* (Toronto: University of Toronto Press, 2005).

Showalter, Elaine, 'Dinah Mulock Craik and the Tactics of Sentiment: A Case Study in Victorian Female Authorship', *Feminist Studies*, 2/2–3 (1975), 5–23.

Shteir, Rachel, *Striptease: The Untold History of the Girlie Show* (New York: Oxford University Press, 2004).

Siebers, Tobin, *Disability Theory* (Ann Arbor, MI: University of Michigan Press, 2008).

Skorupski, Tadeusz, 'Health and Suffering in Buddhism: Doctrinal and Existential Considerations', in J. R. Hinnells and R. Porter, eds, *Religion, Health and Suffering* (London: Kegan Paul International, 1999), 139–165.

Smellie, William, *A set of anatomical tables, with explanations, and an abridgment of the practice of midwifery; with a view to illustrate a treatise on that subject, and collection of cases* (Edinburgh: Charles Elliot 1780).

Souvais, Michel, *La Goulue: Mémoires d'une insolente* (Paris: Bartillat, 1998).

——, *Moi, La Goulue de Toulouse-Lautrec: Les mémoires de mon aïeule* (Paris: Publibook, 2008).

Sparks, Tabitha, 'Dinah Mulock Craik's *Olive*: Deformity, Gender and Female Destiny', *Women's Writing*, 20/3 (2013), 358–69.

Squier, Susan, 'Meditation, Disability, and Identity', *Literature and Medicine*, 23/1 (2004), 23–45.

Staves, Susan, 'Money for Honor: Damages for Criminal Conversation', *Studies in Eighteenth-Century Culture*, 11 (1982), 279–297.

Steedman, Caroline, *Master and Servant: Love and labour in the English industrial age* (Cambridge: Cambridge University Press, 2007).

Steele, Robert, ed., *Medieval Lore: An Epitome of the Science, Geography, Animal and Plant Folk-Lore and Myth of the Middle Age: Being Classified Gleanings from the Encyclopedia of Bartholomew Anglicus on the Properties of Things* (London: Elliot Stock, 1893).

Stephens, Frederic George, *Catalogue of Prints and Drawings in the British Museum, Division I. Political and Personal Satires. Vol. IV: A.D. 1761 to circa A. D. 1770, Prepared by, and containing many descriptions by Edward Hawkins* (London, 1883).

Stevens, George Alexander, *The History of Tom Fool*, 2 vols (London: T. Waller, 1760).

Stoddard Holmes, Martha, *Fictions of Affliction: Physical Disability in Victorian Culture* (Ann Arbor, MI: University of Michigan Press, 2004).

——, 'Intellectual Disability', in *Victorian Review*, 40/1 (2014), 9–14.

Stone, Lawrence, *Road to Divorce* (Oxford: Oxford University Press, 1990).

Straub, Kristina, *Domestic affairs: intimacy, eroticism, and violence between servants and masters in eighteenth-century Britain* (Baltimore, MD: Johns Hopkins Uuniversity Press, 2009).

Stuurnamn, Siep, 'The Voice of Thersites: Reflections on the Origins of the Idea of Equality', *Journal of the History of Ideas*, 65/2 (2004), 171–189.

Sullivan, Arabella Jane, 'The Hampshire Cottage', in Lady Dacre, ed., *Tales of the Peerage and Peasantry* (New York: Harper & Brothers, 1835).

Sweetman, David, *Toulouse-Lautrec and the fin-de-siècle* (London: Simon & Schuster, 1999).

Tarnowsky, Pauline, *Étude anthropométrique sue les prostituées et les voleuses* (Paris: E. Lecrosnier et Babé, 1889).

Taylor, John, *Wit and mirth* (London: J. Dawson, 1640).

Taylor, Stephen, 'Hay, William (1695–1755)', *Oxford Dictionary of National Biography* (Oxford: Oxford University Press, 2004). Accessed 15 September 2015.

Thalmann, W. G., 'Thersites: Comedy, Scapegoats, and Heroic Ideology in the Iliad', *Transactions of the American Philological Association*, 118 (1988), 1–28.

Thomas, D. B., ed., *The Book of Vagabonds and Beggars* (London, 1932).

Thomas, Keith, 'The place of laughter in Tudor and Stuart England', *Times Literary Supplement* (21 January 1977).

Thomson, Richard, 'The Circus', in Phillip Dennis Cate, Richard Thomson and Mary Weaver Chapin, eds, *Toulouse-Lautrec and Montmartre* (Washington, DC: National Gallery of Washington, 2005), 237–253.

——, 'Representing Montmartre', in Claire Frèches-Thory, Anne Roquebert and Richard Thomson, eds, *Toulouse-Lautrec* (London: South Bank Centre, 1990), 225–277.

Thongbunnum, Kampol, *Bright and Shining Mind in a Disabled Body* (Bangkok: Friends of Morak Society, 2007).

Tierney, Brian, 'The decretist and the deserving poor', *Comparative Studies in Society and History*, 1 (1958/1959), 363–4.

Todd, Margo, *Christian Humanism and the Puritan Social Order* (Cambridge: Cambridge University Press, 1987).

Trimmer, Sarah, *The Guardian of Education conducted by Mrs Trimmer* (London, 1802–1806), 130.

Trumbach, Randolph, *Sex And The Gender Revolution, Volume 1: Heterosexuality And The Third Gender In Enlightenment London*, vol. 1 (Chicago: University of Chicago Press, 1998).

Tsurumi, Ryoji, 'Between hymnbook and textbook: Elizabeth Hill's anthologies of devotional and moral verse for late charity schools', *Paradigm*, 2/1 (2000), n.p.

Turner, David M. *Disability in Eighteenth-Century England: Imagining Physical Impairment* (New York: Routledge, 2012).

——, 'Disability humour and the meanings of impairment in early modern England', in A. Hobgood & D. Houston Wood, eds, *Recovering disability in early modern England* (Columbus, OH: Ohio State University Press, 2013), 57–72.

Virmaître, Charles, *Trottoirs et lupanars* (Paris: H. Perrot, 1893).

Visconti, Will, 'Playtime at the Moulin Rouge', *Essays in French Literature and Culture*, 50 (2013), 107–122.

Wacha, Georg, 'Tiere und Tierhaltung in der Stadt sowie im Wohnbereich des spätmittelalterlichen Menschen und ihre Darstellung in der bildenden Kunst', in

Das Leben in der Stadt des Spätmittelalters (Veröffentlichungen des Instituts für mittelalterliche Realienkunde Österreichs Nr. 2: Vienna, 1977), 229–60.

Walker Gore, Clare, 'Noble Lives: Writing Disability and Masculinity in the Late Nineteenth Century', *Nineteenth-Century Contexts*, 36/4 (2014), 363–375.

——, '"The Right and Natural Law of Things": Disability and the Form of the Family in the Fiction of Dinah Mulock Craik and Charlotte M. Yonge', in Duc Dau and Shale Preston, eds, *Queer Victorian Families: Curious Relations in Literature* (New York and London: Routledge, 2015), 116–133.

Wallace, Miriam L., 'Constructing Treason, Narrating Truth: The 1794 Treason Trial of Thomas Holcroft and the Fate of English Jacobinism', *Romanticism on the Net* (2007).

Walters, Alisha R., 'Affective Hybridities: Dinah Mulock Craik's *Olive* and British Heterogeneity', *Women's Writing*, 20/3 (2013), 325–343.

Weber, Louise, *Mémoires de Louise Weber dite la Goulue* (Paris: Archives du Moulin Rouge, n.d.).

Wendell, Susan, *The Rejected Body: Feminist Philosophical Reflections on Disability* (New York: Routledge, 1996).

Wentz, Jed, 'Deformity, Delight, and Dutch Dancing Dwarfs: An Eighteenth-Century Suite of Prints from the United Provinces', *Music in Art*, 36/1–2 (2011), 161–200.

Wheatley, Christopher J., 'Shadwell, Durfey and Didactic Drama', in Susan J. Owen, ed., *A Companion to Restoration Drama* (Oxford: Blackwell, 2001), 340–354.

Whitehead, William, *An Essay on Ridicule* (London: Printed for R. Dodsley, and sold by M. Cooper, 1743).

Wilde, John, *An Address to the Lately Formed Society of the Friends of the People* (London: Printed for T. Cadell and Peter Hill, Edinburgh, 1793).

Williams, Helen Maria, *Letters Containing a Sketch of the Politics of France, from the Thirty-first of May 1793, Till the Twenty-eighth of July 1794*, vol. 1 (London: Printed for G. G. and J. Robinson, 1795), 127–128.

Windemuth, Marie-Luise, *Das Hospital als Träger der Armenfürsorge im Mittelalter* (Stuttgart: Sudhoffs Archiv Beihefte 36, 1995).

Wolfe, Jessica, *Homer and the Question of Strife from Erasmus to Hobbes* (Toronto: University of Toronto Press, 2015).

Wood, P. H. N., *International Classification of Impairments, Disabilities and Handicaps: A Manual of Classifications Relating to the Consequences of Disease* (Geneva: Springer, 1980).

Wortley Montagu, Mary, *Verses Address'd to the Imitator of the First Satire of the Second book of Horace* (London: Printed for A. Dodd, [1733]).

Zola, Irving Kenneth, 'Self, Identity and the Naming Question: Reflections on the Language of Disability', *Social Science & Medicine*, 36/2 (1993), 167–173.

Notes on Contributors

KEVIN BERLAND is Professor Emeritus of English and Comparative Literature at Pennsylvania State University. He has a special interest in the recovery and reinvention of classical tradition in the eighteenth century. He has published on the uses of philosophical history (especially involving Socrates), John Dryden, Henry Fielding, Frances Brooke, the history of physiognomy, newspaper poetry, the Virginia planter William Byrd and a variety of other topics. He is currently working on a book dealing with covert fictionalizing in the midst of eyewitness reports of colonial travel, as well as another on the methodology of physiognomy from classical times to the nineteenth century.

EMILE BOJESEN is Senior Lecturer at the University of Winchester, where he runs the MA in Philosophy of Education and sits on the university Senate. He is also co-convenor of the Centre for Philosophy of Education and branch chair of the South Coast branch of the Philosophy of Education Society of Great Britain. His current research is on the history of educational theory and philosophy in Elizabethan England. He has published articles in journals such as *Educational Philosophy and Theory*, *Ethics and Education*, *Philosophy Today*, *Studies in Philosophy and Education* and the *Journal of Black Mountain College Studies*. He has several articles and book chapters forthcoming in 2016, including *Against Value in the Arts and Education*, which he has co-edited. He sits on the editorial boards of *Studies in Philosophy and Education* and *Policy Futures in Education*. He is currently co-editing a special issue of *Studies in Philosophy and Education* titled 'Education, in spite of it all'.

STAN BOOTH is a student at the University of Winchester. He worked for many years as a local government manager, advising members of the community of a disadvantaged area of London. Seeing the credit crunch coming and the obvious impact it would have, he returned to learning, undertaking an MSc in Health and Disease and from there re-entered academia. His PhD project explores the discourse of physical paralysis in the eighteenth century with a cultural studies emphasis that allows scope to explore individuals and to go beyond the notion of the typical and predicted models.

ADLEEN CRAPO is a doctoral candidate in the University of Toronto's Comparative Literature programme. Her research focusses on disability in the writings of John Milton, Paul Scarron and Miguel de Cervantes. Her work considers the link between early modern authorship and citizenship through the prism of the disabled body. She has also written on women's embodiment and motherhood in French literature of the twentieth century. In the classroom, Adleen applies her research to questions of early modern colonialism and Canadian politics.

SIMON JARRETT is a Wellcome Trust doctoral researcher at Birkbeck, University of London. He writes about idiocy, and how a conceptual shift over the eighteenth and nineteenth centuries saw those labelled 'idiots' moved from community to asylum. His publications include 'The history of intellectual disability: Inclusion or exclusion?' in R. Jackson (ed.), *Community Care, Inclusion and Intellectual Disability* (2016) and '"Belief", "opinion" and "knowledge": The idiot in law in the long eighteenth century' in C. F. Goodey, P. McDonagh and T, Stainton (eds), *Intellectual Disability: A Conceptual History from the Medieval Law Courts to the Great Incarceration* (forthcoming).

KATHARINE KITTREDGE is Professor of English at Ithaca College. She is the editor of *Lewd and Notorious: Female Transgression in the Eighteenth-Century*, and his written numerous articles on Anglo-Irish diarist Melesina Trench.

IRINA METZLER is a leading expert on cultural, religious and social aspects of disability in the European Middle Ages. She has combined the approaches of modern disability studies with historical sources to investigate the intellectual framework within which medieval cultures positioned physically impaired persons, which resulted in her first book. Two monographs on cultural, social and economic conditions of medieval disability were published in 2006 and 2013. Her most recent project examined notions of intellectual impairment in the Middle Ages, and resulted in the publication of *Fools and Idiots? Intellectual Disability in the Middle Ages* (2016). Her wider research interests revolve around medieval notions of history and the past, perceptions of the natural world, and historical anthropology. She gained her PhD from the University of Reading in 2001 and joined the University of Swansea as a Wellcome Trust-funded Research Fellow in 2012.

CHRIS MOUNSEY worked for several years in theatre before an accident and four months of immobility, in which reading was the only possible occupation, led to an academic career. Degrees in Philosophy, Comparative Literature and English from the University of Warwick followed, and a doctorate on Blake founded an interest in the literature of the eighteenth century. He now teaches at the University of Winchester and is the author of *Christopher Smart: Clown of God* (2001) and *Being the Body of Christ* (2012). He has also edited *Presenting Gender* (2001), *Queer People* (2007), *The Idea of Disability in the Eighteenth Century* (2014) and *Developments in the Histories of Sexualities* (2015).

BEE SCHERER is Professor of Religious Studies and Gender Studies, as well as the Director of the Intersectional Centre for Inclusion and Social Justice (INCISE), at Canterbury Christ Church University, United Kingdom (<www.canterbury.ac.uk/INCISE>). An expert in Buddhism and queer theory, Bee has authored more than a dozen monographs and edited volumes in German, Dutch and English. Bee is the founder of 'Queering Paradigms' and the editor for Peter Lang's *Queering Paradigms* book series.

WILL VISCONTI completed a joint PhD in French Studies and Italian Studies at the University of Sydney. His main areas of research include the intersections of gender, representation, performance and transgression, particularly in Europe during the late nineteenth and early twentieth century. Of additional interest is the enduring legacy of women like La Goulue, and their influence on contemporary visual and performing arts around the world.

CLARE WALKER GORE recently completed her PhD at Selwyn College, Cambridge. Her thesis explored disability in the nineteenth-century novel, with a particular emphasis on the work of Charles Dickens, Wilkie Collins, Charlotte M. Yonge and Dinah Mulock Craik. She now holds a Junior Research Fellowship at Trinity College, Cambridge, and is working on her first book manuscript. She has published work in *Nineteenth-Century Gender Studies*, *Nineteenth-Century Contexts* and *Women: A Cultural Review*.

MIRIAM L. WALLACE is Professor of English at New College of Florida, where she has previously served as Director of the Gender Studies programme and is incoming Chair of the Division of Humanities. She has written extensively on the English Jacobin and anti-Jacobin novel and on the radical writers of the 1790s, which are the subject of her book *Revolutionary Subjects in the English 'Jacobin' Novel* (2009). More recently, she was co-coordinator, with Katharine Jensen, of a special issue of *PMLA* on 'Emotions' (October 2016). Her current project, *Speaking Subjects and Criminal Conversations*, focuses on specific sites of 'speech' between 1780 and 1815 that authorize counter-discourses, from trial testimony and 'legal fictions' to cross-class ventriloquizing literary genres. A fellowship at the Lewis Walpole Library of Yale University in July 2012 developed her interest in visual images (particularly satirical prints) as another site for elaborating speaking and variable bodies. She maintains a scholarly interest in British modernism and Virginia Woolf, as well as a personal one in birdwatching.

Index

QUEERING PARADIGMS

Series Editor

Bee Scherer, Canterbury Christ Church University, UK

Queering Paradigms is a series of peer-reviewed edited volumes and monographs presenting challenging and innovative developments in Queer Theory and Queer Studies from across a variety of academic disciplines and political spheres. *Queer* in this context is understood as a critical disposition towards the predominantly binarist and essentialising social, intellectual, political, and cultural paradigms through which we understand gender, sexuality, and identity. *Queering* denotes challenging and transforming not just heteronormativity, but homonormativity as well, and pushing past the binary axes of homo- and hetero-sexuality.

In line with the broad inter- and trans-disciplinary ethos of queer projects generally, the series welcomes contributions from both established and aspiring researchers in diverse fields of studies including political and social science, philosophy, history, religious studies, literary criticism, media studies, education, psychology, health studies, criminology, and legal studies. The series is committed to advancing perspectives from outside of the 'Global North'. Further, it will publish research that explicitly links queer insights to specific and local political struggles, which might serve to encourage the uptake of queer insights in similar contexts. By cutting across disciplinary, geographic, and cultural boundaries in this way, the series provides a unique contribution to queer theory.

Published volumes

Burkhard Scherer (ed.)
Queering Paradigms
2010. ISBN 978-3-03911-970-7

Burkhard Scherer and Matthew Ball (eds)
Queering Paradigms II: Interrogating Agendas
2011. ISBN 978-3-0343-0295-1

Kathleen O'Mara and Liz Morrish (eds)
Queering Paradigms III: Queer Impact and Practices
2013. ISBN 978-3-0343-0939-4

Elizabeth Sara Lewis, Rodrigo Borba, Branca Falabella Fabrício and Diana de Souza Pinto (eds)
Queering Paradigms IV: South-North Dialogues on Queer Epistemologies, Embodiments and Activisms
2014. ISBN 978-3-0343-1823-5

María Amelia Viteri and Manuela Lavinas Picq (eds)
Queering Paradigms V: Queering Narratives of Modernity
2016. ISBN 978-3-0343-1924-9

Bee Scherer (ed.)
Queering Paradigms VI: Interventions, Ethics and Glocalities
2016. ISBN 978-1-906165-87-1

+ +

QP: In Focus

Chris Mounsey and Stan Booth (eds)
The Variable Body in History (QP In Focus 1)
2016. ISBN 978-1-906165-72-7